W9-AZL-817

Postwar America:
1945–1971

The
History of American Society

EDITED BY JACK P. GREENE

HOWARD ZINN

Postwar America: 1945–1971

THE BOBBS-MERRILL COMPANY, INC.
Indianapolis and New York

The author and publisher wish to thank the following for permission to reprint selections:

From *Malcolm X Speaks*. Copyright © 1965 by Merit Publishers and Mrs. Betty Shabazz. Reprinted by permission of Pathfinder Press, Inc.

From *The Orangeburg Massacre* by Jack Nelson and Jack Bass. Copyright © 1970 by Jack Nelson and Jack Bass. Reprinted by permission of the World Publishing Company, the authors, and The Sterling Lord Agency, Inc.

From *Dark Ghetto* by Kenneth Clark. Reprinted by permission of Harper & Row, Publishers, Inc.

From *Once* by Alice Walker. Copyright © 1968 by Alice Walker. Reprinted by permission of Harcourt Brace Jovanovich, Inc.

From "Ballad of the Landlord" in *Montage of a Dream Deferred* by Langston Hughes. Copyright © 1951 by Langston Hughes. Reprinted by permission of Harold Ober Associates Incorporated.

From "The Times They Are A-changin'" by Bob Dylan. Copyright © 1963 by M. Witmark & Sons. Reprinted by permission of Warner Brothers Music.

Copyright © 1973 by The Bobbs-Merrill Company, Inc.
Library of Congress Catalog Card Number 72–88273
Printed in the United States of America
ISBN–0–672–51687–X
ISBN–0–672–60936–3 (pbk)
First Printing
Design: Starr Atkinson

to Dave Dellinger

WHO HAS WORKED SO HARD,
THROUGH ALL THE YEARS COVERED
IN THIS BOOK, AGAINST WAR,
AGAINST INJUSTICE—ALWAYS
WITH THAT RARE COMBINATION
OF REVOLUTIONARY COURAGE AND
CONCERN FOR ALL HUMAN BEINGS.

Contents

Editor's Foreword

The historian's traditional preoccupation with political history, a noted French historian has recently suggested,* is traceable to an understandable fascination with great public figures and noble deeds and events. Because the realm of politics in all its aspects—"theoretical politics, practical politics, politicians"—is by definition and in virtually all societies "the realm of the elite," political history, he has observed, is necessarily history in the "aristocratic style," inevitably preoccupied with the study of the public stage and the most prominent actors upon it: kings and presidents, ministers and senators, diplomats and generals. In view of the elitist orientation of political history, it is perhaps somewhat ironic that historians of the United States, the first large modern republic that has never had a true aristocracy, should have persisted in their emphasis upon political history far longer than those of any other major Western nation. That "economics, society and culture seem to have monopolized historians' attention for the last half-century" is probably true for every other group of national historians; it does not, however, apply to those of the United States, where, despite some impressive shifts of attention over the past decade, politics continues to be the central object of concern.

The *History of American Society* series is an attempt to break free from this emphasis. It represents an effort to look at the American past from the wider perspective of the development of American society as a whole. It proposes not to neglect politics, and the other familiar aspects of the history of American public life, but to put them in their broad social context. Because so few specialized and dependable studies have been made of any of the many complex components of American social development—values, economic and religious organization, aspirations, social structure, and internal tensions—this series is obviously somewhat preliminary in character. Without the kind of precise information about aggregate social

* Jacques Le Goff, "Is Politics Still the Backbone of History?" *Daedalus* (Winter, 1971), pp. 2–3.

behavior and long-term social developments that can only be supplied by an enormous amount of detailed study, the volumes in the series will necessarily be highly impressionistic and illustrative, more speculative analyses of the meaning of contemporary social perceptions than confident syntheses of hard data with firm conclusions about the changing character of the American social system. Despite the tentative nature of this undertaking, the series may at least provide an expanded conceptual framework for viewing the American past, one that will focus not merely upon elites and their public activities but also, and primarily, upon the preoccupations, behavior, and drift of American society as a whole. Each of the seven volumes in the series will outline in broad strokes for a specific period the main thrust of American economic, social, and cultural development and the interaction between that development and American political and public life; each will also provide the reader with a guide to the specialized historical literature on that period.

The second volume to be published, Professor Howard Zinn's extraordinarily powerful and moving reading of the recent American past *Postwar America,* is, chronologically, the seventh and last volume of the series. It is not a conventional work of American history, not the traditional success story, not a chronicle of the social, material, political, and diplomatic achievements of the American nation over the past quarter of a century. It is not even—and makes no pretense to be—what historians would regard as a balanced and "objective" account. Polemical in tone and informed throughout by a sense of passionate and urgent conviction, it is, rather, a stinging indictment of the dominant groups within American society for their failure to live up to the principles on which this nation was founded, a relentless and probing revelation of the glaring discrepancies between the rhetoric of American liberalism and the facts of American life in foreign affairs, social organization, corporate behavior, race relations, the administration of justice, and the toleration of dissent. Yet, this book is obviously not the product of despair. On the contrary. In the questioning of the previously unquestionable norms of American society first by blacks, then by the young, and finally even by a growing number of people at the very center of the American Establishment, Professor Zinn sees the possible beginnings of a sweeping revolution in values and behavior with the potential to mobilize the American public in a successful quest for those great elusive goals of the Declaration of Independence: life, liberty, and the pursuit of happiness. This revolution, then, and the painful failures of American society—more especially those of its predominant liberal credo—are the central and complementary themes Professor Zinn employs to lead his readers through this shattering yet vital and creative period in the *History of American Society.*

Jack P. Greene

Johns Hopkins University

Acknowledgments

To Abby Dunlop, Judith Mandelbaum, Betsy Neal, and Joan Tighe, for indispensable help. To Susan Hartman, for finding material on the treatment of women during World War II. To the Rabinowitz Foundation, for aid at a certain crucial time in the production of this book. To William Hoth, a perceptive and indefatigable editor. To Bill Hackett, for wanting me to do this. To Roz, as always, for wise counsel and encouragement.

H.Z.

Boston University

Introduction:
The American Creed

Any book of history is, consciously or not, an interpretation in which selected data from the past is tossed into the present according to the interest of the historian. That interest, no matter how much the historian's mind dwells on the past, is always a present one. My own interest in writing this short history of the United States in the twenty-five years following World War II is to explore two questions, in the hope that the reader will be stimulated to take a more active part in the making of an American history different from what we have had so far.

First, why did the United States, exactly as it became the most heavily armed and wealthiest society in the world, run into so much trouble with its own people? From the late fifties to the early seventies, the nation experienced unprecedented black rebellion, student demonstrations, antiwar agitation, civil disobedience, prison uprisings, and a widespread feeling that American civilization was faltering, or even in decay.

And second, what are the possibilities, the visions, the beginnings, of fresh directions for this country?

I begin the discussion of the first question in my opening chapter, with Hiroshima, in 1945, when an entire city was annihilated by American technology in a burst of righteous brutality, with no protest from the American public. I raise the second question in my final chapter with the scene at Bunker Hill, 1971, when veterans of the Vietnam War assembled to protest similar brutality in Indochina.

Running through these questions, and this book, is the theme of an American creed at odds with itself. The common distinctions made between promise and performance, theory and practice, words and deeds, do not represent the situation accurately. The promise itself is ambiguous, the words contradictory. And so with the performance—in which greed and violence are mixed with just enough nobility and heroism to confuse any simple characterization of

"America." For America is not only warrior-presidents, insatiable industrialists, servile intellectuals, and compliant victims, it is also men and women of courage, organizers and agitators of dissent and resistance.

In the pages to follow, I distinguish between the warring elements of the American creed. There is the *rhetorical* creed, represented best by the words of the Declaration of Independence: "all Men are created equal . . . unalienable Rights . . . Life, Liberty, and the Pursuit of Happiness . . . whenever any Form of Government becomes destructive of these Ends, it is the Right of the People to alter or to abolish it. . . ." There is the *working* creed, those beliefs that, whether or not written into the Constitution and the laws, are embedded in the minds of the American people by constant practice, reinforced by church, family, school, official pronouncements, and the agents of mass communication: that all men are created equal, except foreigners with whom we are at war, blacks who have not been singled out for special attention, Indians who will not submit, inmates of prisons, members of the armed forces, and anyone without money; that what are most alienable are the lives of men sent off to war and the liberties of people helpless against authority; that whenever members of any group of people become destructive of this working creed, it is the right of the government to alter or abolish them by persecution or imprisonment.

In this sense, American history is a long attempt, so far unsuccessful, to overcome the ambiguity in the American creed, to fulfill the principles of the Declaration of Independence.

Ambiguity has always been useful to those who run societies. It joins a working set of rules and beliefs necessary to keep the system going with a set of ideals that promise something better in the future and soften the harshness of the present. In the great liberal revolutions of modern times—England in the seventeenth century, the United States and France in the eighteenth century—this ambiguity became more necessary than ever before. Large numbers of people had to be mobilized to overthrow the old regimes and to participate actively in the complex economic and parliamentary-party systems born of those revolutions. The ideals spurred the people; the rules controlled them. Religion, education, the mass media took turns in communicating both the ideals and the rules.

The industrial states that emerged from these revolutions have all claimed to represent great progress over pre-modern societies. The claim is enormously exaggerated. Elections and parliamentary systems have not done away with the concentration of decision-making power in the hands of the few; they have permitted only token participation in government by a largely uninformed and powerless electorate. The capitalist system has not done away with the crass division of society into rich and poor that obtained in feudal times; indeed, it has deepened that division on a global scale, and within the rich nations it has disguised the maldistribution of wealth by an intricate set of contractual relationships enforced by law. Modern constitutional due process and bills of rights have not changed the basic truths of pre-modern societies: that justice in the courts and freedom of expression are rarely available to those without money or position. Mass literacy, science, and education have not eliminated deception of the many by the few; rather, they have made it possible for duplicity to be more widespread.

The rise of national states in modern times has been viewed as a progressive development, as an advance over the splintered world of monarchs and popes, tribal chiefs and feudal lords. But the new order, disappointing for most people within the new nations, was lethal for those outside; nation-states were able to organize empires, dispense violence, and conduct war on a level far beyond the reach of the old regimes. The "rule of law" that developed inside the modern nations was accompanied by the rule of lawlessness on the world scene. Nation-states armed with nuclear warheads diverted national wealth to war and preparation for war, while controlling their people at home by police rule and token benefits.

This is not to deny the reality of progress in medical science and technology, in literacy, and political participation. But these pre-requisites for a good society have thus far been perverted by war, nationalistic ambitions, and private profit. What is called progress has meant mostly the sharpening of tools not yet used for human purposes, the sowing of expectations not yet realized.

The United States, as the most modern of modern countries, epitomizes all these characteristics of the twentieth-century nation-state. It has been the most effective in utilizing its rhetorical creed, in conjunction with its working creed, to sustain control over its own people and to extend control over other parts of the world.

In America, the use of ambiguity has been most successful. One reason is that the distance between the rhetoric and the rules has been constantly blurred by symbols of change and reform. To the grand claims of progress wrought by modern revolutions, the United States has added the assertion of progress within its own constitutional system. It has passed civil-rights laws for blacks and welfare laws for the poor; it has widened the suffrage and reformed its political structure; it has extended the rights of the accused and voted economic aid for foreign peoples. All these symbols of change and reform have kept alive the notion that progress is attainable within the rules of the American system—by voting for the right men, passing new statutes, getting new Supreme Court decisions, and accepting the system of corporate profit.

The American system has allowed enough change to ease discontent, but not enough to change the fundamental allocation of power and wealth. That which can be termed progress has taken place within the narrow boundaries of an economic system based on profit-motivated capitalism, a political system based on the paternalism of representative government, a foreign policy based on economic and military aggressiveness, and a social system based on a culture of prejudices concerning race, national origin, sex, age, and wealth.

So far, the major political conflicts in the United States have stayed within these boundaries. The American Revolution itself, while winning independence from a foreign ruling group, substituted the rule of a native group of slave owners, merchants, lawyers, and politicians; the new Constitution legitimized the substitution and created a larger arena for the elites of race and class that already dominated the colonies. With the Civil War, the nation outlawed slavery, while maintaining a general climate of racial subordination. Farm and labor movements succeeded in achieving reforms, but mostly for privileged minorities within their constituencies, and inside a larger framework of corporate control of the nation's wealth. The political fluctuations, even the violent clashes represented by the farm and labor upheavals, had the look but not the reality of a choice between radically different alternatives.

All that I have said here supports the "consensus" interpretation of American history, which states, I believe, a profound truth about our society, that its great "progress" and its political clashes have kept within severe limits. What is missing in the consensus analysis is the persistent strain of protest that shows up repeatedly in American history and should not be ignored—the voices, the ideas, the struggles of those who defy the American working creed, who will not let the nation forget the rhetorical promises, who keep alive the vision, the possibility of a society beyond capitalism, beyond nationalism, beyond the hierarchies that are preserved in a man-eat-man culture. The existence of this strain justifies the work of the "conflict" school of American history, which insists that Americans not forget the black abolitionists, the Wobblies, the Socialists, the anarchists, that we keep in mind Tom Paine, John Brown, Emma Goldman, Eugene Debs, Malcolm X.

In the postwar years, these two strains, consensus and conflict, became most pronounced; the gap between the rhetoric of the American creed and its working rules became most obvious. The traditional successes of the American system, in crusades abroad and reforms at home, were at their greatest in World War II and in the years that followed. But so was the realization of failure. For the first time, the symbols of achievement and progress began to look false to growing numbers of Americans.

The Second World War, after a quarter of a century, is not as glorious as it once seemed. The war revealed the American system of liberal capitalism at its best: enormously efficient in technology, abundant in jobs and money, united in struggle against a reprehensible enemy, pulsating with noble declarations and marvelous intentions for the nation and the world. But the war also revealed that, at its best, the system's declarations against the brutality of the enemy were accompanied by mass slaughter—Dresden and Hiroshima; that at its best the crusade against fascism covered up our own racism—segregation in the armed forces; that at its best America's generosity toward its allies masked nationalist expansion: we aided the British while replacing them as the oil men of the Middle East. At its best, the economy was built on profiteering through war contracts, and the political system was built on conformity: those outside the political pale—Trotskyists and pacifists—were put in prison, and those outside the racial pale—Japanese-Americans—were put in concentration camps.

An atmosphere thick with the righteousness of combat against

Hitler concealed these ironies from everyone except a few cynics and rebels, so tainted by the majority as to make them untrustworthy. Thus, Americans entered the postwar era with great confidence in their system, and with quadrupled power and wealth to back up that confidence.

Not until the sixties did this confidence begin to break down, as crisis after crisis—in race relations, in the distribution of resources, in foreign policy—indicated that something was terribly wrong. The Great Depression had been overcome, fascism defeated, the Ku Klux Klan and McCarthyism subdued, but within the nation a malaise grew. The troubles of American society could no longer be attributed to departures from the liberal creed—to youthful imperialism or southern racism or corporate exploitation or political witchhunts. The nation had passed its youth, defeated the Confederacy, replaced the robber barons with the welfare state, and reaffirmed the Bill of Rights by enlightened Supreme Court decisions. We had saved the liberal creed from its external enemies, cleansed it of its interior impurities, and yet infections grew.

Was it possible (and what could be more frightening than this thought? yet the outbursts of blacks, the inexplicable resistance of Asian peasants, the revulsion of former admirers all over the world, the sudden anger of our children, made us think wild thoughts) that the liberal creed itself was faulty? That is, the *working* creed, not the rhetorical visions of the Declaration of Independence and the pledge of allegiance. Was it possible that the ideas, the values, the symbols, the priorities of American life were wrong? Was it possible that Americans had scraped away certain repugnant layers of their past —the crude imperialism of the Spanish-American War, the lynchings of blacks, the shooting of strikers, only to find that what was left was still ugly?

The turmoil of the sixties planted the suspicion that by the early seventies was stronger than ever: that the most cherished beliefs of liberal democratic capitalism were working to produce those very evils that Americans had always attributed to momentary departures from the liberal creed. The suspicion grew that transgressions on human rights in the United States were not occasional eccentricities; they occurred when we were on dead center; they were normal. The nation's difficulties did not stem from violations of the working creed of American liberalism but from compliance with it.

It is the faith in this working creed that has now begun to waver —faith in achieving racial equality through constitutional amendments, statutes, and Supreme Court decisions; faith in the system of corporate profit as modified by trade unions and the welfare state; faith in due process, the Bill of Rights, the courts, and the jury system as the means of securing justice and freedom of expression for every American; faith in voting, representative government, and the two-party system as the best way in which to guarantee democracy; faith in police to keep peace at home and protect the rights of all, and in soldiers and bombs to keep law and order abroad; faith in what is perhaps the crucial element in the modern system, in the idea that a paternalistic government will take care of its citizens without their day-to-day exercise of judgment or criticism or resistance.

This book intends to show how this faith has been mistaken, how, in the twenty-five years since World War II, the working creed of the American system has produced a crisis of culture and politics. But it also intends to show that out of this crisis has come at least the beginning of an attempt to act out what was promised, two centuries ago, in the Declaration of Independence.

We start from that enthusiastic moment of victory, when the war ended, to see if there were clues even then, as the nation stood at its summit, to why it began its long fall from grace. Or to see if, indeed, the great war itself—the best of wars—was part of that fall.

Postwar America:
1945–1971

1

The Best of Wars

JAPAN SURRENDERS, END OF WAR!
EMPEROR ACCEPTS ALLIED RULE;
M'ARTHUR SUPREME COMMANDER;
OUR MANPOWER CURBS VOIDED

The *New York Times,* Wednesday, August 15, 1945. In the second paragraph of the lead story under these eight-column headlines, Arthur Krock wrote that "the bloody dream of the Japanese military caste vanished in the text of a note to the Four Powers accepting the terms of the Potsdam Declaration of July 26, 1945. . . ."

Two million people gathered in Times Square after the announcement of Japan's surrender was flashed on the electric sign of the Times Building at 7:03 p.m., August 14. Wrote a reporter in another page-one story: "The victory roar that greeted the announcement beat upon the eardrums until it numbed the senses. For twenty minutes wave after wave of that joyous roar surged forth." "The metropolis," he wrote, "exploded its emotions . . . with atomic force."

With one exception, his was the only conspicuous reference in that day's *New York Times* to atomic power. It was eight days after the first atomic bomb had been dropped on Hiroshima, five days after the second one had been dropped on Nagasaki. The exception appeared on page three. Emperor Hirohito, in his radio speech to the Japanese people announcing surrender, explained:

> . . . the enemy has begun to employ a new and most cruel bomb, the power of which to do damage is, indeed, incalculable, taking the toll of many innocent lives. Should we continue to fight, it would not only result in an ultimate collapse and obliteration of the Japanese nation, but also it would lead to the total extinction of human civilization.

On this last day of war, according to another story on page one, Japanese aircraft approaching the Pacific Fleet off Tokyo were still being shot down. Admiral William Halsey was quoted: "It looks like the war is over, but if any enemy planes appear, shoot them down in friendly fashion." It seemed hard to shake off the martial spirit; just before the surrender announcement, the *Times* reported, the Japanese had sunk the American heavy cruiser *Indianapolis,* killing all 1,196 men aboard.

President Harry S. Truman, in declaring a two-day victory holiday, said: "This is a great day. . . . This is the day when fascism and police government cease in the world." His mother told newspapermen: "I'm glad Harry decided to end the war. He's no slow person. He gets where he's going in short order."

The Vatican announced that it was glad the war, in which fifty million people had died, was over. In Buenos Aires, in crowds assembled before the United States embassy to celebrate the end of the war, shouts of "Death to Franco" were heard. Syngman Rhee, president of South Korea, declared his gratitude to the United States government and to Chinese President Chiang Kai-shek, and said Korea was entering the world of free nations in the name of peace, justice, and democracy.

On this last day of the war, France sent notes to the United States, Britain, and the U.S.S.R. suggesting early agreement on France's administrative take-over of Indochina.

Joy was reported among thirty-three Americans of Japanese descent living together in a relocation hostel in New York, after having been released from relocation centers in the West.

In Moscow, General Dwight D. Eisenhower said the United States and Russia should be the best of friends, and hoped Russia would understand that in his country, "under the principles governing our affairs, there is no censorship of the press. . . . I, like every other soldier of America, will die for the freedom of the press. . . ." Alongside the general's observations appeared the announcement that the Office of War Information, which had handed out official propaganda stories to newspapers throughout the war, was about to disband. Elmer Davis, the OWI director, spoke of the "psychological warfare" that had taken place during the struggle; he now voiced hope for "an era of free exchange of information and ideas among all peoples of the world." Another story announced the closing of the United States Office of Censorship.

Hanson W. Baldwin, the *Times*'s military editor, wrote on page 10: "War, to the United States, has been conducted as a big business —not a game of chess. . . ."

A man was electrocuted at a Barnum & Bailey circus. One of the fighting Murphys, seven brothers from Great Falls, Montana, was missing in action. The public was warned about a polio epidemic, and advised that it could now look forward to luxuries and certain essentials it was deprived of during the war. Books published on this day included *Freedom's People: How We Qualify for a Democratic Society* by Bonare W. Overstreet.

A playground was being built in Lancashire in memory of thirty-eight schoolchildren who had died when an American bomber crashed into their school. British children, in New Zealand for the war, were on their way home.

Field Marshal General Wilhelm Keitel said he was still loyal to the Führer, and that he knew nothing about atrocities until the end of the war. The Führer gave all the commands, the story reported him saying, and he "merely saw to it that they were carried out by the Wehrmacht."

A list of "latest war casualties" was given on page 13.

Rehearsals began for "Girl from Nantucket." She was to join, among others, "Bloomer Girl," "Up in Central Park," "Follow the Girls," "Oklahoma!" and "Hats off to Ice." Motion pictures: "Military Secret," "Anchors Aweigh," "Rhapsody in Blue," "Junior Miss." Mayor Fiorello La Guardia conducted the Philharmonic in a group of marches.

On the sports page, Arthur Daley looked back sadly on the decline of sports during the war, but eagerly anticipated a new era with the return of healthy young men from the war zones. In the business section, Senator Claude Pepper of Florida was reported off to Europe and the Middle East to check on business possibilities for Americans.

That day in August, 1945, the United States was powerful and confident. It had built up a colossal industrial apparatus, it had entered a war proclaiming the right of all sovereign nations to be free of foreign domination, and it had defeated the war machines of Germany and Japan. The people of the United States had never been more fully employed, more prosperous, more united in a single cause. Then what happened? What happened within the span of one generation? Peter Berger, a social philosopher, wrote in 1968:

> ... in 1945, almost everywhere in the world, an American uniform represented the armed might of justice, liberating men from one of history's darkest tyrannies. . . . Around 1960 American society still seemed a massive and massively stable structure. Today one has the feeling that the whole structure may come tumbling down at any moment; that even our most basic values are tottering.

The war itself, if Americans had stopped to think, could have told so much about that structure. But the United States was overcome with the grandeur of its mission. It was, all Americans acknowledged—omitting the handful of Nazi sympathizers, and the few pacifist fanatics who went to jail—the most just of wars. Only a master inventor of horror tales could have concocted an enemy as grotesquely evil as Adolf Hitler and the sieg-heiling, goose-stepping Nazi myrmidons. Who could have trumped up, even with the most fiendish imagination, the blitzkrieg conquest of Europe; the figures of Goering, Goebbels, and Himmler; the frozen Russian corpses in the snow as the German armies rolled eastward; the Stuka dive bombers screaming down on London and Warsaw and Rotterdam; the gas chambers, the ghastly operating rooms at Dachau and Auschwitz? Or the Japanese slaughter of Chinese in Nanking and Shanghai, the stunning attack on Pearl Harbor? The total evil of the Axis side certified, without question or condition, the total righteousness of the Allies.

World War II was a perfect example of that one-dimensional moral judgment so characteristic of human history: all evil on one side, all virtue on the other. Without a second thought, the dagger must be plunged not only into the foe but into everybody and everything remotely associated with him.

But what is the cost of a psychology of vengeance, in a war presumably waged for humanity? And what are the real interests of the victors, behind their speeches? World War II was fought, we all assumed, to preserve life, to end tyranny, to foster equality. Did it? And what values, what states of mind were strengthened by the war? Were they the values of peace and friendship?

Complicating factors are forgotten in the glow of a crusade. Thus, the Revolutionary War emerges from our history books without the viewpoint of the black slave, whose condition grew worse after that glorious victory for freedom. And what was the real point of the Civil War, in which more than six hundred thousand died? To slightly simplify and exaggerate: it was fought so that a single economic market could develop the most rapacious capitalism in world history, and so that a single political power from one ocean to another could become the most domineering nation in the world. The black person, presumed beneficiary of that crusade but really the pawn in a game in which competing interests vied with one another, was removed from one state of subjugation to another—one that was less crass, more flexible, more firmly anchored to the social structure.

All wars of the United States were not splendid crusades, perhaps; Americans admit doubts about the Mexican War, the Spanish-American War, and even World War I. But not about World War II; it was the third of America's unquestionably virtuous wars.

Even Hiroshima did not succeed in breaking the spell of righteousness. Indeed, in a strange way, it made the spell more durable. For those who were appalled that Americans had aimed a terrifyingly destructive new weapon at the entire population of a city, the bomb dropped on Hiroshima was explained as something that was quite different from all the other bombs dropped by the good Allies. The event itself was treated as brand new, as an abrupt departure from ordinary devastations—as if it were not a technical extension of the fire-bombings of Tokyo, in which 80,000 were killed, and Dresden, in which 125,000 were killed; as if it were not a logical extension of the cruelty of the whole war.

Hiroshima was, despite all the earnest self-searching after the fact, the final affirmation of the ability of the best of civilizations— that of liberal, rational, enlightened Judeo-Christian society—to commit the worst of war's acts. After Hiroshima, every atrocity short of nuclear death could be accepted as ordinary. And nuclear war itself could be envisioned for extraordinary situations. On August 6, 1970, the twenty-fifth anniversary of Hiroshima, American planes, after dropping three million tons of bombs on Vietnam —more than had been dropped on Germany and Japan in

World War II—were still flying over Vietnamese rice fields and destroying peasant villages. Israelis and Egyptians were still dropping bombs on each other. Russians and Americans were still increasing their stockpiles of atomic weapons, which now equaled about fifty tons of TNT for each inhabitant of the earth.

What Hiroshima showed was that, even if Hitler was at that moment ashes, even if the corpse of Benito Mussolini had dangled upside down in front of a Milan gas station, even if plans were being made to execute Japanese generals and admirals one by one, the only possible result that could justify the death of fifty million people had not been achieved: a change in the minds of men or in the institutions that set those minds. The basic premises of a world that had given birth to fascism—the notion of "superior" beings having the right of life and death over "inferior" beings, the idea that the victory of one nation over another in war is important enough to justify any unspeakable act—were affirmed in the Hiroshima bombing.

The debate itself over the bombing proved a point. Could any truly civilized nation *debate* gas chambers for Jews or slavery for blacks? Would it matter who won the debate? The concession that these were debatable was enough. And after Hiroshima, the use of atomic bombs was debatable, the extermination of villages and cities debatable, modern wars of annihilation debatable.

In this sense, Hitler won the Second World War in the same way the South won the Civil War: the signs and symbols were surrendered—the swastika in the one case, slavery in the other—but the evils they represented remained. The most extreme positions were yielded to enable a retreat to secondary positions, where the fundamental malevolence—nationalism and war for Hitler; racism for the Confederacy—could be kept alive in more acceptable form. Or, to put it another way, despite important differences in style, in rhetoric, in the degree of cruelty—the extermination of Jews in death camps versus the incineration of Japanese and German civilians—neither side represented a clear break from the idea that war itself is an acceptable means of solving disputes over political power.

The defensive arguments for the atomic bombings of Japan are therefore more important than mere historical facts; they anticipate the whole postwar rationale for preparing for nuclear war, and the justification for the most devastating non-nuclear wars. (In Korea, more than two million were killed in a "conventional" war.) The arguments illustrate a larger question: the extent to which the behavior and thinking of the United States, as one of the victors in World War II, epitomized certain qualities that were to bring about a national crisis in postwar America.

The bomb dropped on Hiroshima turned into powder and ashes the bones and flesh of 100,000 to 150,000 (no one is yet sure) Japanese men, women, and children—in a few minutes. It left tens of thousands blinded, maimed, and poisoned by radiation, either to die soon after the explosion or to live on as its relics. The bomb dropped on Nagasaki three days later killed between 35,000 and 75,000 (here, too, no one knows exactly).

Harry Truman took office in April, 1945—four months before Hiroshima—following the sudden death of Franklin D. Roosevelt. He was then told, by Secretary of War Henry Stimson, about the Manhattan Project for the development of the atomic bomb in New Mexico. In his *Memoirs* Truman justified the dropping of the bomb, and one of his points was that an advisory committee appointed by him had carefully considered the question and approved the dropping of the bombs on populated cities. This was the Interim Committee headed by Stimson; it included Secretary of State James Byrnes, three scientists, and three other civilian officials. "It was their recommendation," Truman said, "that the bomb be used against the enemy as soon as it could be done. They recommended further that it should be used without specific warning and against a target that would clearly show its devastating strength. I had realized of course that an atomic bomb explosion would inflict damage and casualties beyond imagination. On the other hand, the scientific advisers of the committee reported: '. . . we see no acceptable alternative.' " Truman said that "the top military advisers to the President recommended its use, and when I talked to Churchill, he unhesitatingly told me that he favored the use of the atomic bomb if it might aid to end the war."

The decision apparatus on the dropping of the atomic bomb was a perfect example of that dispersed responsibility so characteristic of modern bureaucracy, where an infinite chain of policy-makers, committees, advisers, and administrators make it impossible to determine who is accountable. By comparison, the sly double action of the Inquisition—the church holding the trial, the state carrying out the execution—was primitive. Truman created the impression that expert advisers gave him no choice; the experts—Stimson's Interim Committee—claimed in turn that they depended on the advice of even greater experts, the four scientists on the Scientific Panel: J. Robert Oppenheimer, Arthur Compton, Enrico Fermi, and Ernest Lawrence.

The four scientists, it turned out later, did not know certain important facts: that the Japanese were negotiating for surrender through the Russians; that the invasion of Japan, which had been projected before the appearance of the bomb, was not scheduled until November; and that the Japanese were militarily close to total defeat. Oppenheimer, testifying after the war before the Atomic Energy Commission, said: "We didn't know beans about the military situation in Japan. We didn't know whether they could be caused to surrender by other means or whether the invasion was really inevitable. But in back of our minds was the notion that the invasion was inevitable because we had been told that." Yet, the Scientific Panel told the Interim Committee: "We see no acceptable alternative to direct military use."

Early in July Leo Szilard, who had helped persuade Roosevelt to start the atomic-bomb project, circulated a petition among his fellow atomic scientists, which sixty-seven signed, including Ralph Lapp, asking Truman to withhold dropping the bomb while other steps were taken to induce the Japanese to surrender. According to Compton, the Scientific Panel, at the request of Brigadier General Leslie Groves of the Manhattan Project, then took a secret poll among scientists at the Metallurgical Laboratory in Chicago, which had helped make the bomb. Compton, in an article published three years later, wrote of the poll: "There were a few who preferred not to use the bomb at all, but 87 per cent voted for its military use, at least if after other means were tried this was found necessary to bring surrender." But it was precisely these "other means" that were not brought forth as alternatives by the Scientific Panel. The exact figures on the poll given in Compton's article show that only 15 per cent of the 150 scientists surveyed were for full use of the bomb as dictated by military strategy. Forty-six per cent were for demonstrating the bomb in Japan in such a way as to give the Japanese a chance to surrender "before full use of the weapons," and 26 per cent were for a demonstration in the United States, with Japanese representatives present.

The key to Compton's interpretation of the polls is in what he said several years after his 1948 article:

> One of the young men who had been with us at Chicago and had transferred to Los Alamos came into my Chicago office in a state of emotional stress. He said he had heard of an effort to prevent the use of the bomb. Two years earlier I had pursuaded this young man, as he was graduating with a major in physics, to cast his lot with our project. The chances are, I had told him, that you will be able to contribute more toward winning the war in this position than if you should accept the call to the Navy that you are considering. He had heeded my advice. Now he was sorely troubled. "I have buddies who have fought through the battle of Iwo Jima. Some of them have been killed, others wounded. We've got to give these men the best weapons we can produce." Tears came to his eyes. "If one of these men should be killed because we didn't let them use the bombs, I would have failed them. I just could not make myself feel that I had done my part." Others, though less emotional, felt just as deeply.

Behind the polls, behind the panels, behind the committees, behind the advisers and the interpretations of advice, behind the decision-makers, a persistent basic belief seemed to quash all doubt about using the bomb. This view is summed up by Compton's young friend: "If *one* of these men should be killed," the failure to drop the bomb would be damnable. Tears at the thought of even *one* American death. But what of the tens of thousands, the hundreds of thousands of Japanese victims of the bomb?

The dispersion of responsibility for evil, Hiroshima proved, is as insidious in a liberal, capitalist state as in a socialist state or a Fascist state. The proliferation of advisers, committees, and polls on the use of the atomic bomb allowed for enough participants so that the entire procedure might deserve the honor of being termed "democratic." But not all the participants were equals; as the Scientific Panel's ignorance of military matters demonstrates, not all had equal access to information, which is fundamental to real democracy. Further, the liberal state in modern times, like the socialist or Fascist state, is limited in its thinking by national borders; its "democracy" excludes, without a thought, those outside its boundaries. There was no sounding of Japanese opinion on the question of the bomb; indeed, the question sounds absurd in the self-oriented atmosphere created by the nation-state. It seems absurd not just because America and Japan were at war—it would seem just as absurd to suggest that the Greeks should be polled before making a policy decision on whether or not to recognize the Papadopoulos military junta—but because the national limits of democracy are ingrained in our thinking.

Hiroshima showed us that the broad spread of participation in decisions, which presumably marks a "democratic" country like the United States, is also deceptive. Not only did some of the participants have access to information that others did not, some people in the configuration had immeasurably more power than others. Scientists who opposed the dropping of the bomb, like Szilard, who with Fermi had supervised the first controlled atomic chain reaction at the University of Chicago, did not have as powerful a voice as Groves, an army engineer who built the Pentagon and was in charge of building the bomb. The Szilard petition to the president never reached Truman; it was kept for two weeks by Groves. That Szilard's statement and those of others against the immediate use of the bomb were held up by Groves and his staff did not become known until 1963, when the files of the Manhattan Project were opened.

The petition was a forecast of the postwar atomic race:

The development of atomic power will provide the nation with new means of destruction. The atomic bombs at our disposal represent only the first step in this direction and there is almost no limit to the destructive power which will become available in the course of their future development. Thus a nation which sets the precedent of using these newly liberated forces of nature for the purposes of destruction may have to bear the responsibility of opening the door to an era of devastation on an unimaginable scale.

If after this war, a situation is allowed to develop in the world which permits rival powers to be in uncontrolled possession of these new means of destruction, the cities of the United States as well as the cities of other nations will be in continuous

danger of sudden annihilation. All the resources of the United
States, moral and material, may have to be mobilized to prevent the advent of such a world situation. Its prevention is at
present the solemn responsibility of the United States—singled
out by virtue of her lead in the field of atomic power. . . .

Hiroshima pulled all the elements of America's decision-making
process—including notions of right and wrong, nationalism, polling,
secrecy, and absence of information—toward indiscriminate violence for national goals, without any conscious conspiracy or evil
intent by individual leaders. As Groves said, after the war, it was
not a matter of Truman's making the decision to drop the bomb, but
rather of his not altering a decision already made, of keeping a commitment hardened by the expenditure of money and men over years.
Groves, who pictured Truman as "a little boy on a toboggan," said
of the president's action: "As far as I was concerned, his decision
was one of non-interference—basically, a decision not to upset the
existing plans. . . . As time went on, and as we poured more and
more money and effort into the project, the government became increasingly committed to the ultimate use of the bomb. . . ."

It was not that Americans at this point in their history lacked
humanitarian feelings. They did not. That is why they needed explanations that showed lives were *saved* by dropping the bomb. But
because the humanitarianism was vague, while the urge to national
power was sharp, the explanations needed only to be made by national leaders in order to be accepted without question or scrutiny.
Thus Truman could talk in his *Memoirs* of General George C.
Marshall telling him "it might cost half a million American lives
to force the enemy's surrender on his home grounds." (Marshall's
opposition to using the bomb without warning was not known until
the Manhattan Project papers were unlocked; they disclosed that at
a meeting in Stimson's office May 29, 1945, Marshall had urged
that the Japanese be advised about the bomb's targets so people
could be removed and only military installations obliterated.) Similarly, Byrnes could say that he had passed on to Truman the estimate of the Joint Chiefs of Staff that "our invasion would cost us a
million casualties." The president, Byrnes said, then "expressed the
opinion that, regrettable as it might be, so far as he could see, the
only reasonable conclusion was to use the bomb."

That this was not "the only reasonable conclusion" is evident on the basis of only one additional fact, which Truman knew at the time he made the decision on the bomb. He knew that the first invasion of Japan would be on the island of Kyushu, that American casualties there were expected to be about 31,000, and that the Kyushu assault was not scheduled until November—allowing three months for the wobbling nation to surrender. Japan was already beginning to press for peace through her emissary in Moscow, as Truman and the American high command also knew through the interception of Japanese cables. There was, therefore, no immediate need to use the bomb to save lives. Hanson Baldwin summarized the situation as follows:

> The atomic bomb was dropped in August. Long before that month started our forces were securely based in Okinawa, the Marianas and Iwo Jima; Germany had been defeated; our fleet had been cruising off the Japanese coast with impunity bombarding Japan; even inter-island ferries had been attacked and sunk. Bombing, which started slowly in June, 1944, from China bases and from the Marianas in November, 1944, had been increased materially in 1945, and by August, 1945, more than 16,000 tons of bombs had ravaged Japanese cities. Food was short; mines and submarines and surface vessels and planes clamped an iron blockade around the main islands; raw materials were scarce. Blockade, bombing, and unsuccessful attempts at dispersion had reduced Japanese production capacity from 20 to 60 per cent. The enemy, in a military sense, was in a hopeless strategic position by the time the Potsdam demand for unconditional surrender was made on July 26.
>
> Such, then, was the situation when we wiped out Hiroshima and Nagasaki.
>
> Need we have done it? No one can, of course, be positive, but the answer is almost certainly negative.

Confirmation of the argument against the Truman-Byrnes "only reasonable conclusion" thesis was supplied by an official government committee, the United States Strategic Bombing Survey, established by Stimson in 1944 to study the results of the aerial attacks on Germany. After Japan surrendered, the survey committee interviewed hundreds of Japanese civilian and military leaders on many matters, including the effects of the atomic bombing. Its report concludes:

Based on a detailed investigation of all the facts and supported by the testimony of the surviving Japanese leaders involved, it is the Survey's opinion that certainly prior to 31
December 1945, and in all probability prior to 1 November
1945, Japan would have surrendered even if the atomic bombs
had not been dropped, even if Russia had not entered the war,
and even if no invasion had been planned or contemplated.

Truman's and Byrnes's talk of saving lives in the future by destroying lives in the present has been the supreme defense of mass
killing in modern war. As "humanitarian" rationale, it has been the
most persuasive justification for the American depredations not only
in World War II but in Korea and Vietnam. It is a rationale epitomized best by that quintessential liberal Woodrow Wilson when
he described World War I, which cost ten million lives on the battle-
field, as a war to "bring peace and safety to all nations." In the
1950s the destruction of Korea and its people was justified by vague
speculation about preventing some possible conflagration in the future. In the 1960s the continued American bombing of Indochina,
with a million casualties, and millions more driven from their hamlets, was justified by Lyndon Johnson and Richard Nixon as necessary to prevent a larger war.

Truman's other reason for dropping the bomb—that Hiroshima
was a military base—is even more untenable than his talk of saving
"half a million" American lives or Byrnes's talk of preventing "a
million casualties." On August 9, the day on which the bomb was
dropped on Nagasaki and the Japanese were warned to surrender
or be destroyed, Truman declared: "The world will note that the
first atomic bomb was dropped on Hiroshima, a military base. That
was because we wished in this first attack to avoid, insofar as possible, the killing of civilians." In the face of the enormous toll of
civilian life in the bombing of Hiroshima, Truman's statement might
seem to be one of the most mendacious uttered by any political
leader in modern times. Not only were tens of thousands of civilians
killed in this "military" bombing, but the official report of the United
States Strategic Bombing Survey said that "Hiroshima and Nagasaki
were chosen as targets because of their concentration of activities
and population."

Truman's statement, however, had to be made because of an
important political fact: the American population needed such re-

assurance, and it depended for its information on the president and other government leaders. It is one of the ironies of modern "democracy" that the public, which is supposed to weigh the claims of its leaders, depends on its leaders for its information. In the Vietnam War, American political leaders continued to speak to the public, with considerable success, about bombing only military targets, as if American bombers pinpointed their loads on these targets with only occasional, accidental failures resulting in civilian casualties. Among themselves, military men spoke more frankly, as one naval officer did in a *Naval Review* article in 1969:

> One naturally wonders why so many bombing sorties are required in order to destroy a bridge or other pinpoint target. . . . However, with even the most sophisticated computer system, bombing by any mode remains an inherently inaccurate process, as is evident from our results to date in Vietnam. Aiming errors, boresight errors, system computational errors and bomb dispersion errors all act to degrade the accuracy of the system. Unknown winds at altitudes below the release point and the "combat degradation" factor add more errors to the process. In short, it is impossible to hit a small target with bombs except by sheer luck. Bombing has proved most efficient for area targets such as supply dumps, build-up areas, *and cities.* (My emphasis.)

Hiroshima was not an unfortunate error in an otherwise glorious war. It revealed, in concentrated form, characteristics that the United States had in common with the other belligerents—whatever their political nomenclature. The first of these is the commission and easy justification of indiscriminate violence when it serves political aims. The second is the translation of the system's basic power motives into whatever catchall ideology can mobilize the population—"socialism" for socialist states, "democracy" for capitalist states, "the master race" for Fascist states. The common denominator for all has been the survival of the system in power—whether socialist, Fascist, or capitalist. What dominated the motives for war among all the belligerents were political ends—power, privilege, expansion—rather than human ends—life, liberty, the pursuit of individual and social happiness.

This is not to deny that political ends—power, the survival and growth of particular social systems—have human consequences, and that the survival of certain social systems may be highly desirable in human terms. But the overlapping of political and human ends has been, so far, a matter of chance. And the reason why it has been a matter of chance is because no society in the world, including the American, has as yet reached the point where its political leaders are subject to the informed power of the people whose interests they claim to represent. As a result, the decisions of the leadership are motivated primarily by the aggrandizement of its own power and wealth, with token payments made in behalf of human rights when necessary to maintain control, and violations committed against such rights when they conflict with national political power.

The motivation behind dropping the bomb on Hiroshima, despite the death and suffering of the Japanese, and despite the consequences for the world of that atomic terror forecast by the Szilard petition, was political; the "humanitarian" aspect of the decision to drop the bomb is dubious. That political motive was to keep the Russians out of the Pacific war so that the United States would play the primary role in the peace settlement in Asia. The circumstantial evidence for this conclusion, Truman and Byrnes notwithstanding, is that the strictly military need to end the war did not require such instant use of the bomb. Admiral William Leahy, Truman's chief of staff; General Henry Arnold, commanding general of the air force; General Carl Spaatz, commander of the Strategic Air Force; as well as General Douglas MacArthur, commander of the Pacific theater; and General Eisenhower, did not think use of the bomb was necessary.

The political motive was first pointed out by the British scientist P. M. S. Blackett in his book *Fear, War, and the Bomb.* Blackett wondered about the rush to drop the bombs, and concluded that it was to beat the Russian entrance into the war against Japan, which was scheduled for August 8. The Russians had promised at Yalta and Potsdam to attack Japan three months after victory in Europe, which was May 8. Blackett says: "One can imagine the hurry with which the two bombs—the only two existing—were whisked across the Pacific to be dropped on Hiroshima and Nagasaki just in time, but only just, to insure that the Japanese Government surrendered to American forces alone." Blackett points to an article by Norman

Cousins and Thomas K. Finletter, in the *Saturday Review of Literature,* June 15, 1946, in which they ask why the United States did not first warn the Japanese by a demonstration of the atomic bomb. According to Cousins and Finletter, a demonstration would have taken some preparation, and there was no time for making such arrangements before the Russian invasion:

> No; any test would have been impossible if the purpose was to knock Japan out before Russia came in. . . .
> It may be argued that this decision was justified; that it was a legitimate exercise of power politics in a rough-and-tumble world, that we thereby avoided a struggle for authority in Japan similar to what we have experienced in Germany and Italy, that unless we came out of the war with a decisive balance of power over Russia, we would be in no position to checkmate Russian expansion.

Blackett adds:

> The hurried dropping of the bombs on Hiroshima and Nagasaki was a brilliant success, in that all the political objectives were fully achieved. American control of Japan is complete, and there is no struggle for authority there with Russia. . . . So we may conclude that the dropping of the atomic bombs was not so much the last military act of the second World War, as the first major operation of the cold diplomatic war with Russia now in progress.

Blackett's conclusion is supported by Gar Alperovitz's meticulous research of the Stimson papers and related documents. Alperovitz points out that at Potsdam Winston Churchill told his secretary of state for foreign affairs, Anthony Eden, that "it is quite clear that the United States do not at the present time desire Russian participation in the war." Secretary of the Navy James Forrestal, in his diary entry for July 28, 1945, said Secretary of State Byrnes "was most anxious to get the Japanese affair over with before the Russians got in." Byrnes's own memoir, *Speaking Frankly,* is full of frankness: "As for myself, I must frankly admit that in view of what we knew of Soviet actions in eastern Germany and the violations of the Yalta agreement in Poland, Rumania, and Bulgaria, I would have been satisfied had the Russians determined not to enter the war." He then adds a much franker statement: that at the January,

1945, Yalta Conference the United States agreed on Russian entrance into the war because then "the military situation had been entirely different"; now with Japan near defeat and with the United States in possession of a brand-new deadly weapon, there was no reason to give Russia the added psychological and physical power in Asia that a major share in defeating Japan would afford.

What Hiroshima suggests is not that a liberal, humane society can make a *mistake* and commit mass murder for political ends, but that it is *characteristic* for modern societies to do so. The evidence for this harsh conclusion is in the explanations for the atomic bombings, advanced by the government and generally accepted by the American public, and it is reinforced by the behavior of the United States prior to and after Hiroshima. Granted that Hitlerism was a monstrous evil, were the attitudes toward human life demonstrated by the Allies during the war, and perpetuated after the war, such as to make the difference between theirs and Hitler's worth fifty million corpses?

In World War II the two nations credited with being the most enlightened, liberal, democratic, and humane—the United States and England—agreed on the efficacy of saturation bombing of the German civilian population. As early as 1942 the British Bomber Command staff, according to the United States Strategic Bombing Survey's official report, "had a strong faith in the morale effects of bombing and thought that Germany's will to fight could be destroyed by the destruction of German cities. . . . The first thousand-bomber raids on Cologne and Essen marked the real beginning of this campaign." At the Casablanca Conference in January, 1943, this faith was affirmed as Allied strategy; larger-scale air attacks would be carried out to achieve "the destruction and dislocation of the German military, industrial and economic system and the undermining of the morale of the German people to the point where their capacity for armed resistance is fatally weakened."

It was the same strategy Mussolini had used in dropping bombs on civilians in the Ethiopian campaign and the Spanish Civil War, and it was the same strategy used in bombing civilian populations from Kiev to Coventry—all to the horrified outcries of the liberal, democratic, capitalist nations of the West. The only difference in the two strategies was that the English and American attacks on German,

French, Czechoslovakian, and other cities made the Fascist bombing of civilians seem puny.

World War II did not end, but rather sustained, the Fascist notions that war is a proper mode of solving international political problems, and that, once a nation is at war, any means whatsoever justify victory. The saturation bombing of Vietnamese villages by American bombers dropping napalm and cluster bombs, which are deliberately intended for people, not bridges or factories, and leave particularly cruel wounds, has been in accord with the thinking of the Allies in World War II—that "the morale" of the enemy could thereby be destroyed. In 1968 Daniel Ellsberg, at the time an official in the Department of Defense, publicly described this psychological objective in the strategic bombing of Vietnam. But Vietnam is only another example of the post-World War II acceptance of mass slaughter. When British historian A. J. P. Taylor was asked how he could place Hitler in the same broad context of evil shared by other nations, in view of the killing of six million Jews, he responded that those nations that had defeated Hitler were now stockpiling weapons capable of killing far more. American strategist and governmental adviser Herman Kahn suggested in his book *On Thermonuclear War* that atomic warfare did not necessarily mean the end of the human species; it might result in only thirty million American deaths.

Would thirty million American deaths be too high a price to pay for megadeaths among enemy civilians? By the end of the 1950s, the idea of nuclear war was becoming acceptable in the United States. All that people required was a reasonable provocation. In one nationwide poll conducted in 1961 among twelve hundred students, 72 per cent agreed that the United States "must be willing to run any risk of war which may be necessary to prevent the spread of Communism." During the Berlin crisis in the summer of 1961, polls taken in various American cities, including Denver and Atlanta, indicated that most people were willing to risk atomic war with the Russians over the status of West Berlin.

All societies justify the most cruel acts of war by pointing to their superior culture. Thucydides, without making the accusation himself, shows Athens guilty of such arrogance. But whatever differences there are in the qualities of nations—and one can say there were differences between Sparta and Athens, as one can say there were differences between Nazi Germany and the United States—the act of total war reduces and sometimes obliterates these differences. Even if a society waging war possesses admirable features—the welfare system of the Soviet Union, the Bill of Rights in the United States—it is a fallacy to think that war is a valid means of spreading the good features to other nations in the process of "liberating" them from the enemy. Socialism did advance after World War II, but most effectively in those countries (China, Yugoslavia, Vietnam) where the local population fought its own guerrilla warfare and was not dependent on the massive strength of the Red Army. The Soviet Union supported socialist revolutions in certain places (Czechoslovakia, Poland, Hungary, Rumania, Bulgaria), but was reluctant to support them in others (Greece, Italy, France, China) because its main concern was its own national power, not changes in social systems. The historian Gabriel Kolko writes in *The Politics of War:* "The Russians had not created the left and they ultimately could not stop it, though they might try. . . . The two genuinely popular communist parties to take power—in Yugoslavia and in China—did so over Soviet objections and advice. . . ."

Similarly, the United States supported democratic institutions in Japan and undemocratic institutions elsewhere—Greece, Turkey, the Middle East, Latin America, and South Africa. Its main priority was not the social welfare or the human rights of the local populations, but whether the existing government would support and augment the power of the United States in the world. The strange combination of regimes supported by the Soviet Union and the United States is proof enough that their major postwar aims have been to buttress their own national power. It is easy for Americans to accept this realpolitik as Soviet policy—they *know* Communist states are ruthless. It is harder to accept the same truth about themselves.

The romantic aura surrounding sociopolitical theories—the enthusiasm for "socialism," "fascism," "democracy," "liberalism"—has obscured the fact that all ideologies in modern times have been morally limited by national boundaries. This has enabled political leaders to pass off external conflicts over *national* power as conflicts between ideologies, that is, between good and evil. Nationalist feelings are played upon too, of course; in the Soviet Union it was a war for the motherland as well as for socialism, and in the United States it was a war for national identity as well as for democracy. But nationalism came into the modern world as an ambiguity—it meant the safety and unity of people formerly divided or formerly controlled, as well as the rule by national leaders over their own people, and over others.

It was not the actions of Japan, Germany, and Italy against *other* people that prompted the United States to go to war. The United States had maintained neutrality while the Fascist powers destroyed a moderately left-wing parliamentary democracy in Spain; it did not protest against the deliverance by France and England of part of Czechoslovakia to Hitler; it continued to send scrap iron to Japan even after the Japanese slaughter of Chinese in Nanking and Shanghai. True, the United States did begin to give material aid to the Allies after the fall of France in June, 1940. But it did not fully enter the conflict against the Axis until the American naval base at Pearl Harbor had been attacked by the Japanese.

It was this challenge to the national power of the United States, which meant the power and the prestige of those who held office and wealth in America, that was the main reason America entered World War II. The welfare of the American people—or of any people, as American inaction in rescuing Jewish refugees in Germany attests—was not the chief concern of America's wartime leaders. The rhetoric might deal with fighting for freedom, but the reality was expressed by Henry Luce, the multimillionaire publisher of *Time, Life,* and *Fortune;* in a *Life* editorial in 1941, entitled "The American Century," Luce said it was time "to accept wholeheartedly our duty and our opportunity as the most powerful and vital nation in the world and in consequence to exert upon the world the full impact of our influence, for such purposes as we see fit and by such means as we see fit."

This bald assertion of power as the justification for American involvement in World War II was avoided in the language of Roosevelt and other national leaders. Nonetheless, the behavior of the United States during the war was clearly in line with Luce's ideas about "the American Century," and after the war the phrase "world responsibility" became the prime euphemism for what the British had called "empire."

The economic base for America's postwar "world responsibility"—that is, for the American Empire—was laid during the war. The nation's objective was simply to move into the vacuum that would be left by the collapse of British imperial power, and to become the undisputed economic leader of the nonsocialist world. Roosevelt's Secretary of State Cordell Hull declared early in the war:

> Through international investment, capital must be made available for the sound development of latent natural resources and productive capacity in relatively undeveloped areas. . . . Leadership toward a new system of international relationships in trade and other economic affairs will devolve very largely upon the United States because of our great economic strength. We should assume this leadership, and the responsibility that goes with it, primarily for reasons of pure national self-interest.

"No other problem, without exception, received as much space in the Department of State Bulletins during 1944 and 1945 as postwar foreign economic policy," Kolko notes. Vice President Henry Wallace, who became secretary of commerce in 1945, said after a world tour in July, 1944—one month after the Allies had invaded western Europe and victory did not appear too far off: "The new frontier extends from Minneapolis . . . all the way to Central Asia." (Was Kennedy, in making "The New Frontier" the slogan for his administration in the sixties, aware of this earlier use of the phrase? His administration was also conscious of the international reach of American business.)

The war did in fact prove to be an opportunity for the United States to take control of the huge Middle East oil resources from England. Great unexploited oil reserves existed, for instance, in Saudi Arabia. Roosevelt met with its king, Ibn-Saud, after the Yalta Conference, and later recalled telling him, as a State Department summary put it, "that essentially he, the President, was a businessman. . . . and that as a businessman he would be very much interested in Arabia." Forrestal, then secretary of the navy, wrote in his diary that he had told Byrnes about the importance of spending money in Saudi Arabia to promote American over British interests. "I told him that, roughly speaking, Saudi Arabia, according to oil people in whom I had confidence, is one of the three great puddles left in the world. . . ." A Department of State Bulletin put the issue succinctly:

The desirability of control by American nationals over petroleum properties abroad is based on two considerations: (a) that the talent of the American oil industry for discovery and development is historically demonstrated so that results are likely to be better according to the extent to which American private interests participate, and (b) that other things being equal, oil controlled by United States nationals is likely to be a little more accessible to the United States for commercial uses in times of peace and for strategic purposes in times of war.

The postwar outlook for foreign trade and foreign investment of American private capital was extremely important to leaders of the government. Lloyd Gardner in his detailed study of economic foreign policy in these years, *Economic Aspects of New Deal Diplomacy,* says of Harry Hopkins, Roosevelt's chief adviser: "No conservative outdid Hopkins in championing foreign investment, and its protection." Gardner quotes Hopkins as saying in 1944:

Whoever borrows must see to it that expropriation will be impossible. The people of this country have a right to expect that kind of protection from their Government. It must be further agreed that money lent by the Government to other nations must be spent for purchases in this country. . . . And it is highly important that business and government have an early meeting of minds as to general policy governing private investments abroad.

In that same year, however, poet Archibald MacLeish, then assistant secretary of state, spoke critically of what he saw shaping up in the aftermath of a war filled with grand pronouncements about the common man:

As things are now going, the peace we will make, the peace we seem to be making, will be a peace of oil, a peace of gold, a peace of shipping, a peace, in brief, of factual situations, a peace without moral purpose or human interest, a peace of dicker and trade, about the facts of commerce, the facts of banking, the facts of transportation, which will lead us where the treaties made by dicker and trade have always led.

Throughout the war, England and the United States dickered and bickered about the shape of international trade in the postwar world, with the United States anxious to acquire equal access to the raw materials in the British-dominated nations. The rapidly expanding manufacturing apparatus of the United States would desperately require more raw materials than were to be found within its continental limits. America's "open door" policy was similar to that under William McKinley at the turn of the century, a policy of pretending to want nothing but fairness for all while being intensely concerned with American economic access to regions formerly controlled by older empires. At the Bretton Woods Conference of July, 1944, England and the United States set up the International Monetary Fund to regulate international exchanges of currency; voting in the fund, however, was to be roughly proportional to capital contributed, thereby assuring American dominance. The International Bank for Reconstruction and Development was presumably established to help reconstruct war-destroyed areas; but in its own words one of its first objectives was to "promote private foreign investment" all over the world. Herbert Feis, a State Department analyst, wrote: "The United States could not passively sanction the employment of capital raised within the United States for ends contrary to our major policies or interests. . . . Capital is a form of power."

Kolko's judgment of the Roosevelt-Hull doctrine of concern for private profit seems caustic. Yet it is supported by events:

> Nothing in this doctrine suggested a serious preoccupation with the problems of post-war reconstruction outside the context of a renovated world capitalist economy, and Washington's planning focused on its trade goals rather than emergency aid to a starving Europe that was fighting the war with far greater sacrifices than those of American businessmen, farmers, and exporters anxious over their future profit margins.

One fact supporting Kolko's view is that the United States tried to keep down the reparations taken by the Allies from the Axis powers in order that the vanquished would be more dependent on American aid and trade. In November, 1944, the State Department told the Kremlin that "reparations payments should be scheduled in such a way as to interfere as little as possible with normal trading relations."

In the public mind, the foreign-aid program that started during and continued after the war was a humanitarian venture. In the minds of the public's leaders, there were other objectives: the welfare of the business community and the political influence of the

American government in postwar Europe. As Averell Harriman, then United States ambassador to Russia, said in early 1944: "Economic assistance is one of the most effective weapons at our disposal to influence European political events in the direction we desire and to avoid the development of a sphere of influence of the Soviet Union over Eastern Europe and the Balkans."

Similar concern with power lay behind the founding of the United Nations—in spite of the sentimental hopes of those who believed, as its charter declared, that it might save the world "from the scourge of war." At the Tehran Conference in 1943, Roosevelt had proposed a postwar organization at the top of which would be the "Four Policemen"—England, the United States, the Soviet Union, and China. The policemen were to enforce law and order in the world, by military intervention if necessary. Ultimately, something approximating this plan was adopted, with France as the fifth policeman dominating the Security Council, and with each able to veto any important action by the council. It was the United States that first proposed the veto power; the Soviet Union, watching the UN take shape as an American-dominated group, later embraced the idea eagerly. Senator Arthur H. Vandenburg, top-ranking Republican on the Foreign Relations Committee, and former isolationist, who had much to do with creating Republican-Democratic unity on major issues of foreign policy, wrote about the United Nations Charter in his diary:

> The striking thing about it is that it is so conservative from a nationalist standpoint. It is based virtually on a four-power alliance. . . . This is anything but a wild-eyed internationalist dream of a world State. . . . I am deeply impressed (and surprised) to find Hull so carefully guarding our American veto in his scheme of things.

In other ways, too, the UN organization reflected the nationalist interests of the big powers rather than the dreams of freedom that many thought the war would make real. The trusteeship system—by which former Japanese and German territories were to be supervised by the big policemen—was a way of delaying independence for those territories. As for the colonies held by the West European Allies, they were to move only gradually, if at all, toward independence. Hull wrote in his *Memoirs:* "At no time did we press Britain,

France, or the Netherlands for an immediate grant of self-govern-
ment to their colonies. Our thought was that it would come after
an adequate period of years, short or long. . . ." From the American
point of view, as Kolko points out, the "concept of trusteeship
blended well with United States desires to acquire bases in the
Japanese Pacific islands and elsewhere. . . ."

World War II fell upon a world dominated by a few imperial
nations. In liberating people from the special brutality of the Axis,
they were concerned with their own influence over these people, and
with the perpetuation of the traditional prerogatives of empire. So
it was with the English in India, Burma, Malaysia, Egypt, Palestine,
East Africa; the French in Indochina, Algeria, West Africa; the
United States in the Philippines and Latin America; the Dutch in
Indonesia; the Belgians in the Congo. As for the Russians, they
created a new "socialist" empire of their own, embracing Finland,
Poland, Rumania, Hungary, Czechoslovakia, and Bulgaria. The
Western powers and the Soviet Union cooperated in maintaining
hegemony in their respective spheres.

Furthermore, the so-called advanced liberal nations not only extended their control over other peoples, they maintained economic
systems at home that labor strife and years of economic crisis after
1929 had proved both inefficient and unjust. They carried "democracy" only to the point of elections and parliamentary governments,
but without the real day-to-day participation of popular bodies in
decisions. If the war were to justify the deaths of tens of millions of
people, it would seem reasonable to expect that its end would bring
the liberation of subordinate peoples everywhere as well as critical
changes in the societies of those nations that had waged the war.
Instead, the victors continued to be much more concerned with
maintaining the status quo.

For the United States, this meant that its national political leaders,
during the war, never evinced any great interest in moving away from
prewar conceptions. American society as a whole stuck to its traditional values. What were some of these traditional values? The idea
of Manifest Destiny—the rightness of America's growing power
over other countries; white superiority in a population that was
10 per cent black; the inviolability of capitalism, the profit system,
and corporate power and privilege.

Racism, ostensibly, was one reason the war was fought—to wipe out the race doctrines of Hitler. But in the United States, the idea of white supremacy in the North and South proved greater than the libertarian enthusiasm generated by the war. The most striking and bitter irony was that black soldiers fought in the war in segregated units, in separate and unequal situations. When soldiers were jammed onto the *Queen Mary* for transport to the European combat zone, the black soldiers not only ate and slept apart, they were consigned to the lower depths of the ship, near the engine room. On the home front, similar ironies occurred. Donations of blood to the armed forces were separated by race in the Red Cross blood banks, with government approval. (A black physician, Charles Drew, had been largely responsible for the blood-bank system; he died years later for want of blood after being denied admittance to a "white" hospital.) Blacks seeking employment in defense industries encountered the hostility of trade unions, the prejudice of fellow workers accustomed to seeing blacks as domestics and laborers, the discriminatory policies of business firms, and the complacency of the government. One West Coast aviation factory spokesman said: "The Negro will be considered only as janitors and in other similar capacities. . . . Regardless of their training as aircraft workers, we will not employ them." Roosevelt did not issue Executive Order 8802 setting up a Fair Employment Practices Committee until black labor leader A. Philip Randolph in 1941 threatened a mass demonstration in Washington. The FEPC, as it turned out, was not powerful enough to enforce its own orders.

The war created the conditions—blacks moving into northern cities and into new jobs—for exposing the magnitude of racism in America; it did not stimulate eagerness in either the government or the public for dealing with the causes of racism. Poverty and overcrowdedness in the cities, bigotry in the minds of the people continued to exist. Two race riots occurred during the war. One was in Detroit in June, 1943, where white-black conflicts led to looting and property damage by blacks, police action, and the deaths of twenty-five blacks and nine whites. In Harlem that same year, blacks rioted when a white policeman tried to arrest a black woman. During the looting and burning that followed, six people died and five hundred were injured.

The war against fascism not only did little to curtail the power of customary racism in the United States, it did little to change the traditionally subordinate status of American women. One of the distinguishing features of the Fascist societies was the avowedly inferior role played by German, Italian, and Japanese women; their status was based on the recognition of men as the primary workers, and although women might work as society required—certainly in the home, and sometimes out of it—neither their status nor their wages were the same as those of men. The anti-Fascist crusade of World War II paid little attention to the similar status of American women.

In 1940 an attempt to get labor leader Sidney Hillman, a member of the National Defense Advisory Commission, to appoint a woman to his staff was rejected. "It was apparent," says a government report published in 1952 by the Women's Bureau of the United States Department of Labor, that the commission "did not favor the participation of women in the development of policy with respect to women's expanding integration into the labor market."

When the War Manpower Commission was set up in 1942 to coordinate the use of the home-front labor market, the effort of women to join the policy-making group was rebuffed—even though women were needed for the work force and were entering it in large numbers. Mary Anderson, director of the Labor Department's Women's Bureau, asked the manpower commission's Management-Labor Policy Committee to appoint one or two women as members; the proposal was turned down. Rather—on the request of the Federation of Business and Professional Women's Clubs—a women's advisory committee was appointed to the War Manpower Commission. Despite a promise from the commission's executive director that the chairman of this advisory committee would have voting membership on the Management-Labor Policy Committee, this voting right was not granted. Moreover, the chairman initially sat on the sidelines at policy meetings, and only after several sessions was she invited to join the others at the conference table.

The 1952 Women's Bureau report, commenting on the subsequent work of the advisory committee, raises the question as to why the committee "did not concern itself to a greater extent with problems pertaining to wages and hours for women workers. . . ." The report conjectures that the "Committee may have felt that it was necessary to subjugate the interests of special groups to the needs arising from the national emergency." Nevertheless, the bureau report expresses cautious criticism of this neglect of the equal-pay problem:

> . . . it is believed by some reviewers in retrospect that a good opportunity was overlooked by the Committee to gather more data and develop important information on the subject of equal pay, since this was a period in which women were entering the labor market to an unprecedented degree and performing many jobs held before almost exclusively by men. There is evidence that discriminatory pay and work opportunity practices did exist; the issue of equal pay and its corollary, equal opportunity, may have helped to create obstacles to the fullest possible integration of womanpower at a time when the labor supply was most critical. Although the Committee embodied the equality principle in all of its basic policy and program releases, there was comparatively little emphasis on equal pay.

Here was shown the traditional view that women should be reticent and avoid vigorous protest. The bureau report says "women were wary of attracting unpopular attention to issues in their own behalf," adding that "in the climate of war crisis," it was easy for men of the national administration to dismiss the requests for action as unnecessarily feminist—thereby reacting in accordance with tradition. The report also notes the existence of "doubts and uneasiness" on the War Manpower Commission "concerning what was then regarded as a developing attitude of militancy or a crusading spirit on the part of women leaders. . . ."

The conservatism of the women's advisory committee—in the face of the intransigence of the males on the War Manpower Commission—is indicated in the bureau report, which says the committee's work "should set at rest the alarm of those who wince at the memory of objectives ascribed to the early feminists as seeking to usurp the traditional masculine role or seeking special privileges which have no justification." The committee, rather, "demonstrated that it could hold to its purpose, that, in addition, it could quietly go about its business, without offending propriety or tradition, and, finally, that its purpose embraced larger objectives than special privilege."

Once again, therefore, needed changes in America's social structure—action toward achieving equal rights for women—were subordinated to the need to vanquish fascism. Once again, the fore-stalling of change meant that the evils Americans were presumably fighting to overcome would continue at home after the military campaign abroad was over.

The war brought full employment and decisively ended the Depression of the thirties, as Roosevelt's New Deal measures had failed to do. Still, it left intact the same basic features of the American economic system, which had produced, throughout American history, poverty amidst abundance, profiteering by big business, and alliances between giant corporations and the government at the expense of the American public. In *The Crucial Decade,* Eric Goldman writes:

> The America of V-J was prosperous, more prosperous than the country had been in all its three centuries of zest for good living. The boom rolled out in great fat waves, into every corner of the nation and up and down the social ladder. Factory hands, brushing the V-J confetti out of their hair, laid plans for a suburban cottage. Farmers' children were driving to college classes in glossy convertibles. California border police, checking the baggage of Okies returning east, came across wads of hundred-dollar bills.

Goldman exaggerates the reality; there were also the decaying slums, the shortage of housing, the ghettos, the unsatisfying jobs held by most people. He is closer to the truth when he talks of the "tonic sense of new possibilities" that many people felt. Yet the trouble was that even though trade unions, representing only a fifth of the working population, had become stronger during the war, the power of large corporations had increased in much greater proportion. The war accentuated the traditional American economic scheme in which business profit and power were the first considerations.

The alliance between big business and government has been a keystone in the American system ever since Alexander Hamilton's economic program was presented to Congress during the nation's first, peacetime administration. In wartime, the alliance has always become tighter, and World War II was no exception. The mobilization of production was essential to waging and winning the war, and this required the cooperation of those who controlled production—the executives of industry. Roosevelt, in one of his boldest speeches, had denounced the "economic royalists" of America, although his administrations did little to dislodge them from power. As historian Bruce Catton saw it from his post in the War Production Board: "The economic royalists, denounced and derided through two terms of the administration, had a part to play now. . . ."

In his book *The War Lords of Washington,* Catton described the process by which industrial mobilization during the war was carried on in such a way as to leave the economic status quo untouched. The United States began a drastic increase in war production after France's defeat, and according to an official report of the Office of Production Management, as early as 1941 three-fourths of the total dollar value of military supply contracts was concentrated in the hands of fifty-six corporations. A year after the fall of France, on the eve of Pearl Harbor, the auto industry had received $4 billion in war contracts; it was, however, delaying the fulfillment of those contracts while it brought out the 1942 model cars, decorated with more chromium than had ever been used before —and chromium was one of the scarcest and most critically needed materials.

Hitler might be on the rampage, but American businessmen were concerned mostly with business. Moreover, they went to Washington in large numbers as dollar-a-year men to direct industrial mobilization; they drew no salary but they maintained profitable corporate connections. The alliance between America's governmental and business leaders, in effect, was not going to permit the war to cause any basic changes in the American capitalistic system. The government's decision to employ dollar-a-year men, as Catton says,

> grew logically out of the fundamental decision that while we were fighting an all-out war we were going to fight it for limited objectives—which is to say, for purely military objectives— and it was a decision of the most far-reaching importance. In effect, even if not by conscious intent, it was a decision to cling to the status quo.
>
> For the decision to keep on using dollar-a-year men did nothing less than preserve the existing corporate control of American industry; not just because the dollar-a-year man did things on purpose to safeguard that control, but because the possible alternatives to the dollar-a-year man system were all so far-reaching.

"Far-reaching" alternatives might have included giving the rank-and-file workers in industry an important say in economic decisions, and reducing corporate profit in order to give the benefits to the nation's low-income groups. If the war was to bring about any genuine extension of democracy at home as well as abroad, it would have to do something about industrial democracy—at the point of production, where trade unions had fought for a small voice in conditions of work. (Walter Reuther, president of the United Automobile Workers, did suggest labor's participation in production decisions, and ultimately labor-management committees were set up in about five thousand factories; but they came to function as devices for increasing production and cutting down absenteeism—that is, as disciplinary groups rather than as forums for democratic decision-making.)

A report submitted shortly after the end of the war to the Senate Small Business Committee, entitled "Economic Concentration and World War II," noted that the government spent a billion dollars during the war years for scientific research in industry, aside from money spent on atomic research. The billion dollars went to two thousand corporations, with sixty-eight of them getting two-thirds of the total and the ten largest corporations in the United States getting 40 per cent of the total. Furthermore, in 90 per cent of the contracts, the patents for new developments were handed over to the contractor, who then controlled the commercial applications of the government-financed research.

Catton, recollecting his experiences in war mobilization, writes: "We had been put in the position of fighting for the preservation of the status quo; the status quo at home, where reaction had found its voice again, and, by logical extension, the status quo abroad as well. . . . The big operators who made the working decisions had decided that nothing very substantial was going to be changed." One of the most important elements of the status quo was that, despite all the self-congratulatory talk in the United States about democracy, decisions would continue to be made at the top. Whether conservatives or liberals were in power in Washington, the decision-making process and the intent of the decisions would remain the same. As Catton describes it: "Hidebound businessmen had one approach and doctrinaire New Dealers had another. Different as they were, both groups shared one controlling emotion: a distrust of the naked processes of democracy."

This distrust manifested itself in something which, much later in the postwar period, during the Vietnam War, was termed the "credibility gap"—a growing realization that the government was concealing facts, distorting truths, and just plain lying. The war-time government became obsessed with what was said and shown to the people, rather than what was actually done. It seemed easier to get the people to believe that something had been done than to do it; the most important consideration was what became known as "image." In November, 1942, a dollar-a-year consultant on the staff of the War Production Board wrote a memo entitled "Public Relations." It proposed the use of advertising men to promote public goodwill, and suggested: "The deficiencies of WPB are naturally seized upon by press and radio with more glee than its successful achievements. Methods must be found, therefore, to give true value to WPB's really significant results."

As suggested earlier, though the Allied powers won the war, anti-democratic, even totalitarian, ideas dominated the postwar world to a significant degree. One of these ideas was that dissenters from the government policy—especially in wartime—should be silenced by intimidation and, if they refused to remain silent, put in jail. On the eve of war, in 1940, Congress passed, and Roosevelt signed, the Alien Registration Act, known as the Smith Act, which made it a crime to advocate the overthrow of the government by force and violence in speech or writing, or to "affiliate" with organizations urging such action. It was therefore made a crime to advocate what Thomas Jefferson and the Founding Fathers had advocated in the Declaration of Independence. In the midst of the war to end repression, the American government prosecuted and sent to prison a number of leaders of the Socialist Workers Party (Trotskyist) for violating the Smith Act by what they wrote and said. What the government was anxious about was not the imminence of revolution—the Socialist Workers Party was tiny and weak—but the fact that the party criticized the war, questioning its objectives and arguing that its real intent was to preserve capitalism at home and imperialism abroad.

The government not only punished speechmakers and writers during World War II, it put in detention camps (some called them concentration camps) tens of thousands of Japanese-Americans, including those born in this country—not for doing anything, but simply for being of Japanese descent. The argument was that they were potential threats to the war effort. Both the Smith Act prosecutions and the removal of the Japanese families from their homes into camps were ultimately approved by the Supreme Court. In World War II, as in previous wars, civil liberties were put aside at a time when freedom of discussion about life-and-death issues was most urgently needed.

The reconsideration of World War II in this chapter does not mean to ignore the fact that the war destroyed one of the most cruel governments in history—that of the Nazis', as well as the aggressive imperialisms of Italy and Japan. It does not mean to deny that the war had tumultuous effects on many parts of the world, leading to the overthrow of old, oppressive regimes and to the development of revolutionary movements for independence and change. Nor does this reassessment mean to deny that the war created an atmosphere of hope that may have been an instrumental factor in the struggles for freedom that have taken place in many parts of the postwar world, including the United States. The intention here has been to show that these undoubted results must be weighed against other facts: that while the war enlisted the energies and sacrifices of tens of millions of ordinary people, it was directed by power elites in a few major nations. The chief concern of these elites was the expansion of their own power, the perpetuation of their own systems at home, and the extension of their domination over other parts of the world—facts as true of the United States as of the Soviet Union.

The intention has also been to show that the war not only left intact the existing systems, not only concentrated world power even more tightly than before, but that it perpetuated the identical values the victors claimed to be fighting against. The stockpiling of weapons continued; so, too, did the system of military alliances. Indiscriminate war on civilian populations as an instrument of international politics did not cease, nor did governmental control of information, the political use of racial hatred, the monopolization of wealth by a few, and the destruction of civil liberties—facts as true of the "totalitarian" Soviet Union as of the "democratic" United States.

There is no point, now, in answering the question: Should Americans therefore have fought the Nazis? Historians need to be concerned more with the future than with the past, and no crisis

appears in exactly the same form twice. But there are phenomena
that, if not exactly alike, have the same general characteristics at
different times and places in history, and to know this may help us
make the specific decisions that any particular situation requires.
One of the characteristics of war is that it always represents a
multiplicity of interests within each fighting nation. Also, the dominant values in American society may be so close to those the United
States claims the enemy represents as to call into question how much
human sacrifice can be justified for the traditional objective of military victory. As Yossarian said in *Catch-22,* when it was suggested
that his anti-military talk was "giving aid and comfort to the enemy":
"The enemy is whoever wants to get you killed, whichever side he's
on." And in a play by Bertolt Brecht, there is a frightening line of
dialogue for all people called to war: "Let's go fishing, said the
angler to the worm."

The problems America sees now in the postwar period are not
dramatic deviations from that time of idealism and victory that was
World War II; they were visible in wartime America, if anyone had
cared enough to look. In World War II, despite the rhetoric of a crusade, the United States retained its basic historical characteristics: its
arrangements of power and privilege, its traditional ideas and values.
After the war, these characteristics emerged so sharply as to bring,
in the 1960s, a national crisis, with tumultuous conflict, agonizing
disillusionment, and a movement for change beyond anything the
nation had ever seen.

2

Empire

When President Roosevelt returned to the United States from his
meeting with Marshal Joseph Stalin and Prime Minister Winston
Churchill at Yalta in early 1945, the end of the war now in sight,
he said that the Big Three Conference

> . . . ought to spell the end of the system of unilateral action,
> the exclusive alliances, the spheres of influence, the balances
> of power, and all the other expedients that had been tried for
> centuries—and had always failed.

It sounded good—as had Wilson's phrases of the same sort twenty-
five years earlier. But his words represent an exact measure of how
the postwar world failed to curb the same modes of international behavior of which both liberal and illiberal nations had been guilty for
centuries. The foreign policy of the United States after the great war
is almost a precise reproduction of what Roosevelt spoke of ending:
unilateral action (in Lebanon, Cuba, the Dominican Republic, Vietnam, Laos, Cambodia), exclusive alliances (the North Atlantic
Treaty Organization, the Southeast Asia Treaty Organization, the
Central Treaty Organization, the Rio Pact), spheres of influence
(Latin America, the Middle East, Taiwan, the Philippines, Thailand,
Japan), balances of power (war in Korea, conflict over Berlin, the
Cuban missile crisis).

The idea of intervention abroad became more acceptable during
World War II, primarily because it seemed so clearly justified by
Hitler's invasions in Europe and Japan's in Asia. After the war, it
became easier to broaden the concept of interventions, responding
not necessarily to invasions but to internal revolutions. Counter-
revolutionary intervention was not something new. Since the turn of
the century, the United States had sent armed forces into various
countries in the Caribbean area (Cuba, Haiti, the Dominican Republic, Colombia, Mexico, Nicaragua) to prevent political changes
or the inception of economic policies opposed by the American

government or American business interests. After World War II, however, the methods of intervention and the justifications for intervention became far more sophisticated. Arms were now shipped, military and police advisers were sent in as coaches, counter-revolutionaries were trained, undercover operations were conducted by the Central Intelligence Agency—all of which left overt armed intervention by United States forces a policy of last resort. The justifications for intervention were firmly supported by a whole bag of symbols related to communism: "the Red menace," "the Soviet threat," "the Chinese hordes," "the world communist conspiracy," "we 'lost' China," "the danger of internal subversion," "better dead than Red," and more. The postwar interventions were especially palatable because, while supported by conservative Republicans like Eisenhower and Nixon, most of them were carried out by the liberal Democratic administrations of Truman, Kennedy, and Johnson, and could therefore be effortlessly fitted into the liberal tradition.

It has taken a long time for a critical view of this policy of intervention to become widespread in America, perhaps because what is wrong with modern liberal society resembles Yossarian's jaundice:

> Yossarian was in the hospital with a pain in his liver that fell just short of being jaundice. If it became jaundice, they could treat it. If it didn't become jaundice and went away, they could discharge him. But this just being short of jaundice all the time confused them.

If evil were unmitigated and consistent, Americans might recognize it easily and unite to get rid of it. But the modern liberal state runs its course jaggedly, especially with regard to war and the justifications for war. About once in each century the United States has fought a war in such a fire of idealistic benevolence as to shroud in smoke not only that war's own sins and ambiguities, but all other wars and foreign policies for the next several decades. The self-glorification accompanying the Revolutionary War for independence lasted long enough to blur the expansionist sentiment behind the War of 1812 and the Mexican War. The half-truth that the Civil War was a noble war to end slavery made it easier for Americans to believe that their war with Spain over Cuba, and the accompanying seizure of Puerto Rico, the Philippines, and Hawaii, were untainted.

Similarly, World War II gave to the United States such a powerful feeling of righteousness as a fighter for "the free world" that Americans came to think fondly of themselves for the next twenty-five years as the saviors of oppressed peoples on every continent. The American interventions in Korea in the fifties and Vietnam in the sixties were both justified by the need to "stop communism." The slogan was similiar to that used in World War II. The names were switched, the language and uniform of yesterday's "enemy" were modified, but "Stopping the Russians" was an easy substitute for "Stopping the Germans"; "Stopping the Chinese" readily replaced "Stopping the Japanese." In none of these uses of substitute enemies was any attention paid to the possibility that the older, unquestionable crusade may have been at least half-questionable.

The historian Frederick Merk says that the various acts of American expansionism in the nineteenth century were "never true expressions of national spirit" but "traps into which the nation was led in 1846 and 1899, and from which it extricated itself as well as it could afterward." Historian Arthur Schlesinger, Jr., has spoken similarly of the Vietnam War. Is Vietnam another act of expansion that does not express America's normal benevolence, its real "national spirit"? Is Vietnam the momentary aberration of the modern liberal democratic capitalist state? Or are expansionism and aggression persistent characteristics of America as of other states, whether liberal or illiberal, capitalist or socialist? Is it possible that Vietnam was not a deviation but a particularly blatant manifestation of power seeking, of which the American nation is as guilty as any other nation?

The liberal tradition educates us to think well of the modern liberal state, to think that this new phenomenon in world history emerging out of the British, French, and American revolutions of the seventeenth and eighteenth centuries, with its widespread educational opportunities, its technical proficiency, its parliamentary government and constitutional rights, its long history of "reform," would be free of that accusation Plutarch made of ancient societies: "The poor go to war to fight and to die for the delights, riches, and superfluities of others." But why should the modern liberal state be different? Is not war in good part the result of a fragmented, chaotic world, in which constellations of nations vie, jostle, and kill for territory, wealth, and power? The rise of nation-states in the world, to replace city-states and feudal kingdoms, did not change this fact. Indeed, international chaos has heightened considerably through the centuries, because the newer constellations became larger, more fearsome, more aggressive, and commanded greater and greater resources than the older ones. Liberalism and nationalism both came into the world at roughly the same time in the modern epoch; and nationalism creates both the right geographical boundaries and the right spirit for barbarous warfare.

A simple economic explanation for wars need not be accepted, but it is hard to deny that the quest for profit—even in so flamboyantly religious a military venture as the Crusades—has played a considerable part in international warfare. The advent of capitalism—which, like nationalism, accompanied the birth of liberalism, and paid for the delivery—only added the fierce libido of profit seeking to other factors and thereby increased the probability of war. This is not to absolve noncapitalist countries of aggressive nationalism, but to point to the special impetus of business profit. And if liberalism is accompanied by the machine age, should it not be expected that wars would be more destructive than ever before through man's sheer technical competence for mass murder?

Also, if liberalism is accompanied by mass education and mass communication, should it not be expected that the age-old method of getting people to war by enticing slogans and symbols would be improved enormously in the modern era? The beauty of Helen of Troy seemed a sufficient symbol to justify the ten-year war between Greece and Troy. By 1914, a world war costing ten million lives required a bigger public-relations budget and a more grandiose symbol: Woodrow Wilson's war to make the world "safe for democracy." Only an insistent probing beneath the symbols might lead to the conclusion of Demokos, in Jean Giraudoux's *Tiger at the Gates,* that "war has two faces"—that of Helen, but also "the bottom of a baboon: scarlet, scaly, glazed, framed in a clotted, filthy wig."

That the modern liberal state means voting and representative government, and bills of rights and constitutions—that it grants certain formal rights to its citizens—has obscured the nature of its deportment abroad. The history of Western civilization is clear on this point: it was the liberal democratic nations of the West, with their bills of rights and voting procedures, that enslaved and exploited Asians, Africans, and Latin Americans to a degree unparalleled in world history; it was these Western liberal nations that made the imperialism of Greece and Rome seem piddling and kindly by comparison.

The democracy of liberal states, embodied in their constitutions, bills of rights, and representative assemblies, is reserved for certain constituencies at home, not for peoples abroad. For the United States this restriction is recognized explicitly in its constitutional arrangement, which denies any voice to those abroad affected by its foreign policy. Furthermore, its constitutional arrangement denies a voice to those at home on external matters. De Tocqueville saw this fact back in the 1840s when he wrote:

> We have seen that the Federal Constitution entrusts the permanent direction of the external interests of the nation to the President and the Senate, which tends in some degree to detach the general foreign policy of the Union from the control of the people. It cannot therefore be asserted with truth that the external affairs of State are conducted by the democracy.

In the 1930s, the distinction between democracy as applied to domestic affairs and democracy as applied to foreign affairs was underscored by the United States Supreme Court. The Court ruled in the Curtiss-Wright case that whereas in domestic policy the powers of government were limited by the Constitution, in foreign policy it was different:

> The broad statement that the federal government can exercise no powers except those specifically enumerated in the Constitution, and such implied powers as are necessary and proper to carry into effect the enumerated powers, is categorically true only in respect of our internal affairs. . . .

The modern liberal capitalist state, by its essential economic and political characteristics, tends to intensify and expand aggressive warfare. It justifies its actions with its own appealing rhetoric, finding successive, specific epithets for "the enemy," and decorating its objectives with talk of liberty, democracy, and, above all, peace.

American intervention in Greece was the first important postwar instance in which rhetoric was used by the United States to defend large-scale interference in another nation's internal affairs. It was accomplished without dispatching troops. It was accompanied by economic aid, and it was justified as anti-communism. Greece exemplified the *working* creed of liberal America's postwar policy: the drive to extend the national power of the United States into other parts of the world, the compulsion to make the capitalist dollar profitable and secure everywhere, the insistence that Americans know what is best for other people, and the willingness to use mass violence to accomplish these purposes. Technically, American military intervention in Greece was successful; ultimately, it was disastrous not only for democracy in Greece but for any faith in the proposition that American foreign policy was truly devoted to its own stated ideals. In many ways, Greece was the model of the later American intervention in Vietnam.

Before World War II, Greece had been a right-wing monarchy and dictatorship. Its wartime occupation by Hitler stimulated several resistance movements, the strongest of which was the left-wing EAM (National Liberation Front), a coalition dominated by Communists. With the Germans gone, civil war broke out in 1944 between the EAM and the reassembled monarchist Greek army. By the end of that year, the EAM had liberated and controlled two-thirds of Greece. It was popular, with a membership of two million in a population of seven million, and it probably would have won— if the British army had not moved in with 75,000 men. (British political analyst Hugh Seton-Watson said afterward that "without British action, Greece would have had the same regime as Yugoslavia.") Two British divisions were flown in by American planes piloted by Americans. An American observer, newsman Howard K. Smith, wrote later:

> One would prefer to be generous to the British and say that they attempted to bolster what middle-way and democratic forces there were in order to create compromise and a basis for democracy. Unfortunately, there seems little evidence to support

this, and one is forced to conclude that the British were determined to break EAM and install in power the discredited monarchy and its blindly vengeful rightist supporters.

Churchill's instructions to General Ronald Scobie, head of the British forces in Greece, were: "Do not . . . hesitate to act as if you were in a conquered city where a local rebellion is in progress."

The EAM was defeated in a few months. Elections were held in early 1946, which were boycotted by the left, and, to no one's surprise, the monarchists won. Smith said he was told by peasants in a village outside Athens shortly after the election that they were threatened with having the village burned down if the monarchists did not get a majority. During this early postwar period of British control, a right-wing dictatorship came to power in Athens. The elected leadership of the trade unions was replaced by government-appointed rightists; dissident university professors and government officials were fired; opposition leaders were put in jail; and corruption spread as the war-ravaged nation became desperate for food. Under the government of Constantine Tsaldaris, half the expenditures were for the army and the police; only 6 per cent for reconstruction.

In the face of imminent arrest, many former leaders of the ELAS (National Popular Liberation Army, the military arm of the EAM) went into the hills and began arming small guerrilla groups. By the fall of 1946, it had 6,000 men under arms, and was carrying on hit-and-run raids in northern Greece. With international criticism becoming increasingly sharp, the British asked Premier Tsaldaris to liberalize his oppressive regime; instead, he eliminated all opposition parties from the cabinet. The civil war intensified. The ELAS rebels received small arms from Yugoslavia, used Albanian and Yugoslavian territory as sanctuaries, stepped up their raids, and executed hostages. As the jailing and murder of the opposition by the government increased, the rebel forces rose to 17,000 fighters, 50,000 active supporters, and perhaps 250,000 sympathizers.

At this point, with the rebels gaining more and more support and the government having more and more difficulty in putting them down, the British informed the United States State Department that they could no longer continue either economic or military aid to the Greek government. One State Department career man, Joseph

Jones of the policy planning staff, later commented that "Great Britain had within the hour handed the job of world leadership, with all its burdens and all its glory, to the United States."

It was the administration of Harry Truman, heir to New Deal liberalism, that now acted to save the rightist Tsaldaris government of Greece from revolution. The State Department career officers were eager to take over from Britain, and the high-ranking military men agreed that the Greek rebels must be put down. Truman's popularity was at a record low in the country, and his Democratic party had just lost the 1946 congressional elections to an overwhelming Republican majority. It has been argued that the domestic political situation was a factor in Truman's decision to move. Whether or not it was, he called congressional leaders to the White House to sound them out on the idea of military and economic aid to Greece, and it was Under Secretary of State Dean Acheson who supplied the most persuasive argument: stopping world communism. Jones recorded Acheson's argument as follows:

> Only two great powers remained in the world, the United States and the Soviet Union. We had arrived at a situation unparalleled since ancient times. Not since Rome and Carthage had there been such a polarization of power on this earth. . . . It was clear that the Soviet Union was aggressive and expanding. For the United States to take steps to strengthen countries threatened with Soviet aggression or Communist subversion was to protect the security of the United States.

The argument carried, and the decision was made to give aid to Greece. As was to become a common pattern in such situations, a request for such aid was drafted in Washington by the State Department and suggested to the Greek government, which then made a formal request.

The Truman Doctrine was the name later attached to the speech Truman made before Congress, March 12, 1947, in which he asked for $400 million in military and economic aid to Greece and Turkey:

> The very existence of the Greek state is today threatened by the terrorist activities of several thousand armed men, led by Communists, who defy the Government's authority. . . . Meanwhile, the Greek Government is unable to cope with the situation. . . .

At the present moment in world history nearly every nation must choose between alternative ways of life. . . .

One way of life is based upon the will of the majority, and is distinguished by free institutions, representative government, free elections, guarantees of individual liberty, freedom of speech and religion, and freedom from political oppression.

The second way of life is based upon the will of a minority forcibly imposed upon the majority. It relies upon terror and oppression, a controlled press and radio, fixed elections, and the suppression of personal freedoms.

I believe that it must be the policy of the United States to support free peoples who are resisting attempted subjugation by armed minorities or by outside pressures.

I believe that we must assist free peoples to work out their own destinies in their own way.

I believe that our help should be primarily through economic and financial aid, which is essential to economic stability and orderly political processes. . . .

If Greece should fall under the control of an armed minority, the effect upon its neighbor, Turkey, would be immediate and serious. Confusion and disorder might well spread throughout the entire Middle East. . . .

There were at least three questionable elements in Truman's speech. First, his description of the "second way of life . . . terror and oppression, a controlled press and radio, fixed elections, and the suppression of personal freedoms," while it might conceivably fit some imagined future left-wing regime in Greece, at that time most accurately described the right-wing government for which Truman was asking support. Second, the connection between the Greek rebellion and the "outside pressures" of world communism ran counter to one basic fact: although the Greek rebels were getting some useful aid from Yugoslavia, their manpower was Greek; internal conditions and indigenous support made it a Greek affair. The "outside pressures" were largely British; they were about to become American.

Back in the fall of 1944, in Moscow, Churchill and Stalin had agreed on the division of Eastern Europe into spheres of influence; Rumania, Poland, and Bulgaria would be in the Soviet sphere, and Greece in the British. When the British were suppressing the ELAS rebellion in 1945, the Russians sat by. They studiously refrained from giving aid to the insurgents. Churchill wrote later that Stalin had "adhered strictly and faithfully" to their agreement to give the British a free hand in Greece. Historian and biographer Isaac Deutscher has pointed out that in 1948 the Soviet Union expelled Yugoslavia from the Comintern and President Tito closed the border to the Greek rebels. Tito's aide, Milovan Djilas, reported that in early 1948 Stalin told the Yugoslavs that "the uprising in Greece must be stopped, and as quickly as possible," that it did not have a chance of succeeding. The "international communism" excuse for American intervention ignored the fact that Soviet communism was as nationalistic as American communism, and that like the United States, the Soviet Union preferred revolutions it could control.

The third questionable element hidden by the moralistic language of the Truman Doctrine was that the traditional interests of political power and economic profit were involved in the American decision to keep a rightist government in power in Greece. Presidential adviser Clark Clifford had suggested that Truman's speech to Congress should also say that "continued chaos in other countries and pressure exerted upon them from without would mean the end of free enterprise and democracy in those countries and that the disappearance of free enterprise in other nations would threaten our economy and our democracy." But Acheson decided this language, with its disguised reference to saving capitalism, might embarrass the new Labor government of Britain. Also kept out of the message was another Clifford suggestion that Truman refer to "the great natural resources of the Middle East." What Clifford had in mind here, of course, was oil. When Field Marshal Sir Bernard Montgomery of Britain, in the fall of 1946, asked the U.S. Chiefs of Staff how important Middle East oil was to them, "their immediate and unanimous answer was—vital." In his book *Greece and the Great Powers,* Stephen Xydis concludes that at least one motive in the Greek intervention was to "contribute to the preservation of American oil concessions " in the Middle East.

It did not take long, once Congress rubber-stamped the Truman Doctrine, for American military equipment to begin pouring into Greece: 74,000 tons was sent in during the last five months of 1947, including artillery, dive bombers, and stocks of napalm. Other factors also worked against the rebels. The Tito-Soviet split of 1948 led to factionalism among the Greek Communists, poor military tactics, and ugly, desperate measures against villagers whose support they needed. A group of 250 U.S. Army officers, headed by General James Van Fleet, advised the Greek army in the field; Van Fleet also initiated a policy of removing thousands of people from their homes in the countryside to try to isolate the guerrillas. The final blow to the rebel cause came when Yugoslavia closed its border in the summer of 1949. A few months later they gave up—two years after the first American guns had arrived. What was won for Greece by American intervention? Richard Barnet summed it up in his book *Intervention and Revolution:*

> For the next twenty years the Greeks struggled to solve the staggering economic and social problems that had led to the bloody civil war. Despite massive U.S. economic and military aid the Greek government has remained unable to feed its own population. . . . Despite improvement in the economy, the same basic conditions of the forties—widespread poverty, illiteracy, shortage of foreign exchange, repressive and ineffective government—remained in the sixties, leading to a series of constitutional crises and, most recently, to a particularly brutal and backward military dictatorship. . . .
>
> From 1944 to 1964 the United States gave Greece almost four billion dollars, of which a little over two billion dollars was in military aid. . . . Although private U.S. capital had flowed into Greece from such U.S. companies as Esso, Reynolds Metal, Dow Chemical, and Chrysler, and large sections of the economy are effectively controlled by U.S. capital, the financial health of the country remains precarious.

Twenty years after the first American guns arrived to fight against "the suppression of personal freedoms" in Greece, a military dictatorship, this time under the leadership of Colonel George Papadopoulos, took over the country. Roy C. Macridis, a political scientist and specialist in European politics, wrote shortly after the 1967 coup:

> Last Sunday, May 28, free elections were scheduled for Greece. Instead, a military junta is in power, thousands of political prisoners are in jail, the newspapers are under control, and local representative institutions are set aside. . . .

Two years later, an American journalist interviewed two hundred persons, some still in Athens, others who had escaped, who told sickening stories of torture in Greek prisons. Special military courts sentenced hundreds of Greeks to years in jail for being guilty of distributing leaflets stamped LONG LIVE DEMOCRACY.

On September 19, 1970, the *New York Times* reported that the United States, which was supposed to have diminished its aid to the Papadopoulos regime in the midst of the horror stories that came out of Greece, was now resuming full-scale military aid. In return, Greece was to institute a "liberalization" program, ending the special military courts. The military junta, however, would maintain the state of siege in order that security cases could still be referred to military courts. Two weeks after the *Times* report appeared, the release of formerly secret testimony before the Senate Foreign Relations Committee by State and Defense department officials disclosed that the United States had sent $168 million worth of military aid to Greece during those three years in which the government had publicly announced a selective arms embargo against that country's military rulers. The committee transcript includes the following exchange between Robert J. Pranger, deputy assistant secretary of defense, and Senator J. William Fulbright, committee chairman:

> FULBRIGHT: Do we supply the Greeks with ammunition?
> PRANGER: Yes, sir. . . .
> FULBRIGHT: You have no practical way to prevent the Greek forces from using your ammunition for internal security purposes, have you?
> PRANGER: Sir, as far as the ammunition which we are supplying today, no.
> FULBRIGHT: In other words, we can supply the bullets which they used to kill their own citizens, can they not? I mean, we do.
> PRANGER: Well, sir, that is not our intention.

The statement *"that is not our intention"* tells the story of modern civilization, which has so institutionalized cruelty that it takes place without "intention." It also tells the story of American foreign policy after World War II. Behind a liberal language so persuasive it often gulled its users lay the working creed of the United States: the drive to extend its power—national, economic, and political—into other parts of the world, and the use of "such means" as it deemed "fit" to do it successfully. For the public, American aggressiveness was rhetorically disguised as "stopping communism" or "saving the free world."

What this verbal device concealed was that Americans came to use the word "communism" to represent a wide variety of situations: actual Communist invasions, such as those by Soviet Russia in Hungary and Czechoslovakia; civil wars between Communist and non-Communist areas, as in Korea; popular Communist uprisings, as in China and Vietnam; and left-liberal movements, as in Guatemala and the Dominican Republic. Americans have used the phrase "the free world" in connection with a few western democracies, but they have also applied it to dozens of military dictatorships in Europe, Asia, and Latin America.

This same contradictory relationship between promise and performance was to characterize American foreign policy in the twenty years following intervention in Greece. And this was true—with slight variations in language, or in tactics—whether the administration in Washington was Republican or Democratic, conservative or liberal. The parallel between American intervention in Greece and American intervention twenty years later in Vietnam is striking. Although the Greek intervention was on a much smaller scale, it had begun with a small group of "advisers" and military aid to prop up an unpopular, corrupt, dictatorial government. In Greece the United States took over the imperial burden from the British, in Vietnam from the French. In both cases, the justification was based on the need to suppress a Communist-led rebellion, one reason being that if Red uprisings succeeded in one country, they would trigger revolts in others.

The policy of the United States toward China is another example of the breach between the promises of its rhetoric and the results of its working creed. In his memoirs just after the war, Secretary of State Byrnes said:

> If we regard Europe as the tinderbox of possible world conflagration, we must look upon Asia as a great smoldering fire. There, civilization faces the task of bringing a huge mass of humanity, the majority of the people on this earth, from the Middle Ages into the era of atomic energy.

Through the rhetoric of a secretary of state, America is here citing the usual task of Western imperialism in its more paternalistic mood: to "civilize" backward peoples, in this case Asians. No doubt the secretary missed—as the survivors of Hiroshima would not—the tragic irony of mentioning the need to bring Asia "into the era of atomic energy," but his statement exemplifies the kind of official justification used to support the tyrannical regime of Chiang Kai-shek while "stopping communism" at the same time.

China after World War II endured four years of civil war between the Nationalist government of the Kuomintang party, headed by Chiang Kai-shek, and the Communist forces spread out from the north central province of Shensi, led by Mao Tse-tung and Chou En-lai. At the end of 1945, Truman sent General Marshall to China to negotiate peace between the Communists and the Kuomintang, and to try to establish a coalition government under Chiang Kai-shek. The mission did not succeed; distrust between the two forces was too deep. Moreover, as Kenneth Latourette, an authority on Far Eastern history, put it in explaining the subsequent victory of the Communists: "A major reason for the Nationalist defeat was that the Kuomintang, the national government run by it, and Chiang Kai-shek had completely lost the confidence of the Chinese people."

The State Department White Paper on China, issued at the time of the Communist victory in 1949, declared:

> The historic policy of the United States of friendship and aid toward the people of China was, however, maintained in both peace and war. Since V-J Day, the United States Government has authorized aid to Nationalist China in the form of grants and credits totaling approximately 2 billion dollars. . . . In addition . . . the United States Government has sold the Chinese Government large quantities of military and civilian war surplus property with a total procurement cost of over a billion dollars. . . .

Further along, the White Paper also describes the Nationalist government as "a Government which had lost the confidence of its own troops and its own people." Thus, American "friendship and aid toward the people of China" was translated into several billion dollars for the Nationalist government of China, which, according to official documentation, was not supported by the people of China. The reason for the nonsupport was that the Kuomintang was brutal, corrupt, inefficient, and dictatorial. It was dominated by the rich and the reactionary, and it was subservient to Western power—all those factors that the Chinese Nationalists themselves had hoped to eradicate after the 1911 revolution.

The "historic policy" of the United States had not been one of "friendship and aid to the people of China," as the White Paper asserted. Long before the Communists came to power, American policy was based not only on strategic interests but on commercial interests, as the treaty arrangements following the Opium War and the "Open Door" policy testify. What was abhorrent to the United States about the Communists running China was not that intellectual and political freedom were limited—this was certainly true under Chiang—but that a powerful independent China, which the Communists were creating, would lend itself neither to the West's traditional commercial dealings with the huge China market nor to political and military control.

After Mao's victory, United States policy toward China remained consistent through five administrations. Its principal elements were: maintenance of a military base on Taiwan, to which Chiang had fled and where he now planted a dictatorship over the eight million Taiwanese; pressure on smaller states in the United Nations to keep Chiang in China's seat on the Security Council and to keep Communist China out of it; refusal to give diplomatic recognition or economic aid to Peking; construction of a ring of military bases around China, with American troops, planes, and weapons, in Korea, Japan, Okinawa, the Philippines, Taiwan, South Vietnam, and Thailand.

America's China policy was not conducted in a vacuum. All major episodes of American foreign policy in the postwar period show the same fanatical anti-communism. This obsession was due less to ideological-moral disagreement than to the fact that Communist nations posed an especially tough obstacle to the normal drives of liberal nationalism: for expansion, for paternalism, for maximum profit. These nationalist ambitions have always been presented to the public in the guise of protecting national security or promoting peace or defending other nations against aggression or helping backward nations to modernize—justifiable objectives that have lent moral passion to the most ferocious technology of death ever devised. In the actual practice of American policy, this combination of moralism and technology has supported a willingness to use massive violence, to break the peace, to exhaust the national resources, and, finally, to threaten the internal cohesion of the United States itself—in other words, to have effects totally different from those promised.

The remainder of this chapter summarizes some of the major aspects of American foreign policy in the postwar period. They are discussed under the general headings of Intervention, Economic Penetration, Militarization, Vietnam. All are discussed in the light of the discrepancy between liberal rhetoric and liberal nationalism in action.

I. INTERVENTION

A. Korea, 1950–1953

On June 25, 1950, the armies of Communist North Korea crossed the 38th parallel into South Korea; the next day, President Truman, presumably to help the South Koreans defend themselves against the attack, announced the use of American air and sea forces in Korea. His announcement was made in response to a UN resolution asking the invaders to withdraw to the 38th parallel. "A return to the rule of force in international affairs would have far-reaching effects," said Truman. "The United States will continue to uphold the rule of law."

If the rule of law was represented by the United Nations, American military action stretched it to the breaking point. The UN resolution on Korea had recommended "such assistance to the Republic of Korea as may be necessary to repel the armed attack and to restore peace and security in the area." The United States, with General MacArthur in command of a largely American "United Nations" force, went further; after pushing the North Koreans back across the 38th parallel, it moved all the way up through North Korea to the Yalu River, on the border of China—an action that provoked the Chinese into entering the war. They swept southward until the war was stalemated at the 38th parallel.

To call American intervention a blow to "the rule of force" must have seemed bitterly ironic to the Koreans, North and South; in three years of war, American bombers reduced Korea to a desolate, corpse-strewn shambles, with perhaps two million Koreans, North and South, dead. Napalm was used, and a BBC correspondent described the result:

> In front of us a curious figure was standing, a little crouched, legs straddled, arms held out from his sides. He had no eyes, and the whole of his body, nearly all of which was visible through tatters of burnt rags, was covered with a hard black crust speckled with yellow pus . . . He had to stand because he was no longer covered with a skin, but with a crust-like crackling which broke easily . . . I thought of the hundreds of villages reduced to ash which I personally had seen and realized the sort of casualty list which must be mounting up along the Korean front.

The war was a catastrophe for the Korean people. America's intervention illustrated, once again, the common moral failure of international diplomacy, as true of liberal capitalist nations as of others: that transgressions—certain transgressions, of course—must be punished, even if it means supporting an undemocratic regime, and even if the punishment falls with devastating effect on the original victims of the transgression. The effect of intervention in Korea was not rectification but destruction.

Not only was it ironic that America should castigate "force," it was deceitful that it should talk as the champion opponent of aggression. Other cases of aggression in the world did not prompt such a drastic response from the United States. When Arab states invaded Israel in 1948, the United States did not mobilize the UN and its own armed forces for intervention. The fact was that in Korea the United States had a political stake: the dictatorial regime in the south of Syngman Rhee was an American client. Furthermore, America wanted South Korea as a military base on the Asian mainland. It had an eye on Communist China, and it was still operating on the balance-of-power concept that Roosevelt in 1945 thought was outmoded.

Truman's statement of June 27, 1950, announcing the use of American military force to help South Korea, simultaneously ordered the Seventh Fleet to defend the Nationalist Chinese government on Taiwan. It also directed more military aid to the French forces fighting against the Communist Viet Minh insurgents in Indochina. When the long-range effects of the Korean intervention are considered, on the Korean nation and its people, on Sino-American relations (postwar treaties had assumed Taiwan belonged to China), and on the American attitude toward the French imperialists in Indochina, it is difficult to see how the declared aim of the intervention—to bring peace and stability to Asia—was furthered.

B. Guatemala, 1954

What Truman had said at the start of the Korean intervention about the United States upholding "the rule of law" as opposed to the "rule of force" was utterly contradicted in 1954 by the American overthrow, through force, of the legally elected reformist government of Guatemala. On June 18 an invasion force of mercenaries, trained by the United States Central Intelligence Agency at secret bases in Honduras and Nicaragua and supported by four American P-47 Thunderbolts flown by American pilots, invaded Guatemala from Honduras, and put into power Colonel Carlos Castillo Armas, who at one time had received military training at Fort Leavenworth, Kansas.

The Guatemalan intervention was a violation of the United Nations Charter, which in Article 2, Section 4, says: "All members shall refrain in their international relations from the threat or use of force against the territorial integrity or political independence of any state. . . ." According to the 1968 edition of the *Manual of International Law,* sponsored by the Carnegie Endowment for International Peace, "an indirect involvement of a government in an armed venture outside its territory constitutes a use of force and is governed by the same law as is applicable to open hostilities directed against another state." When an attempt was made to put the Guatemalan invasion on the agenda of the UN Security Council, the United States delegate to the UN, Eisenhower appointee Henry Cabot Lodge, who was then president of the Security Council, kept it off, arguing that it was an internal affair and not within the jurisdiction of the UN.

The rationale for the Guatemalan invasion was supplied by President Eisenhower. "There was a time," he said, "when we had a very desperate situation, or we thought it was at least, in Central America, and we had to get rid of a Communist government that had taken over." But the government the United States got rid of was the most democratic Guatemala had ever had. Communist influence in it was small—only four of the fifty-six seats in Congress were held by Communists, and no member of the presidential cabinet was a Communist—and throughout the country no more than four thousand persons, in a population of three and a half million, were Communists. Communists did hold important posts in the land-reform and education programs. It may be, however, that what really irked the United States was not communism but the actions of the government of Jacobo Arbenz against the United Fruit Company and American oil interests. In one region of Guatemala, Arbenz had expropriated 234,000 acres of uncultivated land owned by United Fruit; he offered compensation for the unused land, but the company turned it down, terming the offer "unacceptable." Meanwhile, Arbenz began action to expropriate 173,000 acres of the company's land in another area.

The ten years of reformist government in Guatemala that preceded the American intervention were described as follows by Ronald Schneider in his study *Communism in Guatemala, 1944–1954:*

> While Guatemalans in general had enjoyed more freedom during the 1944–54 period than ever before, the working class had particular reason to feel loyal to the revolutionary regime. For the first time in Guatemalan history labor enjoyed the right to organize freely, bargain collectively and strike. Never before had they felt free to speak out openly and voice their feelings without restraint, much less be confident of gaining a sympathetic hearing from the government. The lower classes enjoyed the novelty of living in a new atmosphere, officially fostered, in which they were treated with a measure of respect and dignity.

Castillo Armas arrived in late June in American Ambassador John Peurifoy's embassy plane to take over the government; the next day Secretary of State John Foster Dulles said the situation was "being cured by the Guatemalans themselves."

Castillo Armas received ninety million dollars of aid from the

United States in the next two years, compared with six hundred thousand dollars given to Guatemala in the previous decade. He returned the land to United Fruit, and abolished the tax on interest and dividends to foreign investors. He jailed thousands of political critics, eliminated the secret ballot, ruled by decree, and, after three years in power, was assassinated. It would be hard to find a more clear-cut example of where liberal rhetoric about "the rule of law," "opposing aggression," and "stopping communism" concealed the reality, in which the protection of corporate profits and a "sphere of influence" made an absurdity of the liberal promise.

And in 1961 Guatemala itself was used as a base for an American-planned invasion of a real Communist country: Cuba.

C. Lebanon, 1958

Guatemala was not an exception; the policy of armed American intervention abroad was maintained by the Eisenhower administration. On July 14, 1958, thirty-five hundred marines landed in Lebanon. Thousands more followed. The year before, Eisenhower had secured from Congress a joint resolution giving the president authority to use armed force "to secure and protect the territorial integrity and political independence of such nations, requesting such aid, against overt armed aggression from any nation controlled by international communism." This proposition became known as the Eisenhower Doctrine. In broaching it to congressional leaders on New Year's Day, 1957, Eisenhower said: "The existing vacuum in the Middle East must be filled by the United States before it is filled by Russia."

Though the authorization to use armed force against communistic armed aggression would not seem to pertain to internal political strife, the doctrine was used to put down political agitation in Lebanon. Lebanon was the one country in the Middle East which, after the doctrine went into effect, specifically agreed with the United States to accept economic and military aid—and further assistance in case of attack by "international communism."

In his 1952 election campaign, Lebanese President Camille Chamoun had received the effective assistance of the Central Intelligence Agency of the United States. Early in 1958, Egypt and

Syria, and tiny Yemen, banded together as the clearly anti-Western United Arab Republic, with Egypt's dictator Gamal Abdel Nasser as its head. The creation of the U.A.R. stimulated anti-Chamoun, anti-American activity in Lebanon, and some arms were smuggled into the country from Egypt. Rioting broke out, American arms were airlifted to Chamoun's army, and an incipient civil war appeared to be under way. Chamoun then asked for American troops; Eisenhower, invoking his new doctrine, dispatched within the next few days seven thousand marines to the former French mandate, a force equal to the size of the entire Lebanese army.

Communist strength in Lebanon was meager, and it remained an insignificant factor throughout those critical days. Yet in explaining his unilateral action, Eisenhower compared the Mideast situation to Communist threats in Greece, Czechoslovakia, China, Korea, and Indochina. Here, again, the liberal rhetoric was at work: armed intervention was justified as "stopping communism," whereas the real reason for the U.S. invasion of Lebanon was to protect one of America's most vital economic interests: oil.

The "vacuum" Eisenhower had told congressmen the United States must fill had been created by the postwar withdrawal of British power from the eastern Mediterranean. In 1955 America had secured the signatures of Great Britain, Iran, Iraq, Pakistan, and Turkey to the Baghdad Pact, which was designed to stem Egyptian and Soviet influence in the Mideast. The pact, however, had not done much to curb the growing influence of either. Nasser nationalized the Suez Canal in 1956 and appeared to be stronger than ever after surviving the abortive British-French-Israeli armed counterattack. The formation of the U.A.R. and the sudden overthrow of King Faisal's feudal regime in Iraq in July, 1958, posed the greatest threat yet to the western power's rich oil supply. The United States was far less concerned with propping up a questionable democratic government in Beirut than with seeing to it that Mideast oil sources remained available. The coup in Iraq led immediately to the presence of American marines in Lebanon—and British paratroopers in Jordan.

Eisenhower sent Robert Murphy, a veteran State Department diplomat, to negotiate with the various factions in Lebanon. He arranged for a successor to Chamoun—General Fuad Chebab—

who was acceptable to the Lebanese Parliament. With Chebab's "election," fighting in the country died down, and the American marines were withdrawn. Lebanon was a minor intervention as U.S. interventions go, but it was evidence that Republicans would never lag behind Democrats in asserting American power anywhere in the world.

D. Cuba, 1961

Interference by the United States in the affairs of Cuba has always followed the special method America uses for handling its Latin American empire. Outright annexation is renounced. Instead, America offers its southern neighbors paternal protection from others in return for: the establishment of American military bases; American control of key sections of their economy; American support of governments—even those dealing ruthlessly with their own people —that demonstrate concern for American military and economic interests; and, when necessary, American troops.

This approach began with the "liberation" of Cuba from Spain at the turn of the century. At the conclusion of the Spanish-American War, the United States insisted that Cuba accept an agreement for American naval bases on the island, and for the right of Americans to send troops into Cuba whenever the United States considered it necessary to maintain "a government adequate for the protection of life, property, and individual liberty." This was the Platt Amendment to a 1901 army appropriations bill.

Under Franklin D. Roosevelt's "Good Neighbor" policy, the Platt Amendment was repealed, but the naval base at Guantánamo remained, and United States business interests continued to dominate the Cuban economy. By the 1950s, U.S. citizens controlled from 80 to 100 per cent of Cuba's utilities, mines, cattle ranches, and oil refineries. They also controlled 40 per cent of the sugar industry and 50 per cent of the public railways. From 1950 to 1960, the balance of payments between Cuba and the United States added up to a billion dollars—in America's favor. In 1952 Fulgencio Batista, a military dictator whose power in Cuba, either direct or through puppets, went back to the early 1930s, again took over the government in a coup d'etat. For the next seven years Batista continued to serve foreign economic interests while jailing political opposition and using terror and torture to maintain his rule. During this period, the United States sent military missions to Cuba to advise the Batista regime, and gave it substantial military aid.

It was the corruption, the cruelty, and the unpopularity of the Batista government, more than the military strength of Fidel Castro's revolutionary movement, that accounted for Batista's overthrow in 1959. Castro had been imprisoned after leading an unsuccessful attack July 26, 1953, on the Moncado army barracks in Santiago. Released, he went to Mexico to study guerrilla tactics, met Argentine revolutionary Ernesto ("Che") Guevara, and returned to Cuba in December, 1956, with a small group of men, most of whom were either captured or shot. Castro spent the next two years with a handful of guerrillas in the Sierra Maestra jungles, withstanding the onslaught of Batista forces—who were using planes and tanks supplied by the United States. In 1958, Castro's band came out of the mountains, marched across the country from Oriente Province to Havana, and the Batista government collapsed on New Year's Day, 1959.

Castro, in 1957, discussed Cuba and the program of his 26 of July Movement in a Costa Rican publication, *Cuba Libre:*

> Throughout the country, 200,000 rural families are without a square foot of land on which they can support themselves; yet almost ten million acres of untouched arable land remain in the hands of powerful interests. . . . There are about 200,000 huts and shacks in Cuba; 400,000 rural and urban families live crowded in slums without the barest necessities of sanitation. . . . 2,800,000 of our rural and suburban population are without electricity. . . . Only death frees people from such poverty, and in this solution, the state cooperates.

Castro pointed to the natural wealth of Cuba:

> There is no reason, then, why misery should exist among its present inhabitants. The markets should be full of produce; the pantries of our homes should be well-stocked; every hand should be industriously at work. No, this is not inconceivable. What is inconceivable is that there should be men who will accept hunger while there is a square foot of land not sowed; what is inconceivable is that 30 per cent of our rural folk cannot sign their names and that 90 per cent know nothing of

Cuban history; what is inconceivable is that the majority of
our rural families live in conditions worse than those of the
Indians whom Columbus found when he discovered "the most
beautiful land that human eyes have seen."

Castro, once in power, moved quickly to invest money in housing,
schools, and health. Rents and electric power rates were cut, land
was distributed to landless farmers under the Agrarian Reform Law,
and the government took over more than a million acres from three
large U.S. companies.

Relations between Cuba and the United States began to deteriorate soon after January 1, 1959. Castro at that time was not a Communist, and the relations between his revolutionary movement and
the Cuban Communist Party were, by turns, harmonious and trou-
blesome. American foreign policy in the East-West cold war, however, had never made fine distinctions among revolutionaries. Castro
needed a loan to finance his reforms, but he returned from his dramatic visit to the United States in April, 1959, empty-handed.

Just why he did not receive American aid is not clear; it seems
plausible that Castro, being proud, did not ask for American money;
it is equally plausible that the United States was not eager to finance
a program such as Castro's. Cuba's attempt to obtain a loan from
the American-dominated International Monetary Fund failed because the Castro government would not accept the IMF's "stabili-
zation" conditions, conditions that would have impeded implemen-
tation of the revolutionary program.

In October, 1959, the United States officially objected to Cuba's
land-reform law under which property owned by American businessmen had been expropriated. A few months later Cuba signed a
trade pact with the Soviet Union. From that point on, U.S.-Cuban
relations steadily worsened. American-owned oil companies in Cuba
refused to refine Soviet crude oil, and Castro retaliated by seizing
them. In July, 1960, the United States cut the quota of sugar it had
been buying from Cuba, a crucial blow to Cuba's trade needs; within
days the Soviet Union agreed to buy all the seven hundred thousand
tons of sugar that America had slashed from its quota. Quite obviously, revolutionary Cuba and the United States were not "good
neighbors."

In March of 1960, only fifteen months after Castro had come to power, President Eisenhower secretly authorized the Central Intelligence Agency to arm and train Cuban exiles in Guatemala for a future invasion of Cuba. When John F. Kennedy took office the following January, the CIA and the fourteen hundred armed and trained exiles were ready to move. For Kennedy to have then called off the invasion, says Schlesinger, would have involved both "embarrassment" and what Allen Dulles, head of the CIA, called a "disposal problem"—how to stop fourteen hundred demobilized Cuban refugees from blurting out the story of their secret invasion plan, which had been engineered by the United States government.

Schlesinger, who had been called from Harvard to be a Kennedy adviser and court historian, refers to the "Cuban inheritance" as something "bequeathed" to Kennedy by Eisenhower, which is true. But it is also true that Kennedy, not Eisenhower, was then president, and that Kennedy himself had the same basic hostility toward a Cuban revolutionary regime that his Republican predecessor had. In his October 21, 1960, television debate with Richard Nixon during the presidential campaign, Kennedy criticized the Eisenhower administration for not being tough enough with Castro. His remarks drew praise from right-wing columnist George Sokolsky, who wrote about Kennedy as follows:

> He has been speaking in the voice of American history much closer to the spirit of Theodore Roosevelt than Franklin D. Roosevelt. He is closer to the nationalist attitude of the Republican Party than to the internationalism of the Eisenhower Administration. Certainly this country must carry a big stick or we shall become the laughing-stock of the Western world which watches little Cuba mock and twit the great United States that does not know what to do.

At about the time of the Nixon-Kennedy television debates, reports began to appear in the press—in a Guatemala City newspaper, in a Stanford University publication on Latin American affairs, and in the *Nation*—about the secret training base in Guatemala. In January, 1961, the *New York Times* carried a story on the base. In February the *Wall Street Journal,* in a dispatch from Fort Bragg, North Carolina, center for training the army's counter-guerrilla Special Forces, said "it's no secret that this country already is furnishing weapons and supplies to anti-Castro forces in Central Cuba's Escambray Mountains and training counter-revolutionaries in Florida and Guatemala." The State Department denied such goings-on; its spokesman, Lincoln White, told the press: "As to the report of a specific base, I know absolutely nothing about it."

In March—with the invasion only four weeks off—Kennedy asked Schlesinger to draw up a White Paper explaining the administration's position on Cuba. The White Paper was a perfect example of liberal rhetoric masking conservative action. It invoked Oliver Wendell Holmes's phrase—adapting for foreign affairs its previous use by the Justice Department to put domestic dissenters in prison—to call Cuba "a clear and present danger" to the "authentic and autonomous revolution of the Americas." No, Schlesinger would have Kennedy say, the United States is not against revolution, only against *Communist* revolutions. But just how fervently the American-trained Cuban exiles wanted an "authentic revolution" was revealed by the declaration of war issued April 8, 1961, in New York by Dr. José Miró Cardona for the Cuban Revolutionary Council. It berated Castro because "the free-enterprise system has been destroyed. . . . We emphatically assure those who have been unjustly dispossessed that all their assets shall be returned. . . . We shall encourage investment in private property, both national and foreign, and we shall give complete guarantees to private enterprise and to private property." The Cuban exiles, and Kennedy, and Schlesinger, claimed to want a revolution, but one that would not take away "private property"—that is, the land, the assets, the controlling interests, and the oil refineries of American businessmen.

On April 17, 1961, the invasion—with some Americans participating—took place at the Bay of Pigs on Cuba's south shore, ninety miles from Havana. The military result was summed up by presidential assistant Theodore C. Sorensen: "A landing force of some fourteen hundred anti-Castro Cuban exiles, organized, trained, armed, transported and directed by the United States Central Intelligence Agency (CIA), was crushed in less than three days by the vastly more numerous forces of Cuban dictator Fidel Castro." The political result was a blow to American prestige throughout the world. The *Manchester Guardian* wrote: "Everyone knows that the sort of invasion by proxy with which the U.S. has now been charged is morally indistinguishable from open aggression."

Legally, the United States was also culpable. In 1948 it had agreed to Article 15 of the Charter of the Organization of American States, which reads: "No state or group of states has the right to intervene, directly or indirectly, for any reason whatever, in the internal or external affairs of any other state." Furthermore, the CIA and other federal officials were guilty of violating Section 960, Title 18, of the U.S. Code, which charges any American with being a criminal who "provides or prepares a means for or furnishes the money for, or takes part in, any military or naval expedition or enterprise to be carried on from thence against the territory or dominion of any foreign prince or state, or of any colony, district, or people with whom the United States is at peace. . . ." When a group of law professors pointed out to Attorney General Robert F. Kennedy that Americans had violated this law, he shrugged it off by saying that the law was too old to deal with the new situation of the cold war.

American policy toward Castro's Cuba under the conservative Eisenhower administration remained unchanged under the "liberal" Kennedy administration. Both were willing to carry out covert plans to invade a neighboring country in total violation of all treaty pledges and of the laws of the United States. Both had no compunction about the United States financing, organizing, and arming an invasion of another country—so long as it could be done secretly. Kennedy's press-conference remarks on April 12, four days before the invasion, can only be termed, at best, an exercise in deception:

> . . . there will not be, under any conditions, any intervention in Cuba by United States armed forces, and this government will do everything it possibly can—and I think it can meet its responsibilities—to make sure there are no Americans involved in any actions inside Cuba.

Sorensen wrote later that Kennedy, with the invasion obviously failing on the second day, "agreed finally that unmarked Navy jets could protect the anti-Castro force of B-26's" used to provide air cover. As it turned out, American pilots ended up having to man the B-26s; four of them were killed. Sorensen explains the plan:

The exile air arm, other than transports, was composed solely of lumbering B-26's as part of the covert nature of the plan. These World War II vintage planes were possessed by so many countries, including Cuba, that American sponsorship would be difficult to prove, and the prelanding attack on Cuban airfields could thus be attributed to defecting Cuban pilots.

A cover-up story was invented in which one B-26 would fly to Florida claiming to have defected from the Cuban air force.

The deception extended to American statements made at the UN by Ambassador Adlai Stevenson. Schlesinger writes about a White House meeting in the midst of the invasion: "Kennedy, who had been much concerned about the UN aspect of our Cuban operation, told the group in the Cabinet Room that he wished Stevenson to be fully informed, and that nothing said at the UN should be less than the truth, even if it could not be the full truth." Stevenson, who knew about the invasion plans in Guatemala, seems to have been kept in some ignorance by his government about the extent of American participation. A briefing of him a week before the invasion by Schlesinger and CIA agent Tracy Barnes was, Schlesinger wrote later, "probably unduly vague." In any case, Stevenson became a participant in the general dissemination of untruths when he insisted at the UN that no American personnel or planes were taking part in the invasion. Schlesinger reports that while Stevenson was not in favor of the invasion, "if it was national policy, he was prepared to make out the best possible case."

Some influential newspapers and magazines played along with the government's plans by withholding stories on the invasion at official request. A few weeks before the invasion, *New Republic* editor Gilbert Harrison sent the White House galleys of an article on CIA training of Cuban exiles in Florida; Schlesinger turned them over to Kennedy, who asked that the article not be printed, and Harrison complied. About the same time, James Reston and Turner Catledge of the *New York Times* collaborated in keeping out of the *Times* another story from Miami which reported the imminent invasion of Cuba. Schlesinger writes: "This was another patriotic act, but in retrospect I have wondered whether, if the press had behaved irresponsibly, it would not have spared the country a disaster."

The Kennedy liberals reacted to the Bay of Pigs fiasco with regrets that it had failed. They did not raise a question about whether it was right for the United States to have intervened in Cuban domestic affairs. Their reaction is apparent in Sorensen's book *Kennedy* and in Schlesinger's book *A Thousand Days;* Schlesinger even quotes John Stuart Mill about how "free states" cannot give up the doctrine of non-intervention if others do not. As Kennedy himself, in a speech made immediately after the invasion to the American Society of Newspaper Editors, put it:

> Any unilateral American intervention, in the absence of an external attack upon ourselves or an ally, would have been contrary to our traditions and to our international obligations. But let the record show that our restraint is not inexhaustible. Should it ever appear that the inter-American doctrine of non-interference merely conceals or excuses a policy of non-action —if the nations of this hemisphere should fail to meet their commitments against outside Communist penetration—then I want it clearly understood that this government will not hesitate in meeting its primary obligations which are to the security of our nation.

Was Cuba an example of "outside Communist penetration"? The history of the Castro movement hardly bore that out. Was it a threat to the security of the nation? Even Reston wrote shortly after the invasion: "Cuba is not a present danger to the United States." What was true, however, was that an unspoken part of the liberal creed embodied the principle that governments whose policies were revolutionary enough to threaten American property interests were not to be tolerated, least of all in the Western Hemisphere. The Bay of Pigs episode was another in a long line of actions taken by the United States to maintain its Latin American empire.

E. The Dominican Republic, 1965

It was Truman who intervened in Greece and Korea, Eisenhower in Guatemala and Lebanon, Kennedy in Cuba, and in 1965, as if to emphasize the continuity in the aggressive drive of American nationalism, it became Lyndon Johnson's turn. The Dominican Republic in the Caribbean was fixed as the target of yet another American invasion—this one, too, in violation of the Charter of the Organization of American States. Introducing his study of the 1926

American intervention in Nicaragua, Neill Macaulay notes the historical parallel between the Nicaraguan and the Dominican actions:

> The military junta that had overthrown the constitutional government of Juan Bosch in the Dominican Republic was recognized soon after Johnson took office. Then, when popular resentment against the illegal government took the form of armed resistance, President Johnson, in a reckless reaction to a supposed communist threat, landed thousands of American troops in the Dominican Republic—thus duplicating President Coolidge's Nicaraguan exploits of 1926–1927. American intervention prevented a "rebel" victory in the Dominican Republic, but it also resurrected the image of the United States as a trigger-happy vigilante intent on smashing any democratic movement that might be tinged with communism.

The United States had supported the Trujillo dictatorship in the Dominican Republic throughout its thirty-year rule, starting in 1930. The family of Rafael Trujillo Molina came to own about 80 per cent of the Dominican economy. What did a "liberal" foreign policy mean for the United States in the Caribbean? It meant there what it so often meant elsewhere, that a right-wing terrorist regime, dominated by American business, was preferable to any kind of leftist regime, from moderate left, as in Guatemala, to far left, as in Cuba. Schlesinger, from his special observation post in the White House during the Kennedy administration, reported the president's thinking about the Dominican Republic when he took office:

> There are three possibilities in descending order of preference: a decent democratic regime, a continuation of the Trujillo regime, or a Castro regime. We ought to aim at the first, but we really can't renounce the second until we are sure that we can avoid the third.

When Juan Bosch, with much support from the lower classes, won 60 per cent of the vote in the 1962 Dominican election, following the demise of the Trujillo regime, and then taxed sugar profits to provide housing for workers, Washington became uneasy. Florida Senator George Smathers, a close friend of Kennedy's, and of business interests in Latin America, had urged sending marines to Santo Domingo after Trujillo's fall. Said Smathers: "Many Americans

having invested $250 million in the Dominican Republic believe that
Generalissimo Trujillo was the best guarantee of American interests
in the country . . . open intervention must now be considered to protect their property and to prevent a communist coup. . . ." Not sur-
prisingly, the overthrow of the Bosch government by a military coup
in 1963, according to *Time* correspondent Sam Halper, followed
"a wink from the U.S. Pentagon."

The military government did not set well with the Dominicans,
however, and in the spring of 1965 they rebelled. It was this uprising that was seen by special U.S. envoy John Bartlow Martin
as containing a "serious threat of communist takeover," although
the CIA itself had reported "not more than one hundred well-trained,
fully-committed and fully-disciplined" Communists existed in all of
the Dominican Republic. The rebellion led President Johnson to
send in the marines, although the move had already been foreshadowed while Kennedy was president. "I take it we don't want
Bosch back in power," Kennedy had said to Martin on a trip to
Washington for the purpose of consultations; Martin had replied:
"No, he isn't a president."

The underlying assumption of American intervention in the
Dominican Republic was that here, too, the United States could and
should decide who should rule. The rebellion was defeated in the
name of "stopping communism," but the operating factor was
American money and American power. Once the rebels were defeated, and a regime palatable to the United States was again in
power, Barnet reports that

> Private U.S. investment in housing and tourism began to
> flow into the island once more. The shooting had scarcely
> stopped before new Hilton Hotels, Holiday Inns, and housing
> projects sponsored by IBEC, a Rockefeller-family company,
> were being planned. The South Puerto Rican Sugar Company,
> now merged with Gulf and Western Industries, decided to di-
> versify, and use some of its beachfront property for a new
> tourist center.

The Dominican Republic was "stable" once more. It could now receive more than double the highest annual per capita aid of any
country in Latin America: $32.2 compared with $13.4 for Chile.

II. ECONOMIC PENETRATION

The five postwar instances of American military intervention in the affairs of other states, leaving out Vietnam, were part of a foreign policy that embraced another form of American penetration: economic. With the end of the First World War, when the United States became the banker of the war-shattered European nations, the picturization of America as a generous dispenser of economic aid to the needy peoples of the world began to evolve. World War II and its aftermath greatly magnified all the elements of this picture: the war had been the most devastating in history, the scale of postwar American economic programs abroad was larger than ever, and the talk about helping the desperate nations of the world became even more grandiloquent.

The operating reality was somewhat different. In determining which nations received aid, political considerations prevailed from the start. While the economic interest of American business was a principal factor in fixing the direction and the nature of assistance, most of what was called "economic" aid was, quite simply, financial support for the military programs in other nations. And the purpose of this support was, first, to strengthen their war capacities against possible Communist enemies abroad, and, second, to build their armed strength to deal with revolutionary movements—whether Communist or not—at home.

The idea of aid being funneled to nations through an international agency—to avoid domination by the donating country—died early in the postwar years. The United Nations Relief and Rehabilitation Administration—created for just such purposes—was terminated in 1946. The United States delegate argued that the need for further aid was not established, and that it was time for a return to the normal method of international transactions.

Clearly, the need for assistance was there; European nations could neither rebuild their economies nor buy goods from the greatly expanded American production machine without grants of money. The problem for the United States was how to keep such aid under the kind of economic and political controls that would serve America's overall foreign policy, as an international agency was not likely to do. Thus, the Marshall Plan was born. Secretary of State George Marshall, in a speech at Harvard University in mid-1947, called on European nations to formulate a coordinated program of reconstruction, with American aid.

In response, British Foreign Affairs Secretary Ernest Bevin and French Foreign Minister Georges Bidault met in Paris, inviting Soviet Foreign Minister V. M. Molotov to join them. Molotov did join them, but after three days left for Moscow, charging that the conditions for aid would bring American domination of the grantee nations. When England and France then invited the twenty-two nations of Europe to a conference in Paris to formulate integrated programs of economic reconstruction, the six Eastern European nations in the Soviet bloc stayed away. A unified four-year plan was developed at the Paris conference, which asked for $19 billion in American grants.

In the meantime Truman administration spokesmen were working diligently to get Congress to pass the necessary enabling legislation. Marshall was quoted in an early 1948 State Department Bulletin as saying: "It is idle to think that a Europe left to its own efforts . . . would remain open to American business in the same way that we have known it in the past." In April, 1948, Congress passed the bill for the European Recovery Program, authorizing $5.3 billion for the first year; the European Cooperation Administration (ECA) was set up to administer the grants.

In the four years of the Marshall Plan, $16 billion was dispensed to Western European countries. This large sum gave the United States political influence in all these countries—especially in France, Italy, and West Germany. It also allowed the United States to steer the economic policies of these nations into channels beneficial to American industries—such as building up markets for American exports.

The political intent of the Marshall Plan was never denied in Washington. Indeed, it was specified at the plan's inception by Dean Acheson:

> These measures of relief and reconstruction have been only in part suggested by humanitarianism. Your Congress has authorized and your Government is carrying out, a policy of relief and reconstruction today chiefly as a matter of national

self-interest. . . . Free peoples who are seeking to preserve their
independence and democratic institutions and human freedoms
against totalitarian pressures, either internal or external, will
receive top priority for American aid.

When political events dictated, however, the form of American
assistance changed. By 1952 the cold war was intensifying, the
Korean War had extended American military commitments in the
Pacific, and the emphasis in the foreign-aid program now switched
from relief and reconstruction to military aid. In the next ten years,
of the $50 billion in aid granted by the United States to ninety coun-
tries, only $5 billion was for nonmilitary economic development.

Official reference to humanitarianism did not, to be sure, die out
with the Marshall Plan. With Kennedy's launching of the Alliance
for Progress in 1963, the rhetoric of generosity became extravagant.
This economic-aid program for South America was presented as a
bold new plan under which a billion dollars a year would come from
the United States government, with another billion from private investors, over a ten-year period. His emphasis was, of course, on
social reform:

> For unless necessary social reforms, including land and tax re-
> form, are freely made—unless we broaden the opportunity for
> all our people—unless the great mass of Americans share in
> increasing prosperity—then our alliance, our revolution and
> our dream will have failed.

Here, again, the reality was something else. Professor Edwin Lieuwen, an adviser to the government on Latin American affairs,
summed up the Kennedy administration's work in South America
as follows:

> The most unexpected and unintended repercussion of all
> was that military assistance was contributing new political
> strength to an anti-reform institution—the role assumed by
> the armed forces themselves—just when Washington had
> hoped to carry out a broad-scale program of economic and
> social change through democratic constitutional governments.
> By force of arms, six such governments were destroyed dur-
> ing Kennedy's term of office.
>   The administration's policies were not always consistent.
> Its general policy was to encourage the growth of responsible
> apolitical military organizations so that democracy might have

a better chance to function; yet, when it wanted to isolate Cuba, it did not hesitate to make political use of the military against policies of the civilian governments of Argentina and Ecuador. Also, it compromised democratic principles for the sake of expediency in accepting the coups in Guatemala and Ecuador. Finally, it began to veer toward a watered-down definition of democracy by going along with vetoes issued by the military against majority-supported civilian politicians.

The military programs also came under increasingly severe criticism from Latin American civilian parties. Whether or not it was United States aid that had swung the balance in behalf of military intervention, they could not help noting that United States-manufactured tanks and jets were the weapons of the coups and that United States-trained officers were the perpetrators of the coups. In Honduras, for example, the infantry and air force battalions especially developed for defense-of-the-hemisphere missions were the ones used to topple the Villeda Morales government.

In 1969, the *New York Times* summarized the conclusions of a series of United Nations reports on Latin America as follows:

> An exhaustive survey of Latin American development since the establishment of the Alliance for Progress shows that the region has plunged more deeply into foreign debt, has lost ground in world trade and has failed to reduce unemployment.

Despite the promises, the pattern of American aid to Latin America had not varied; most of America's resources were being expended once more to help American business interests, to prop up the continent's military dictatorships, and to stymie revolutionary changes. In 1969 Defense Department figures showed that two hundred thousand Latin American military officers had been trained in the United States since the end of World War II, and that there were American military missions in all Latin American countries except Cuba, Mexico, and Haiti.

In the same year the *Times* published the UN reports, a presidential mission to Latin America headed by New York Governor Nelson Rockefeller urged less criticism by Americans of the military leaders in Latin America and more respect for the police. The Rockefeller report augmented these comments with requests for more aid to the police and military in Latin America. At the same time, the need for improved language was recognized in the report:

"The name 'Military Assistance Program' should be dropped. . . . The program should be renamed the 'Western Hemisphere Security Program.' "

Latin America only partially depicts the dimension of America's economic—and political—penetration in the postwar world. In these years American financial interests abroad became enormous. By 1970 American companies had roughly $70 billion invested overseas. In key areas, the United States replaced older Western imperial nations. For instance, whereas 72 per cent of the control of Middle East oil reserves in 1940 was British, and 10 per cent of it American, in 1967 it was 58 per cent American and 29 per cent British.

One powerful stimulus to American economic and military intervention was the increasing dependence of American business on certain raw materials. Before the war, iron imports were equivalent to 3 per cent of domestic production; by 1966 they had raised to 43 per cent. Before the war the United States imported as much bauxite as it produced domestically; by 1966 it was importing six times as much as it was producing. What economist Harry Magdoff calls a "dramatic reversal in the self-sufficiency of the United States with respect to raw materials" was considered by the President's Commission on Foreign Economic Policy in 1954 as follows: "Both from the standpoint of our long-term economic growth and the viewpoint of our national defense, the shift of the United States from the position of a net exporter of metals and minerals to that of a net importer is of overshadowing significance in shaping our foreign economic policies."

The magnitude of American economic penetration can be demonstrated by several facts. By 1960 United States foreign investments were 60 per cent of the world total; it was no longer merely a matter of American *exports* competing with the products of other nations but of American plants inside those countries competing with their domestic products. By 1963 American firms controlled more than half the British auto industry, 40 per cent of the German oil industry, 40 per cent of the telegraph, telephone, electronic, and statistical equipment business in France. By 1967 the United States Council of the International Chamber of Commerce estimated that the gross value of production by American companies abroad was more than $100 billion a year—equivalent in productive capacity to a third "nation" in the world, just behind the United States and the U.S.S.R.

III. MILITARIZATION

From the end of World War II to 1970, the United States government spent a thousand billion dollars for military purposes. It trained a standing army of three million men; it built four hundred major and three thousand minor military bases in thirty countries overseas; it put seven thousand tactical nuclear weapons in Europe; it kept an undisclosed number of heavy bombers in the air constantly, carrying hydrogen bombs; and it launched forty-one submarines capable of firing more than six hundred nuclear missiles while submerged. With all its armor, however, the United States in 1970 felt less secure than it did in 1945. It continued to plan increases in its military hardware: more submarines, more nuclear warheads, more bombers; even more complicated, more deadly, more expensive weapons. And its arms race with the Soviet Union showed no sign of diminishing.

The insistence of such armaments-minded men as Robert McNamara, Kennedy's secretary of defense, that there was no real defense against a large-scale missile attack was of no avail; the government went ahead anyway with plans for an anti-ballistic-missile system. The cost of the system was estimated initially at $5 billion, but with the final cost of long-term military contracts tending to be three times the early estimates, the price tag on ABM could reach $15 billion. This expenditure would cover what is called a "thin" defense; if the defense should be made "thick," the cost was estimated at $40 billion to $100 billion. Since any anti-missile system would endanger the American population itself, thereby requiring large-scale shelters, the total cost, as estimated by John E. Ulmann, a military electronics expert at Hofstra University, might run to more than $250 billion. Quite understandably, critics of military policy in the 1960s began using the term "missile madness."

The motivation for acquiring all this armament—offensive and defensive—was fear of aggression by the Soviet Union and Communist China against the United States. Between 1953 and 1968, the Soviet Union sent troops into neighboring Communist countries —Hungary, Czechoslovakia, Poland, East Germany—to put down rebellion. In 1959, China took military action against the border state of Tibet and against India along the frontier. Their actions were typical great-power bullying of neighboring states, not much different from American bullying of Latin America; they were quite far from constituting a threat to the United States itself. Neither the Soviet Union nor China had military bases on the borders of the United States; the United States, on the contrary, had bases, with nuclear weapons, all around the borders of both Communist nations. China had no troops stationed in other countries, while the United States had perhaps 750,000 troops and the Seventh Fleet deployed in various parts of Asia.

The one time in which the Communist countries broke through these geographic limits came in the fall of 1962, when Soviet missiles were sent to Cuba, and a serious crisis, involving the threat of nuclear war, enveloped the United States, the Soviet Union, and the world. On October 16, American intelligence overflights disclosed Soviet nuclear missiles in Cuba. Whether they had been placed there on Cuban initiative as a possible deterrence to an attack by the United States or on Soviet initiative to match American missiles near the Soviet Union never became clear. In either case, the Kennedy administration went into a series of crisis meetings, out of which came the policy of blockading Cuba to pressure the removal of the missiles.

Robert Kennedy wrote later that the Joint Chiefs of Staff advocated air strikes against the missile sites and other military targets, and that one of them approved the idea of using nuclear weapons. But the blockade idea prevailed, and was put into effect. After several tense days, the Russians ordered their ships to respect the blockade, and they turned back. On October 26, two messages were sent to President Kennedy from Soviet Premier Nikita Khrushchev. The first offered to remove the missiles if American missiles were in turn removed from Turkey; the Soviet Union offered to guarantee Turkey against invasion if the United States would make a similar guarantee to Cuba. The second message did not mention the missiles in Turkey; it merely asked for a non-invasion guarantee to Cuba.

Kennedy ignored the first message, responded affirmatively to the second, and the missiles on Cuba were dismantled.

Kennedy had successfully forced the Russians to pull back their missile frontier to their own borders. But the United States did no such thing, and the race between the two countries, in missiles, in airplanes, in submarines, in nuclear weapons of all sorts, continued to mount in the sixties. By the spread and number of its weapons and men around the world, the United States was far more of a menace to the Soviet Union and China than those countries were to America. Nevertheless, the United States government, supported by an American public nurtured on fear of communism, made leap after leap in arms expenditures, troop deployment, and weapons inno-vation, while seeking an ever-widening circle of treaty arrange-ments in order to "contain" communism.

This process is carefully traced by Edgar Bottome, an authority on military policy, in his book *The Balance of Terror*. Bottome makes the following points: that the huge American increase in armaments expenditure after 1950 was not a response to the Korean War, but had been in the works before then; that before 1955 the Soviet Union was in no position to threaten the security of the United States, yet America proceeded with its weapons build-up in such a way as to ensure that the Soviet Union would become a threat; that stories told to the American public about a "bomber gap" and a "missile gap" between the U.S.S.R. and the United States were myths, designed to speed American arms production; and that up to 1970 American military policy continued to reflect a paranoia that threatened to become a self-fulfilling prophecy of destruction. Bottome writes:

> With minor exceptions the United States has led in the de-velopment of military technology and weapons production. . . . This constant American superiority in thermonuclear weap-ons and the means to deliver these weapons has meant that throughout the postwar era, only the United States has had the potential to initiate a surprise attack on its opponent. At no time during the past twenty-five years has the United States had less than a two-to-one advantage in nuclear delivery ve-hicles over the Soviet Union and most of the time it has been better than a four-to-one advantage. The Soviet Union has

been placed in a position where all it could do was react to American initiatives in bomber or missile building programs. This American superiority, along with the highly-ambitious nature of American foreign policy, has placed the United States in a position of being fundamentally responsible for every major escalation of the arms race.

Scientist Dr. Herbert York, a high official in the Defense Department under both Eisenhower and Kennedy and an adviser on military policy to Johnson, came to the conclusion by 1970 that a certain madness pervaded United States policy in the postwar period. "Ever since World War II the military power of the United States has been steadily increasing, while at the same time our national security has been rapidly and inexorably decreasing," York wrote in his book *Race to Oblivion.* "The same thing is happening to the Soviet Union. . . . Each of us has lived as the pawn of the other's whim—or calculation—for the past twenty years." He said further:

> Over the last thirty years we have repeatedly taken unilateral actions that have unnecessarily accelerated the race. These actions have led to the accumulation of unnecessarily large numbers of oversized weapons. In short, these actions have led to the present situation of gross overkill. I do not mean to imply by anything I have written that the Soviets are blameless for accelerating the arms race. . . . [But] our unilateral decisions have set the rate and scale for most of the individual steps in the strategic-arms race. . . .

The policy of military overkill was deeply embedded in, and perpetuated by, the fundamental characteristic of the American economy: the profit motive. With an annual governmental military budget soaring into the multibillions—in 1970 it hit $80 billion— fabulous profits were to be made by big corporations. The United States in the 1960s was spending approximately $40 billion a year on weapon systems alone, two-thirds of the money going to twelve or fifteen industrial giants—corporations whose main reason for existence was to fulfill government contracts for death-dealing weapons. Senator Paul Douglas, who understood the situation well from his vantage point of chairman of the Joint Economic Committee, pointed out that "six-sevenths of these contracts are not competitive but what are termed 'single supplier negotiable.' In the alleged interest of secrecy, the government picks a company and draws up a contract in more or less secret negotiations." He also pointed out that despite initial cost estimates "it is customary for the ultimate costs to be double or treble the original estimates."

The closeness of the connection between business profits and military expansion is represented in another way. A report by Senator William Proxmire found that in early 1969 more than two thousand former upper-echelon military officers were employed by the one hundred largest defense contractors—who held 67.4 per cent of the military contracts. Proxmire's report was corroborated in a 1970 study of the Pentagon made by the President's Blue Ribbon Defense Panel; this study revealed that the first eleven of the top one hundred war contractors employed about half of the two thousand former officers in their sample, and were awarded 47 per cent of the prime contracts received by the one hundred contractors. "Clearly, a few firms—primarily in the aerospace business—employ most of the retired officers in defense work," the presidential panel said. The pace of militarization of the economy was also shown in Proxmire's study, which found that the number of retired officers working for the ninety leading firms doing war business with the government had tripled in ten years. Here, indeed, was America's military-industrial complex at work.

IV. VIETNAM

The foregoing summary of American foreign policy in the postwar era is not intended to be a comprehensive history; its purpose is to illustrate the point made at the beginning of this chapter: that the rhetorical values of American liberalism are in contradiction with its operating values, which actually determine policy for the policy-makers. This discrepancy between promise and reality was true for every administration, whether it called itself liberal or conservative, Democrat or Republican. And nowhere was this discrepancy clearer than in America's policy toward Southeast Asia.

The war in Vietnam was the tragic embodiment of all the characteristics of American foreign policy in the postwar period. Every postwar administration played its part in effecting a consistent policy of American intervention in Indochina. The first priority of that policy was to prevent a Communist movement, based on indigenous strength, nationalist fervor, and a desire to make revolutionary changes in a traditionally elitist social structure, from taking power in Vietnam. What the United States wanted was a government in Vietnam that it could dominate or, at the very least, strongly influence.

In Vietnam, the United States could not achieve its objectives without violating a long list of promises and principles that are part of the rhetoric of American liberalism. The revolutionaries in Indochina were fully aware of this from the moment they embarked on their postwar struggle for independence; at the outset, they invoked the language of Thomas Jefferson as part of their own Declaration of Independence, proclaimed in Hanoi on September 2, 1945, from the French. Their declaration begins: "All men are created equal. They are endowed by their Creator with certain inalienable rights, among these are Life, Liberty, and the pursuit of Happiness." They also pointed to the Declaration of the Rights of Man and the Citizen, the great document of the French Revolution, and then went on to list their grievances against the French:

> They have enforced inhuman laws. . . . They have built more prisons than schools. They have mercilessly slain our patriots, they have drowned uprisings in rivers of blood. They have fettered public opinion. . . . They have robbed us of our rice fields, our mines, our forest, and our raw materials. . . . The whole Vietnamese people, animated by a common purpose, are determined to fight to the bitter end against any attempt by the French colonialists to reconquer their country.

Recalling the promises made by the victorious powers of World War II, the Vietnamese also declared: "We are convinced that the Allied nations, which at Tehran and San Francisco have acknowledged the principles of self-determination and equality of nations, will not refuse to acknowledge the independence of Vietnam."

The Allied nations, however, wasted little time in betraying the Vietnamese. At the Potsdam Conference in July and August, 1945, Vietnam was divided into two parts, the southern half given into the temporary custody of the English, the northern half into the custody of the Chinese Nationalists. The English quickly turned over their half to the French, and special instructions went from the American government to Colonel Phillip Gallagher, head of the American military mission in Hanoi, to persuade Chiang Kai-shek to turn the northern half of Vietnam over to the French, too.

Shortly after the Potsdam Conference, Ho Chi Minh, the Communist leader in the north, tried to enlist American support for Vietnamese independence by sending a number of letters to President Truman. (These letters are referred to in the Department of Defense historical study of the Indochina War, released unofficially to the public in 1971 and known popularly as *The Pentagon Papers.*) There is no evidence that Truman ever replied. In late 1946, after the French bombarded the North Vietnam port of Haiphong, killing thousands of civilians, the long war began between the Viet Minh, the Vietnamese independence movement led by Ho Chi Minh, and the French, whose efforts to regain control over Indochina had been manifested in notes sent to London, Moscow, and Washington on the day World War II ended.

Through the late 1940s, the United States moved slowly toward open support of the French. In February, 1947, State Department instructions to the American ambassador in Paris were to assure the French "that we have fully recognized France's sovereign position in that area." And on May 13, 1947, State Department cables to U.S. diplomats in Paris, Saigon, and Hanoi were to assure them that the rhetoric of anticolonialism must give way to the historic realities of America's commitment to the colonial powers of the West:

> Key our position is our awareness that in respect developments affecting position Western democratic powers in Southern Asia, we essentially in same boat as French, also as British and Dutch. We cannot conceive setbacks to long-range interests France which would not also be setbacks our own. . . .
>
> Following relaxation European controls, internal racial, religious, and national differences could plunge new nations into violent discord, or already apparent anti-Western Pan-Asiatic tendencies could become dominant political force, or Communists could capture control. We consider as best safeguard against these eventualities a continued close association between newly-autonomous peoples and powers which have long been responsible their welfare. In particular we recognize Vietnamese will for indefinite period require French material and technical assistance and enlightened political guidance which

can be provided only by nation steeped like France in the democratic tradition and confirmed in respect human liberties and worth individual.

In 1949 the French made an agreement with Bao Dai, who had been the puppet Vietnamese emperor under Japanese rule, to play the same role, in effect, under them. With Saigon as the capital, Bao Dai was made head of a supposedly autonomous "State of Vietnam." In the same year the United States, overwrought by the Communist victory in China, became more overt in aiding the French in their war against the Viet Minh. Bao Dai might be an embarrassment, with his lack of popular support, his corruption, and his preference for long flings on the French Riviera, but, still, he fitted the more sophisticated American approach to colonialism: he offered some semblance of native sovereignty while outsiders retained the real economic, political, and military power. It was the kind of solution that in 1946 had worked out so nicely for the United States in the Philippines.

American military aid to the French mounted rapidly, but to slight avail; the French forces in Indochina found themselves unable to subdue the armed peasant detachments of Ho Chi Minh. In 1950 American aid to the French totaled $10 million; in 1954, the last year of the French military effort, U.S. aid soared to more than a billion dollars—78 per cent of France's war costs. Why? President Truman in a radio talk April 11, 1951, on the Korean War explained to the American public that the Kremlin was leading a "monstrous conspiracy to stamp out freedom all over the world." Yet the State Department, in a secret memorandum of July, 1948, had said, "Dept has no evidence of direct link between Ho and Moscow but assumes it exists, nor is it able to evaluate amount pressure or guidance Moscow exerting." Moreover, the department's Office of Intelligence Research had reported in the fall of 1948: "If there is a Moscow-directed conspiracy in Southeast Asia, Indochina is an anomaly so far."

The nationalist-Communist movement of the Viet Minh had gained strength in the 1940s on the basis of widespread opposition to the imperious rule of both the Japanese and the French, and because the poor people in the countryside needed to be released from the oppressive conditions under which they lived. The fierce, frantic efforts of the French and the United States to maintain the prewar status quo in Vietnam, their public claims to being champions of self-determination notwithstanding, put them in the position of opposing the Vietnamese people's own desire for change.

Did the United States really care what the people of Vietnam wanted? President Eisenhower at a news conference February 10, 1954, described American support to the French as "a case of independent and free nations operating against the encroachment of communism." Was this the liberal rhetoric doing its deceptive work again? Was America truly interested in the rights of the Vietnamese? Or was profit and power closer to the real motivation behind American intervention in Indochina? Was Eisenhower closer to the truth when he told the 1953 Governors' Conference that if "we lose Indochina," Malaya, Burma, India, and Iran would be threatened? "All of that weakening position around there is very ominous for the United States, because finally if we lost all that, how would the free world hold the rich empire of Indonesia? So when the United States votes $400 million to help that war, we . . . are voting for . . . our security, our power and ability to get certain things we need from the riches of the Indonesian territory, and from Southeast Asia."

As the French position in Indochina deteriorated, American government strategists reiterated the "domino theory" that Eisenhower had stressed. A State Department memo of August 5, 1953, said: "Under present conditions any negotiated settlement would mean the eventual loss to Communism not only of Indo-China but of the whole of Southeast Asia." It added: "If the French actually decided to withdraw, the U.S. would have to consider most seriously whether to take over in this area."

In 1954 the failure of the French in Vietnam was dramatized by their defeat at the battle of Dienbienphu. They went to an international peace conference at Geneva to negotiate their way out of Indochina. The French-Viet Minh agreement at Geneva again divided Vietnam into two zones, the northern one under the Viet Minh, the southern zone temporarily under the French, until elections could be held in 1956 to pick the government for a united Vietnam.

The United States made two moves in 1954 to do as the State Department had suggested the previous year: "take over in this area." It established the Southeast Asia Treaty Organization, a predominantly white, anti-Communist "Asian" alliance of Australia, New Zealand, the Philippines, Thailand, Pakistan, France, Great Britain, and America, and it put its money and military power behind a new puppet in South Vietnam, Ngo Dinh Diem. It then encouraged Diem to reject the nationwide elections scheduled for 1956 and to set up a government in Saigon tied to American power. On the eve of the Geneva Conference, March 12, 1954, the Joint Chiefs of Staff had told the Defense Department that intelligence estimates showed "a settlement based on free elections would be attended by almost certain loss of the Associated States [Laos, Cambodia, and Vietnam] to Communist control." Thus, as a Pentagon analyst put it, "South Viet Nam was essentially the creation of the United States."

The Diem regime became increasingly unpopular with the Vietnamese peasants. It favored the landlords, making only the flimsiest efforts in the direction of land reform. It replaced locally selected provincial chiefs with Saigon appointees, more and more of whom came from the ranks of the military. In 1958, 36 per cent of the chiefs were military men; in 1962 the percentage would reach 88. It jailed increasing numbers of Vietnamese who spoke out against the corruption and ineptitude of the regime.

With the Diem government, supported by the United States, exercising broad dictatorial powers, it was hardly surprising that guerrilla activity began to develop in 1958 in several South Vietnam provinces. Two years later the National Liberation Front was formed to unify the opposition to Diem. While the Communist regime north of the 17th parallel, in Hanoi, undoubtedly sympathized with and gave aid to the NLF, its essential strength came from peasants in South Vietnam who found the Diem government unacceptable, and who looked to the NLF for a radical improvement in the day-to-day conditions of their lives. In his study of the NLF, Douglas Pike, an American government researcher, tells of the progressive "record of alienation" of the Vietnamese people from Diem; he also points to the simultaneous achievements of the Viet Cong, in which Vietnamese Communists were playing an important role in bringing "significant social change" to the villages of South Vietnam. To Pike, the NLF is primarily a "social revolution," and only secondarily is it a military force. In the twenty-five hundred villages of the South, he says, the NLF created "a host of nationwide socio-political organizations. . . . This is a significant point. Aside from the N.L.F. there has never been a truly mass-based political party in South Vietnam."

By the late 1950s, the American government, committed to abetting the corruption and ruthlessness of Premier Diem's regime, found itself in the same position the French had been in—working against a popular revolutionary movement. When Kennedy took office in January, 1961, he continued the Far Eastern policies of the Eisenhower and Truman administrations. The Kennedy administration also determined to keep Communist-led native revolutionary groups from power in Indochina, and to do so by supporting the Saigon government with yet more economic and military aid. On the eve of his inauguration, Kennedy met with Eisenhower on Laos, which had been granted independence from the French in the Geneva Accords and in which the revolutionary Pathet Lao and traditionalist forces were fighting for control. A memorandum on that conference in *The Pentagon Papers* notes: "President Eisenhower said with considerable emotion that Laos was the key to the entire area of Southeast Asia. . . . President-elect Kennedy asked the question as to how long it would take to put an American division in Laos." In early May, 1961, Kennedy approved a secret plan for various military actions in Vietnam and Laos, including the infiltration of attack teams in Laos, and the "dispatch of agents to North Vietnam," where "sabotage and light harassment" might take place.

Under the Geneva agreements, the United States was permitted to have 685 military advisers in the southern half of Vietnam. During Kennedy's tenure, the total number of American military men rose to sixteen thousand. Further, they did more than advise; they began to take part in combat operations. And as America's military might rose, the Diem regime's credibility declined; having put many thousands of its political opponents in jail, it was becoming more and more embarrassing to the United States and more and more intolerable to the Vietnamese. Early in November, 1963, an army coup against Diem took place, with the secret approval of the United States, and Diem was killed. The United States, rather obviously, was prepared to shift its allegiance to any side in Saigon that could successfully maintain control while fighting Communists. Up to the time of his assassination, November 22, 1963, Kennedy continually reiterated to the American public his determination to keep using the armed strength of the United States to block a possible Communist victory in South Vietnam.

Under President Lyndon Johnson, America's commitment to a succession of military regimes in Saigon became even deeper. In August, 1964, the United States government used a questionable naval encounter in the Gulf of Tonkin as an excuse to bombard North Vietnam. An American destroyer, the U.S.S. *Maddox,* rigged with electronic spy equipment, was operating close to the North Vietnamese shore, probably within the twelve-mile limit set by the North Vietnamese as their territorial boundary. Secretary of Defense McNamara said that the destroyer was on a "routine patrol in international waters," but his "explanation" of what happened in the gulf was one of several official deceptions regarding the naval incident. On August 2, the *Maddox* claimed it was attacked, although the evidence is that it fired first; in fact, its only damage was one machine-gun bullet mark. On August 4, another destroyer, the U.S.S. *Turner Joy,* reported that it, too, was attacked, but this "open aggression on the high seas," as Johnson put it, seems to have been the product of imagination. Johnson, however, asked Congress that he be authorized to "take all necessary steps, including the use of armed force, to assist any member or protocol state in the Southeast Asia Collective Defense Treaty requesting assistance in defense of its freedom." On August 7, Congress dutifully passed the "Gulf of Tonkin Resolution"; it gave the president carte blanche military powers in Southeast Asia, powers similar to those bestowed by an earlier Congress on Eisenhower for use in the Mideast.

Following passage of the Gulf of Tonkin Resolution, and Johnson's presidential election victory three months later over Republican Barry Goldwater, whom Johnson chided for urging more aggressiveness in Vietnam, the war escalated sharply. During 1965, more than two hundred thousand American military personnel were sent to South Vietnam, and the regular bombing of North Vietnam began. By the time Johnson left office in early 1969, more than five hundred thousand American troops were in Vietnam; American planes had dropped more than two million tons of bombs on North and South Vietnam—about one ton for every three Vietnamese families; and the United States had made hundreds of villages in the south uninhabitable, by bombing, artillery fire, and the burning of huts.

The brutality of the war, in which the most technologically advanced of all nations was destroying the land and the people of one of the most poverty-stricken regions in the world, began to cause revulsion abroad and in the United States. Protests against the continuation of the war mounted as more and more people learned of the bombing of villages and the use of napalm to produce horrible burns on men, women, and children.

The *New York Times* on June 5, 1965, carried this dispatch by Jack Langguth from Saigon:

> As the Communists withdrew from Quangngai last Monday, United States jet bombers pounded the hills into which they were headed. Many Vietnamese—one estimate is as high as 500—were killed by the strikes. The American contention is that they were Vietcong soldiers. But three out of four patients seeking treatment in a Vietnamese hospital afterward for burns from napalm, or jellied gasoline, were village women.

On September 6, Charles Mohr wrote in the *Times* from Saigon:

> In Bien Hoa province south of Saigon on August 15 United States aircraft accidentally bombed a Buddhist pagoda and a Catholic church. . . . it was the third time their pagoda had been bombed in 1965. A temple of the Cao Dai religious sect in the same area has been bombed twice this year.
>
> In another delta province there is a woman who has both arms burned off by napalm and her eyelids so badly burned that she cannot close them. When it is time for her to sleep her family puts a blanket over her head. The woman had two of her children killed in the air strike that maimed her.
>
> Few Americans appreciate what their nation is doing to South Vietnam with airpower . . . this is strategic bombing in a friendly allied country . . . innocent civilians are dying every day in South Vietnam.

Large areas of South Vietnam were declared "free fire zones"; anyone remaining within them—including children—was considered an enemy, and bombs were dropped at will. Villages suspected of harboring Viet Cong were subject to "search and destroy" missions; men of military age in the villages were killed, and women, children, and old people were herded together and sent off to refugee camps, their homes razed or burned by artillery and air strikes. What one American officer said about the village of Ben Tre—"We had to destroy it in order to save it"—was representative of what the American military was thinking and what American firepower was doing in Vietnam.

Though it did not become known for two years, the most publicized act of cruelty was the massacre that occurred in the hamlet of My Lai 4, in Quang Ngai Province, on March 16, 1969. Hundreds of Vietnamese were rounded up, including the very old and women with infants in their arms, and ordered into a ditch where they were methodically shot to death by American soldiers. Lieutenant William Calley, Jr., was court-martialed in 1970 in connection with the My Lai murders. James Dursi, a rifleman in Calley's platoon, testified at the lieutenant's trial, according to the *New York Times,* that

> . . . Lieutenant Calley and a weeping rifleman named Paul D. Meadlo—the same soldier who had fed candy to the children before shooting them—pushed the prisoners into the ditch. . . .
> "There was an order to shoot by Lieutenant Calley, I can't remember the exact words—it was something like 'Start firing.'
> "Meadlo turned to me and said: 'Shoot, why don't you shoot?'
> "He was crying.
> "I said, 'I can't. I won't.'
> "Then Lieutenant Calley and Meadlo pointed their rifles into the ditch and fired.
> "People were diving on top of each other; mothers were trying to protect their children. . . ."

Other soldiers who participated in the My Lai Massacre were also court-martialed, but only in the case of Calley was a guilty verdict returned. While many Americans expressed horror and disbelief over the events at My Lai, many others resented the guilty verdict. President Nixon referred to Calley in a sympathetic way, and ordered him removed from a cell and placed under a kind of house arrest while the verdict was being appealed. What may have accounted for some of the popular sympathy for Calley was that many Americans believed he was not alone in committing atrocities in Vietnam, that My Lai was not a unique incident, that the whole war was full of atrocities. In early 1971 Colonel Oran Henderson, who had been charged with covering up the My Lai killings, told reporters: "Every unit of brigade size has its My Lai hidden someplace."

My Lai was indeed only one aspect of the brutality committed in Vietnam. By the spring of 1968, domestic opposition to the war had grown to significant proportions. One reason for the increasing antipathy was attributable to the savagery of the war being waged by the United States. Moreover, many Americans were ashamed that the United States was engaged in wholesale killing for the dubious purpose of keeping in power an elite of generals and rich landlords in Saigon. A further reason was simply that Americans were tired of fighting a war in which 40,000 American soldiers had been killed and 250,000 wounded, and in which no end was in sight. In early 1968, the National Liberation Front launched its Tet (New Year) offensive; it took Americans by surprise and it was stopped only after Saigon itself was bombed by American planes and the ancient city of Hue ruined by bombing and artillery fire. The NLF did not drive the United States out of its country, but it proved that it could not be defeated by the most powerful military nation in world history. That spring Lyndon Johnson announced he would not seek the Democratic nomination, and four days before the election he halted the bombing of North Vietnam. The bombers, however, merely altered their destination; Laos became the prime target, and soon refugees were pouring out of bombed Laotian villages as they had in South Vietnam. The war was still on when Richard Nixon took office in January, 1969.

Nixon, elected on a pledge to get the United States out of Vietnam, began a scheduled withdrawal of American troops. By February, 1972, less than 150,000 were left, a drop of approximately 400,000 from America's peak strength in Vietnam. Nixon did not at that time, however, give an indication as to when, or even whether, all U. S. troops would leave Vietnam. In the meantime, he had extended the war geographically through a joint American-South Vietnamese invasion of Cambodia in the spring of 1970, and that fall American power backed a South Vietnamese incursion into

Laos. All during this period, American air power continued to bomb South Vietnam, Laos, Cambodia, and, periodically, North Vietnam; in 1971, eight hundred thousand tons of bombs were dropped by the United States on all of Indochina—as much as in the escalating year of 1967. Meanwhile, the Saigon military regime, headed by President Nguyen Van Thieu, continued to keep thousands of its critics in jail.

Since 1968 the United States had been negotiating in Paris with the North Vietnamese and with the National Liberation Front on a peaceful settlement of the war. Little headway had been made by early 1972, however; the United States refused to accept NLF and North Vietnamese demands that it set a date for and begin a complete withdrawal of its armed forces from Indochina, and that it end its support of the Thieu government, in return for the release of American prisoners of war held in North Vietnam. The United States rejected Viet Cong proposals for a coalition of Communist forces to form a new government in the south, which would hold elections and eventually negotiate on unification with the north. And the NFL refused to accept the offer of withdrawal and a cease-fire so long as the American-dominated Saigon government remained in power. The United States had no wish to relinquish its hold on the Saigon government, and this seemed to be the basic factor that kept the war going.

In Vietnam, as elsewhere, the language of liberalism had been converted into an operational reality involving massive violence against millions of people in a far-off country, where American power kept in place an antiquated and despotic government. In Vietnam, as elsewhere, the efforts of a people to determine their national destiny for themselves had been thwarted by America's drive for power and empire.

3

Democracy and Profit

The New Deal inflated the rhetoric of democracy in America: amidst the turmoil of economic crisis, it was now proclaimed that government had to be responsible for easing the misery of Americans who suffered want. The words once again were no match for reality. It took the Second World War, and the exigencies of the battle-front, to bring about full employment and the full utilization of the national resources. The New Deal of Franklin D. Roosevelt, with all its legislative innovations, made no changes in the economic structure of the United States or in the distribution of national wealth, changes necessary to achieve real equality and democracy.

In the twenty-five years that followed the war, popular descriptions of America were overwhelmingly confident. This was "the free society," "the democratic state," "the affluent society"; these were "the people of plenty." Truman spoke of a "Fair Deal," Kennedy described a "New Frontier," Johnson bragged of a "Great Society." Yet the resources of the richest nation on earth were still irrationally allocated to the production of war goods and luxury goods; urgent social needs, like housing, health care, schools, were considered secondary in importance. The distribution of income was still so badly distorted that the upper fifth of the population lived on twenty to thirty thousand dollars a year and the bottom fifth tried to get by on two to three thousand dollars a year. At the top of the economic scale was enormous wealth, at the bottom, poverty—and hunger.

Even the middle three-fifths of the population, which came to enjoy a measure of "prosperity"—automobiles, suburban houses, longer vacations—did not show the ease of mind that might be expected to exist in a good society. These were people frantic for more "security," dissatisfied with their work, with crowdedness on the highways and in the cities, with air and water pollution. These were the people who were also experiencing nagging fears about war, about depressions, about The Bomb, about overpopulation, about the computerization of American life. Accompanying this general discontent was an increasing sense of powerlessness on the part of the average man, a feeling that though he voted, though he could speak freely in his own milieu, all the great decisions of life were being made somewhere, somehow, by people he did not know. More than ever before, the average American had the feeling that he was becoming an invisible atom in a huge country, reading the newspapers, watching television, listening to the radio, a passive recipient of whatever history was being made, but certainly not a vibrant force in making it.

The American claim of political and economic democracy has always been quietly undermined by the working values of American society. The power of corporations and the drive for profit have always been more real than the chatter about a "welfare state." The rule of special interests in politics has always been more real than the glib talk about "representative government." And these working values have prevailed in postwar America whether the administration in power was liberal or conservative, run by Harry Truman or Richard Nixon.

An American economist, Harold Vatter, surveying the postwar economy, wrote: "It became clear to all the world that the United States economy after mid-century was capable of producing enough to provide every man, woman, and child with a minimum-comfort level of living." Some pages later, he commented that, "there remained at the end of the 1950's, a large segment of the population with insufficient income. In 1947, for example, 36 per cent of all spending units had income before taxes of less than $2,000." In 1960, a year in which poverty was being "discovered" all over America, forty million Americans were below the Bureau of Labor Statistics minimum standard of three thousand dollars a year for a four-person family and four thousand dollars a year for a six-person family. In 1968 a Citizens Board of Inquiry into Hunger and Malnutrition in the United States recorded the testimony before them:

> . . . you buy the cheapest meat you can, neck bones and that kind of stuff and have it a couple of times a month.
> And always there are the days without milk for the children.
> No fresh milk?
> No sir.

No milk for the children?
No sir.
Do they get milk, the small ones?
No.
No milk at all?
No.
Ain't no one of them has milk everyday. They lucky to have
it twice a month.
And there are days without meat, or vegetables, or fruit.
And days with only one meal or two—or three, and they aren't
really meals.
And the children go to bed hungry.
Sometimes they cry.

America's ability to produce goods and services increased at an
astounding rate during the postwar years. Measured in gross national product, and tempered somewhat by inflation, it rose from
$212 billion in 1945 to about $900 billion in 1970. But the distribution of this increased wealth continued in the historic American pattern: most of it went to the rich, very little of it went to the
poor; those in the middle-income bracket became somewhat more
prosperous. The concentration of wealth in the hands of a small
number of corporations and a small number of families remained
the most striking fact about the United States economy. Between
1944 and 1961, the lowest fifth of the families received 5 per cent
of all the income; the highest fifth received 45 per cent. In 1953,
about midway in this period, 1.6 per cent of the adult population
owned more than 80 per cent of the corporate stock and nearly
90 per cent of the corporate bonds. Herman P. Miller, an economist for twenty years at the Bureau of the Census, wrote in 1964:
"The stability of income distribution during the past twenty years
is a matter of some concern that has been generally overlooked by
students in the field."

The continued concentration of American wealth at the top char-
acterized the postwar years. About 200 giant corporations—
of the 200,000 corporations in the country—controlled approximately 60 per cent of the manufacturing wealth of the nation. The
net profits of the ten largest companies in America equaled that of
the 490 next largest companies. The biggest companies grew even
bigger, by merging with other companies, so that between 1948 and

1965, some 800 companies with more than ten million dollars in assets were absorbed by even bigger companies. Conglomerate mergers became common; companies swallowed up others that were in completely different fields of activity. International Telephone and Telegraph, as an example, took over a finance company, a furnace company, the Sheraton Corporation, and the Bobbs-Merrill Company.

Reports by the Federal Trade Commission—a relic of the Wilson administration set up to curtail business giantism, but now relegated to charting its growth—detailed the persistence of American oligopoly. Three automobile companies—General Motors, Ford, and Chrysler—made 95 per cent of all the new cars. Three aluminum companies made 90 per cent of all the aluminum. Three steel companies made 60 per cent of all the steel. Four companies made virtually all the copper. Soap, salt, metal cans, computers—the market for these products was also dominated by a few giant corporations. The inevitable result, of course, was price-fixing, at the expense of the consumer, and fabulous profits, at the expense of the worker. In 1965 General Motors made $2 billion in profits, *after* taxes—a sum greater than the general revenue of forty-eight of the fifty states; its sales exceeded the gross national product of all but nine nations in the world.

The control by a few corporations of each major industry also amounted to a form of taxation on the average American. As Adam Smith had stated back in the eighteenth century in *The Wealth of Nations:*

> To widen the market and to narrow the competition is always the interest of the dealers. To widen the market may frequently be agreeable enough to the interest of the public; but to narrow the competition must always be against it, and can serve only to enable the dealers, by raising their profits above what they naturally would be, to levy, for their own benefit, an absurd tax upon the rest of their fellow citizens.

From 1963 to 1968 corporate profits rose from $33 billion to $51 billion. In the latter year, the Standard Oil Company made $1 billion dollars in profits; its chairman made a salary of $289,000 and was then given a bonus of $135,000.

For perhaps forty to fifty million families, life was different. Being rich or poor was more than a statistic; it profoundly determined how an American lived. In postwar United States, how much money Americans had determined whether or not they lived in a home with rats or vermin; whether or not they were cold in the winter, sweltering in the summer; whether or not their home was such that their children were more likely to die in a fire; whether or not they could get adequate medical and dental care; whether or not they got arrested, and, if they did, whether or not they spent time in jail before trial, whether they got a fair trial, a long or short sentence, whether or not they got a parole. How much money Americans had determined whether their children would be born alive. It determined whether or not Americans had a vacation; whether they needed to hold down more than one job; whether or not they had enough to eat; whether or not they could influence a congressman to run for office; whether or not a man was drafted, and what chances a man had that he would die in combat.

The irony John Kenneth Galbraith wrote into the title of his book *The Affluent Society* was never more apparent than in the billions of dollars spent by the United States government to propel astronauts toward the moon while millions went hungry. A dispatch in the *New York Times,* July 13, 1969, read:

> Within the shadow of the John F. Kennedy Space Center, the hungry people sit and watch.
> They sit on wooden porches near Highway 520 each evening and watch the out-of-state cars crammed with tourists stream into Cocoa Beach and surrounding towns of Brevard County.
> They sit and watch the early morning crush of cars filled with engineers and technicians move toward "the Cape," 18 miles north, in the feverish days before the moon launching on Wednesday morning.
> "The irony is so apparent here," said Dr. Henry Jerkins, the county's only Negro doctor. "We're spending all this money to go to the moon and here, right here in Brevard, I treat malnourished children with prominent ribs and pot bellies. I do see hunger."

In the entire postwar period, no progress was made for the bottom tenth of the population—some twenty million Americans—in increasing its share of the national income. In 1947 the bottom tenth was getting 1 per cent of the money income, and in 1968 it was still getting 1 per cent of the money income. In 1945 the top tenth got about 30 per cent of the money income, and in 1968 it was still getting 30 per cent. One Washington economist, Oscar Gass, noted in 1965 that since the end of World War II the greatest income increases were in capital gains for corporations, and that by the end of the period the tax system was worse for the bottom-income groups than it had been in 1945.

Postwar America saw a boom in highways, motels, restaurants, and office buildings to serve the upper and middle classes, while tens of millions worried about the necessities of life. The contrast is described in a story from Mobile, Alabama, in the *Southern Courier*, January 1, 1966:

> When the restaurant opens at the top of the new 33-story First National Bank building in Mobile, diners will be able to see the city dump from their tables. If they've come to the restaurant at night, from the opera or the symphony, and have a pair of those little binoculars that many take to performances, they may be able to see people outlined against the flames of burning trash.
> These people make their living picking paper and metal out of the garbage and selling it to junk dealers. One hundred pounds of paper brings 50¢. Brass, copper, and aluminum bring much more per pound and are also much harder to find.
> About 60 people—mostly middle-aged or elderly men and women—live at the dump in shacks built of trash. Perhaps 200 others, including children, come to the dump regularly to earn what they can.
> Most people say they average $3 or $4 a day and can make $10 on a rare lucky day. . . .
> The younger ones come because they can't make better money at anything else. A 21-year-old man, who left school in the seventh grade, recently quit a job in a restaurant to work at the dump. He made $30 for 72 hours of dishwashing a week.

Another New Year's Day dispatch in the *Southern Courier*, from Boligee, Alabama, reported:

> Six-week-old Chester Washington is dead because of poverty.
> In Boligee, 11 miles southwest of Eutaw, Miss Sara Washington lives in a one-room log cabin with her six remaining children. She has no income, no heat, and no food. . . .

This is the house that Chester Washington was born in a little over six weeks ago. A Negro midwife delivered him. This is the house he died in on a night when the thermometer read eight degrees. His death was probably due to exposure.

Poverty was neither a black nor a Southern rural phenomenon. In New York City, by the early seventies, more than a million people were on the welfare rolls, including 600,000 children. In Connecticut, the third wealthiest state in the country on a per capita basis, 10 per cent of the families in 1964 were earning less than three thousand dollars a year. In San Antonio in 1967, it was estimated by local welfare officials that 100,000 to 150,000 residents suffered from hunger or malnutrition. Many of those on welfare were white; inadequate income was not a black problem alone. True, blacks were disproportionately poor. Twice as many blacks as whites were under the poverty line, relative to population. In 1968, for example, 36 per cent of the black families in America had an income below four thousand dollars a year; the percentage for white families was 14. But of the 9 million families below that poverty line, 7 million were white and 2 million black.

While many of the poor could not work, because of age or illness, or because they were women tied to the home, many of those who could work could not get jobs. It has always been one of the folk myths in middle America that the lower classes, black and white, shun work, when these are exactly the people who do the hardest, dirtiest, most oppressive work, for the least pay—and who have the most difficult time getting work. The following conversation, between a television reporter and a black woman in her shack on a southern plantation, tells much about the folk myth and about reality:

> WOMAN: I've been on this same plantation for seventeen years. No, it's not my home. Not my land. We need work.
> REPORTER: Do you have respect for work?
> WOMAN (*laughing uproariously*): I worked for nineteen years and what do I *have?* You don't know about work, do you?
> REPORTER: I work.
> WOMAN (*again laughing*): You know about cotton? (*She peered at the reporter.*) You don't know anything about cotton, do you?

The contrast between wealth and poverty in postwar America was also reflected in a government medical report. As related in the *New York Times* on January 22, 1969:

> The phenomenon of chronic hunger and malnutrition in a land fat with agricultural surpluses was officially verified for the first time today in a Government medical survey.
> Preliminary findings of an examination of 12,000 Americans selected at random in low-income areas of Texas, Louisiana, New York and Kentucky show an "alarming prevalence" of disease commonly associated with undernourishment.
> They also disclosed the presence of exotic diseases that were thought to exist only among the ill-fed peoples of backward countries. . . .

In sum, the postwar years saw no basic change in the traditional distribution of American income in which the top fifth of the population made ten times the income of the bottom fifth. A 1970 report by a private organization in Washington, the National Bureau of Economic Research, spoke of "the failure of 20 years of unprecedented prosperity and rapid economic growth to produce any significant change in the distribution of income, at least at the lower end."

What was the government of the United States—dedicated, verbally, at least, since the New Deal to the elimination of want—doing in behalf of those in need? What was the government of the United States—dedicated, verbally, at least, since the American Revolution to the precept of equal opportunity—doing to help the disadvantaged?

Was the government seeing to it that all had equal educational opportunities? Without much question, higher education was the path upward in postwar America. Yet for youngsters from low-income families, access to higher education had its difficulties. A New York State survey in the 1960s of high-school students with IQs of more than 130 revealed that if family income was under four thousand dollars, 77 per cent of them planned to continue their education; if family income was more than eight thousand dollars, however, 96 per cent of them made plans to continue. For those with IQs between 110 and 119, the difference was even more striking: in the under-four-thousand-dollar group, 47 per cent planned to go on to college while in the over-eight-thousand-dollar group, 89 per cent had such expectations. In 1967 in Massachusetts, 25 per cent of the students from low-income groups went to four-year colleges, but 55 per cent of the high-income groups went. Class discrimination extended to the IQ tests themselves; sociological surveys indicated they favored the high-income groups. For instance, a question that asked "Symphony is to composer as book is to what?" drew 81 per cent correct responses from higher economic groups, and 51 per cent from lower economic groups. But when the question was "A baker goes with bread like a carpenter goes with what?" 50 per cent got it right in each group.

Was the government's allocation of funds for the poor, the sick, the aged, and the ill-housed comparable to what it was allocating wealthy corporations through subsidies, tax benefits, and contracts? Back in 1932 the historian Charles Beard, in an essay entitled "The Myth of Rugged Individualism," noted that the greatest recipients— and the first—of "welfare" aid from the government were the big businesses of America. This preferential pattern continued in the postwar decades and grew to monstrous proportions.

The war itself had been a bonanza for the big corporations through government contracts. But with the end of the war, many of these corporations were sustained by the government. In 1946 a secret air force guideline said that contracts should be given to aircraft companies in order to keep them in business—even if there was no immediate need for their products. By the 1960s, some of the major aircraft companies depended for 100 per cent of their business on government contracts—and at a tidy profit. Lockheed Aircraft, for instance, made a profit in 1965 of 19 per cent of its net worth, somewhat above the 4 per cent interest the average American drew on his savings. Between 1950 and 1970, the government budget rose from $40 billion to $200 billion, and war-related expenditures from $12 billion to $80 billion. Many of these billions were spent through government contracts with large corporations. In 1966 one corporation alone—General Dynamics—had government contracts totaling $2.2 billion.

Was the government watchful of the needs of the poor farmer, or was it giving fat bonuses to the rich landowners? The agricultural subsidy program was another striking example of government wel-

fare for the rich. Begun under the New Deal for the plausible purpose of helping the ordinary farmer, it became, in the postwar
period, a handsome handout for the landed gentry. In 1969, $3.5
billion in farm subsidies were given out. Half of it went to those in
the top 15 per cent farm-income bracket. The twenty wealthiest
farmers in the nation were getting more from the Department of
Agriculture than the bottom 350,000 farmers. In 1968 one farm—
the J. G. Boswell Company in California—got $3 million in sub-
sidies. That same year Senator James Eastland of Mississippi, a
farmer, got $117,000 from the government in direct payments. In
the Texas district of George Mahon, chairman of the House Appropriations Committee, his brother in Lubbock received $26,000
in subsidies; more than 1,200 other farmers in Mahon's congressional district also received subsidy checks—more than $20,000
each. Kenneth Frick, appointed by President Nixon to administer
the farm-support program, received $88,000 in subsidies in 1968.
An attempt that year to place a $10,000 ceiling on individual farm
subsidies was rejected by the House of Representatives in a secret vote.

Were the government's tax programs aimed at redistributing income toward the low-income groups or maintaining wealth at the
top? The most important single fact about income taxes in the postwar era was that, beginning with wartime policy, they reached down
into the lowest income groups. Whereas in 1940, 7.4 million people
reported taxable income, in 1945, the number was 42 million.
Families living below the official four-per-family, $3,000 poverty
level set by the Department of Labor were paying income taxes.
For instance, in 1967, 2.5 million citizens earning less than $3,000
paid $1.5 billion dollars in taxes—exactly the sum allocated by
Congress that year for the so-called "poverty program." That same
year, 155 persons who made more than $200,000 paid no taxes
whatsoever. The popular notion about the American tax structure
was that the rich paid relatively more in taxes, that the tax rate rose
steeply from the lower to the upper income brackets. The actual tax
rate, as opposed to the nominal one, however, did not change dramatically. While about 75 per cent of the taxpayers making between
$3,000 and $5,000 a year paid 15 to 20 per cent of their income in
taxes, the same proportion of those making $20,000 to $50,000 a

year paid 25 to 35 per cent and those making $1 million or more a year paid 20 to 30 per cent.

The oil industry has been one of the more extraordinary examples of special favors for the rich. For most of the postwar years, oil companies could deduct 27.5 per cent of their gross income from their federal income taxes, up to half of their total tax bill; in 1969 Congress, after years and years of protest, reduced this allowance to 22 per cent. In addition, oil companies have been permitted to deduct many of the costs involved in exploration, drilling, and development, plus most of the royalties they pay to foreign powers. As a result, oil and gas companies have been saving in taxes nineteen times their original investment for the average well. In 1968, while corporations in general were paying 40 per cent of their income in taxes, oil companies paid less than 8 per cent. The federal government has also effectively eliminated foreign competition and enabled the oil companies to raise their prices—at a cost to the American consumer in 1970 of some $5 billion.

Like the rich farmers, the rich oilmen have had powerful pals in Congress, too, including Texan Lyndon Johnson and Russell Long of Louisiana. Long, chairman of the Senate Finance Committee, and a key figure in steering the oil-depletion provisions through the Senate, made more than a million dollars from oil leases from 1964 through 1970, with about $330,000 of this exempt from taxes because of the depletion allowance. Long responded to criticism by saying: "I don't regard it as any conflict of interest." The Nixon administration has followed its predecessors' attitude toward taxation and the rich; in early 1971, Nixon announced tax reductions for business amounting to several billion dollars, applying the depletion-allowance idea to other businesses.

Did the poor have friends in Congress? Was the government acting in their behalf? The Full Employment Act of 1946 had been conceived as a grand attempt to harness the nation's resources for social welfare as it was done for war. Its original language had stressed public investment, but, as passed, it spoke ambivalently about action "to foster and promote free competitive enterprise and the general welfare." In the end, it accomplished little more than the establishment of the three-member Council of Economic Advisers to help the president.

Through Democratic and Republican administrations, from Truman to Nixon, the pattern of government action for low-income groups was basically the same—to increase slightly the basic benefits that had begun during the New Deal: social security for the aged, unemployment insurance, minimum-wage laws, public housing. By 1967 the average monthly payment to retired workers at age 65 was $85, a $25 increase in seventeen years. The average weekly benefit for unemployed workers was $20 in 1950 and $40 in 1967. During the sixties, the welfare rolls increased sharply, particularly in the cities, with the states carrying the largest burden in welfare payments. Fatherless families were the biggest recipients of local welfare, with the average payment to such families in 1968 amounting to only $43 a week. In the fall of 1971, 14 million Americans were receiving welfare payments.

Was the government providing housing for the ill-housed? Care for the sick? Sustenance for the destitute? Most of the postwar housing construction was for upper- and middle-income groups; housing for the lowest third of the population just became shabbier. The Census Bureau in 1960 classified 11 million homes as "deteriorating" or "dilapidated," but between 1950 and 1960, only 278,000 units were built for low-income people out of a total of 14 million units constructed. By 1970, the United States still had no national health program guaranteeing adequate medical care for any person needing it, regardless of income. Between 1950 and 1970, America dropped from seventh in the world to sixteenth in the prevention of infant mortality, in female life expectancy from sixth to eighth, in male life expectancy from tenth to twenty-fourth.

The poverty program initiated by the Johnson administration, and administered through the Office of Economic Opportunity, faltered its way into 1970, plagued by limited funds and control by local politicians, although it was the poor of the communities to whom control had been promised. In April, 1966, a thousand delegates came to the Citizens Crusade Against Poverty in Washington and received a speech by Vice President Humphrey with open hostility. As the *New York Times* reported:

> The mood of the convention was mutinous. Delegates from Harlem, the Mississippi Delta, Appalachia, and the Watts district of Los Angeles expressed outrage at how little was being

done to help them, particularly by the Office of Economic Opportunity, which runs the national poverty program.

"O.E.O. ought to be ashamed of itself and the Federal Government ought to be ashamed of itself," declared Mrs. Unita Blackwell, an official of the Mississippi Freedom Democratic Party. Mrs. Blackwell said she was "tired of beautiful speeches." She charged that "hand-picked people" of white boards of supervisors, plantation owners, and police chiefs were running the local poverty programs in Mississippi. "They're going to see me about my poverty," she said scornfully. "They kept me in poverty."

"We is the people, we is the poor people, we is the people you is supposed to help. The same men who pay us $3 a day and are bent in putting people off the land—that's the men who are on the poverty committee," she declared.

Her charge was confirmed by an executive order issued by Johnson in 1968 putting all job-training programs under federal and local government control rather than the control of community groups.

The gross national product in 1971 approached a thousand billion dollars, and in terms of gadgets and machines, Americans were doing better. Almost everyone—99.8 per cent of the population, said the Census Bureau in 1970—had a refrigerator; roughly 92 per cent of American families had a washing machine, 95 per cent a television set, 91 per cent a vacuum cleaner. For the top third of the population, there were multiple joys: 36 per cent of the population had air conditioners, 38 per cent color television, 30 per cent more than one car, and a freezer. More and more families had speed boats and vacationed in Florida or the Caribbean in the winter. Still, poverty persisted. Still, behind the opulence, there were signs of distress: by 1965, 488,000 persons were in mental institutions, 435,000 outpatients in psychiatric clinics, 9 million were mentally ill; in the mid-sixties, more than a million Americans were chronic alcoholics; several hundred thousand were narcotic addicts; the annual suicide rate was twenty thousand; and one of four marriages ended in divorce. Close to 2 million crimes involving property were committed every year. Despite the thousand billion dollars in GNP, the American system was obviously not using its vast production for humane ends, was not achieving an equitable distribution of resources, was not creating an atmosphere of cooperation and goodwill among the people.

What was wrong? The promise in the Declaration of Independence for equality in the right to life, liberty, and the pursuit of happiness was not even close to fulfillment. Galbraith wrote in 1970: "The economic system does not work and the reforms required to make it work—to make it work uniformly and for individuals and not for corporations—are far more fundamental than anything contemplated by the cheap and soft and easy-going liberalism of these last years."

What is it in the working creed of liberalism that has acted to defeat rhetorical promises from the days of Jefferson to the decades after Roosevelt? I would suggest three factors: nationalism, the profit motive, and the failure of the political system to go beyond a spurious representation to something approaching self-determination.

I. NATIONALISM

Liberalism and socialism have both been at a disadvantage in fulfilling their theoretical promise because they have come to power in the era of the nation-state. Liberalism especially, as the ideology of the new commercial-capitalist class, required the nation-state as organizer of domestic resources and as usurper, through imperialism, of foreign resources. The fierce self-centeredness and aggressive xenophobia of the nation-state has acted in the United States, more acutely than anywhere else, to divert material and human energies toward war and the preparation for war and away from the most fundamental human needs. In postwar America, the thousand billion dollars spent for military purposes could have guaranteed to every American adequate food, housing, education, and medical care.

American culture fed nationalism in every way. Almost the first act of children in school was to pledge allegiance to the flag. Homage to the flag became so ingrained that in 1970 some citizens who wore the stars and stripes on their clothing were sent to jail. Patriotism was sanctified in the United States, as in the other nation-states, with a special force given to it by the overriding concern with "national security." No nation in the world was more heavily armed;

no nation in the world patrolled as much of the rest of the planet as America. Yet no nation trembled so much for its national security or ventured so far abroad in presumed defense of its security. The drain on the country's resources for reasons of "security" might have been intolerably painful, but for the drug of nationalism.

Perhaps the most flamboyant evidence of how enormous resources can be squandered for nationalist purposes was the allocation, all through the sixties, of three billion to five billion dollars a year for the purpose of putting an American on the moon. The transfer of these billions to the National Aeronautics and Space Administration (NASA) culminated in 1969 with the first lunar landing of a man. The scientific value of much of this expenditure was dubious; many scientists pointed out that unmanned lunar landings would yield needed data just as well, and at much less cost. But patriotic zeal, the compulsion to be first in putting a man on the moon—with flag—operated to support the allocation of vast sums of money for national pride rather than for men and women.

II. THE PROFIT MOTIVE AND THE COMPETITIVE SPIRIT

The engine that drives the productive mechanism of the capitalist system is the profit motive. As Marx admiringly noted, it is a powerful engine that at a certain period in history carries man far in using and shaping his environment. But Marx also noted the tendency of the engine to run down after its major contribution had been made. Andrew Shonfield, a specialist in the comparative study of American and European economies, concluded that in the United States "the pace of industrial expansion was significantly slower during the years after the Second World War than it had been in the 1900's."

Socialist critics for a long time have pointed out the tendency of the capitalist system to produce wasteful, harmful, and destructive goods, simply because they have been profitable. The profit motive not only has served as the spur for military production—profits in military-related industries have been consistently 50 to 100 per cent higher than in other production areas—it has diverted resources that would best be used elsewhere. The profit drive in the postwar period was not directed toward building schools, hospitals, playgrounds, or low-cost housing—there was no profitable market there—but toward the production of automobiles. In 1968, General Motors received a return of 25.8 per cent on its investment. The automobile industry alone spent $2 billion in the decade of the sixties advertising its wares, dinning into the ears of every American his need for a new car. In 1968 nine million cars were sold—and six million scrapped; for a population of 200 million, there were 72 million automobiles, one for every three persons in the nation. In October, 1971, a record one million cars were sold.

How much waste did this represent in money, materials, labor? A study by Harvard economists has shown that style changes alone after 1949 cost $4 billion each year. The greatest waste was in lives lost in auto crashes. Highway deaths exceeded fifty thousand a year by the mid-1960s. Safe cars were not the first concern of the auto-mobile manufacturers. Indeed, an October 5, 1969, *New York Times* story, under the headline BUSINESS OF THRILL AUTOMOBILES HIGH ON DETROIT PROMOTION LIST, described how

> . . . the thrill business, or the promotion of muscle cars, as Detroit calls them, is one of the automobile industry's major thrusts today.
>
> These high powered cars, with up to 150 miles an hour top speed, as delivered from the factory, carry names such as Chevrolet's Z-28. . . . Thomas Feaheny, leading engineer at Ford Motor Company, said that 600,000 muscle cars . . . will be sold in 1969, up from 56,000 in 1964. . . . The General Motors Company does not acknowledge publicly that it is in such a business. . . .

In an economy motivated by private corporate profit, the human effects of production are secondary, and social concern is a luxury. Sixty years after Upton Sinclair's *The Jungle* had helped stimulate passage of the Meat Inspection Act, a November 9, 1967, *New York Times* story from Washington read:

> Federal investigators told a Senate subcommittee today of finding filthy conditions and meat infected with parasites as recently as last July in meat-packing plants not covered by Federal meat inspection.

They said that they had also found adulterated meat and the use of additives, including excess water in hams, in meat sold in retail stores throughout the country. . . .

Senator Walter F. Mondale, Democrat of Minnesota, told the subcommittee that some of the country's largest packers had deliberately established plants "out of reach" of the Federal Government, to effect "savings" by passing off sick meat to consumers and by using additives not permitted under Federal regulations.

The most basic need of man—food—was not exempt from corporate greed. The Federal Water Pollution Control Commission estimated that in 1968 fifteen million fish were killed by water pollution. It blamed industrial waste for the death of six million of the fish. By 1970, there were periodic scares about the presence of dangerous mercury in salmon, and other poisons in tuna. And as America polluted its waters it profaned its land. As Adelle Davis, one of the nation's leading nutritionists, remarked in late 1970:

> Our ground has been depleted to the point where even a cow can't get adequate nutrition from the grass it grazes on. Farmers are given $3 billion a year to keep land fallow when the money could be used to build up the ground by growing crops to supply humus. But the Department of Agriculture isn't doing that because nobody's making money on it. The whole country is at the mercy of people who are making money off our food.

As concern grew on the part of many Americans about the pollution of air and water by industrial wastes, the demands of corporate profit created obstacles to regulations for the reduction of pollution. The adoption of national standards for air pollution, urged before a Senate committee in 1967, was opposed by the United States Chamber of Commerce, the National Association of Manufacturers, the American Mining Congress, and the National Coal Association. Automobile companies were reluctant to endanger profits by changes in auto-engine designs to cut exhaust pollution. The oil that polluted California's beautiful beaches early in 1968 was produced by a system in which the oil companies' need for profit had far more weight than a man's need to swim in clean water. And profit at the expense of man and his environment was the first consideration no matter which political party was in power. It was the liberal Secretary of the Interior Stewart Udall in the Kennedy-Johnson administrations who allowed the dangerous oil drilling to go on in California. As one news analyst wrote from Santa Barbara: "It was all signed, sealed, and delivered. No public agency at any level has ever had any power to make the oil companies conform to anything—and that's still the way it is." In January, 1969, sulfur dioxide was pouring out of the tanks of Boston Edison into the city's sky. Headlined the *Boston Globe:* EDISON CITES HIGH COST OF CLEAN AIR. The "high cost" meant $8 million—too dear a price for breathable air when measured against the need for more and more profits.

The rush for profit also stimulated collusion by corporations to maintain high prices on their products in industries where a few giant firms could control the price market. In 1961 officials of three electrical companies, General Electric, Westinghouse, and Allis-Chalmers, were brought to trial in what became known as "the incredible electrical conspiracy." Company officials were charged with fixing prices on circuit-breaking equipment, thereby cheating the public out of what the sentencing judge described as "millions upon millions" of dollars. A few of the officials involved were sent to prison—for thirty days.

In 1959 testimony before the United States Senate disclosed that the drug industry was also selling its products at artificially inflated prices. Penicillin tablets which could have been sold by the manufacturer at $3.75 a hundred, with a good profit, were sold at $14.85 a hundred. Prednisone tablets, sold by one small company at $2.35 a hundred, were sold under another name by three major drug companies at $17.90. Committee accountants estimated that the public was paying $750 million a year in excess prices for drugs.

Senator Estes Kefauver of Tennessee, chairman of the Senate Antitrust and Monopoly Subcommittee, questioned John T. Connor, president of the Merck drug company, on the price of an antiarthritic drug:

> KEFAUVER: I still don't understand why people in London get this drug at the drug stores at $7.53 and our drug stores have to pay $17.90.
> CONNOR: Mr. Chairman, we meet different market conditions in different countries.

Kefauver also questioned Merck's director of marketing, Eugene L. Kuryloski:

> KEFAUVER: How did it happen that you and Upjohn and Schering all arrived at exactly the same price of $17.90?
> KURYLOSKI: Well, sir, we entered the market later following Schering by several months, and, as with any commodity which is identical, we felt it to our advantage to meet their price.

Francis C. Brown, the president of Schering, testified with Alice-in-Wonderland logic: "Undoubtedly some people find it difficult to pay for needed medication. They will also have difficulty in meeting their rent and food bills as well . . . It is a matter of inadequate income rather than excessive prices." In this same vein, Dr. Austin Smith, president of the Pharmaceutical Manufacturers Association, told four hundred representatives of major pharmaceutical companies: "I am sure that all of us feel the greatest compassion for elderly people who find it difficult to pay for medication. If the pharmaceutical industry is at fault here, it is because it has helped create a pool of millions too old to work by prolonging their lives."

This same kind of profit-motive compassion was described in early 1970 by a Stanford University anesthesiologist in the *New England Journal of Medicine*. Dr. John P. Bunker, studying surgery in the United States, England, and Wales, found that there were twice as many surgeons in proportion to population in the United States, and that they performed twice as many operations. Bunker wrote that "with a limited total medical manpower pool, more physicians engaged in the practice of surgery means fewer for other possibly needier medical disciplines. . . . Thus, we have the paradox of a country that provides 'luxury' surgery for the well-to-do but cannot provide basic medical care for the indigent." In an editorial in the same journal issue, Dr. Francis D. Moore, a Harvard surgeon, said that "money may be at the root of it all" and that "among the many reasons for the excessive development of American surgery, as compared to Great Britain, are those based on the laissez-faire system of American medicine, solo practice and fee for service."

In a humanistic society, toys would be produced according to their value in helping children grow into happy, thoughtful people. In a profit-seeking society, such an objective becomes absurd. In

1963 the toy industry's major publication, *Toys and Novelties,* noted: "Military will lead the league this year." That is, military toys would predominate among twenty-eight American manufacturers of toys. One company, Aurora Plastics Corporation, announced that its "output of military and naval equipment could supply all of NATO's needs and then some."

An even grimmer example of the connection between money and death came to light in February, 1969, with an Associated Press dispatch from Tooele, Utah, headlined: UTAH TOWN HAPPILY CO-EXISTS WITH POISON GAS. The army was storing nerve gas just outside the town, but "the people of Tooele generally shrug and accept it. Their discomfort is outweighed by the money the Tooele Army Depot means to the area. About 5,000 of the 15,000 residents work at the depot." According to Tooele's mayor, the town was so completely tied to the military that "it would blow away without it," a rather bizarre comment considering that six thousand sheep had died from the nerve gas one day because of the way the winds blew. In the poison-gas case, it was not corporate profit that was involved but the livelihood of ordinary people; yet a system that could guarantee people their daily bread only at such a risk must surely be deficient.

The neurotic drive of the capitalistic system for profit has fostered its own kind of culture in America. With governmental sanction, the profit motive has been permitted not only to pollute our environment but to befoul our bodies. Why else was the cigarette industry allowed to resist regulation while deaths from lung cancer multiplied? Not until 1970 was cigarette advertising on television banned—at least ten years after the dangers of cigarette smoking were clearly known. The major allocations of resources in American society have been made on the basis of money profit rather than social use. Why else was a private communications satellite system allowed to develop from public expenditures on space projects?

A society that did away with private business profit would still not be free of other corrupting motives, such as power and ambition, but it would at least eliminate an urge that in a capitalist society becomes an obsession: to make almost anything, to do almost anything, to sell almost anything that brings a profit.

III. THE FAILURE OF THE POLITICAL SYSTEM

Just as economic "progress" under liberal capitalism has meant token reforms without coming close to fulfilling the promise of equality, so the political system has dispensed tokens of democracy without giving the mass of people any real power to help make the decisions that govern their lives. One basic reason for America's failure to go beyond the tokens of democracy is because the notion of "democracy" has been confined to the larger arenas of politics, where people vote once every several years for representatives; what has remained outside the realm of democracy are the small chambers of everyday life. The American workplace, for instance, has always been regimented, hierarchical; frustrations, alienation, the loss of identity permeate all levels of work from the factory to the corporation. The home, presumably a haven, has been a microcosm of the larger society, exemplifying the domination of male over female, old over young, money over human feeling. The colleges and universities have been run by absentee lords—trustees, regents, principals, presidents—with policy-making power diminishing steeply as it reaches those for whom the school allegedly exists: the students and the faculty. The courtroom has been the imperial domain of the judge and his retinue of toadies. The city street has belonged less and less to its residents, more and more to those twin enemies—the criminal and the policeman.

In the larger arena of politics, where the promise of democracy has been made loudest, where liberal democracy has taken historic pride, there has been a failure of self-determination, of the individual's opportunity to shape his own life and environment. The American political system is a representative system. Its decisions are made not directly by those affected, but by either representatives—state legislators, congressmen, senators, governors, presidents—or their appointees—administrators, federal and many local judges. The decisions made by these representatives influence the life, liberty, and ability to pursue happiness of each American. Congress and the president decide on the tax structure, which has a direct bearing on the distribution of resources. They decide how to spend the tax money received, whether or not the nation goes to war, who serves in the armed forces, what behavior is considered criminal, which crimes are prosecuted and which are not. They decide what limitations should be imposed on travel, or on the right to speak freely. They decide on the availability of education, health services, public housing.

If the representative system is by its nature undemocratic, then real democracy in the United States has not yet been attained, and will not be unless new institutions, new modes of decision-making can be created. However, because representative government is closer to the people than monarchy, it has been hailed as one of the great liberal features of modern times. Yet at its best it is only a step in the direction of democracy. Its inherent flaws were pointed out by Rousseau in the eighteenth century, Victor Considérant in the nineteenth century, Robert Michels at the start of the twentieth century, and Hannah Arendt in the postwar period. No representative, their argument runs, can adequately speak for another's needs. The representative has a tendency to become a member of a special elite; he has privileges that weaken his sense of concern about the grievances of others. The passions of troubled groups lose force as they are filtered through the representative system—as James Madison noted in *The Federalist Papers;* the elected official attains an experience that tends toward his own perpetuation. Leaders develop what Michels called "a mutual insurance contract" against the rest of society.

The "democracy" that replaced the monarchies of the sixteenth, seventeenth, and eighteenth centuries was only an intermediary step between absolutism and true democracy. The throne also claimed to represent the people. Both Napoleons used plebiscites, as have later dictators; indeed, modern elections are merely modified plebiscities. A majority may bind not only itself but the minority to a form of slavery. As Rousseau put it in *The Social Contract:* "How have a hundred men who wish for a master the right to vote on behalf of ten who do not?" Thoreau saw the limited influence of voting when he said: "Cast your whole vote, not a strip of paper merely, but your whole influence."

In 1956 the sociologist C. Wright Mills, in a book that exerted immense influence on the next generation, *The Power Elite,* pointed to the inadequacy of the American political system. He was reacting to the comfortable, complacent view of American democracy prevalent in the society at large and reflected in textbooks and in popular literature. In this orthodox view, the continued expansion of the suffrage and the two-party system were part of a great "pluralist" system in which no one group dominated American politics, but a multiplicity of interests generated compromises that afforded sufficient benefits to enough people to maintain stability and general contentment.

Mills argued that most people were powerless in the American political system, that a complex elite of political, business, and military leaders ruled the country, operating through institutions: the state, the corporation, and the armed forces. Each of these three institutions had become highly centralized in the twentieth century: the political establishment had concentrated power in a vast executive bureaucracy, the economy was now dominated by about two hundred giant corporations, the military had expanded enormously through the ideology of hot and cold wars. Furthermore, the three institutions were interlocked, with the key positions interchangeable—generals becoming presidents or corporation executives; businessmen becoming cabinet members.

Anticipating, but not deterring, later criticism, Mills repudiated the idea of a conscious conspiracy at the top, but he also rejected the notion of drift. Mills made the point that at crucial moments the hard will of the privileged asserted itself. It was an important point to Mills, because a disjointed leadership, supervising a series of "accidents," could not be held accountable by the public. And Mills insisted on the necessity for such accountability. It was precisely on this question that he and the orthodox liberal political scientists parted. They were often ready to admit the exercise of power in concentrated form at the top, but argued that there were serious restraints from below on this power. Mills, on the other hand, said that power on the middle levels of society was semi-organized, stalemated, and that on the bottom levels it was fragmented, impotent. Analysts who hailed the American system for its checks on power came from the middle levels themselves, Mills said, and at the middle levels the struggle was noisy but rather meaningless.

Looking at politics in the postwar period, Mills saw a decisive shift of power in Washington from Congress to the president. Congressmen were brokers of local power groups, and they tended to straddle important, national issues. They were reinforced in their conservatism by party rule and the seniority system in committees, and they too often deferred to the president. The power of the public to check presidential power was limited, Mills said, by the manipulation of public opinion in the mass media, including education. The mass of people had lost their political will to resist because they saw no way to realize their objectives in the face of the power elite.

Not only radicals like Mills pointed to the inadequacy of the political processes in the United States. Established political scientists of a moderate bent talked bluntly in the 1950s of the limitations of the representative system and electoral politics as a means of ensuring democracy. Robert Dahl's *A Preface to Democratic Theory,* an authoritative statement by an acknowledged leader among professional political scientists, expressed deep doubts about the degree of democracy in the United States, though it also conveyed a certain confidence about the relative superiority of the American system. Dahl noted that the Founding Fathers were much more worried about tyranny by the majority than by the minority, and that the American political system developing out of the Constitution seemed to work against wide participation by the lower classes:

> By their propensity for political passivity the poor and uneducated disfranchise themselves. . . . Since they also have less access than the wealthy to the organizational, financial, and propaganda resources that weigh so heavily in campaigns, elections, legislative, and executive decisions, anything like equal control over government policy is triply barred to the members of Madison's unpropertied masses. They are barred by their relatively limited access to resources, and by Madison's nicely contrived system of constitutional checks.

Dahl's belief that "our society is essentially democratic" is based on low expectations. Even if democracy were to be superficially defined as "majority rule," the United States would not fulfill that, he said, because "on matters of specific policy, the majority rarely rules."

To Dahl "the election is the critical technique for insuring that governmental leaders will be relatively responsive to non-leaders." Yet he goes on to say that "it is important to notice how little a national election tells us about the preferences of majorities. Strictly speaking, all an election reveals is the first preferences of some citizens among the candidates standing for office." Only about 60 per cent of the potential voters in national elections, and about 40 per cent of the voters in local elections, go to the polls. These low percentages cannot be attributed, Dahl believes, simply to indifference. Whatever the reason, "in no large nation-state can elections tell us much about the preferences of majorities and minorities," he says, adding that this absence of detectable preferences is "even more true of the interelection period." In his words:

> If you examine carefully any policy decision, even a very important one, you will always discover, I believe, that only a tiny proportion of the electorate is actively bringing its influence to bear upon politicians. In an area as critical as foreign policy, the evidence is conclusive that year in and year out the overwhelming proportion of American citizens makes its preferences effective, if at all, by no means other than going to the polls and casting a ballot.

Dahl asserts that the election process and interelection activity "are crucial processes for insuring that political leaders will be *somewhat* responsive to the preferences of some ordinary citizens." The italics are mine—to suggest that if an admirer of democracy in America can say no more than that about it, democracy becomes a euphemism.

The election process, Dahl declares, is one of "two fundamental methods of social control which, operating together, make government leaders so responsive to non-leaders that the distinction between democracy and dictatorship still makes sense." Since his description of the election process weakens the claim for one of those two methods, what is the second? "The other method of social control is continuous political competition among individuals, parties, or both." What this means is "not minority rule but minorities rule." Yet there is much evidence to support the contention that "minorities rule" would hardly transform America into a valid democracy: the vastly disproportionate influence of wealthy groups over poorer ones; the lack of democracy among the groups that compose the major political parties; the unrepresentative nature of the major lobbies—the wealthy doctors speaking for all doctors through the American Medical Association, the wealthy farmers speaking for the poor farmers through the American Farm Bureau Federation, the most affluent trade unions speaking for all the workers. Dahl finds some comfort in the American system's "steady appeasement of relatively small groups." If the aircraft industry among these relatively small groups has a greater voice than the aged, the space industry more influence than the poor, the Pentagon far more weight that the college youth, what is left of democracy?

Sometimes the elitism of decision-making is defended by political scientists on the ground that the elite is enacting decisions passively supported by the mass, whose tolerance for these decisions is proof of an underlying consensus in society. However, Murray Levin's studies in *The Alienated Voter* indicate how much nonparticipation in elections is a result of hopelessness rather than approval over what has been done by the elite.

Adequate information for the electorate is a precondition for any kind of action—whether electoral or demonstrative—to affect national policy. As for the voting process, Paul Lazarsfeld and his co-authors state in their book *Voting,* based on extensive empirical research: "One persistent conclusion is that the public is not particularly well-informed about the specific issues of the day." This is corroborated by Angus Campbell and his co-authors in *The American Voter:* "The thinness of the electorate's understanding of concrete policy alternatives—its inability to respond to government and politics at this level—helps explain why it is that efforts to interpret a national election in terms of a policy mandate are speculative, contradictory, and inconclusive."

How well-informed, for instance, is the public on two major issues of the day? One is the tax structure, so bewilderingly complex that only the corporation, with its battalion of accountants and financial experts, is in a position to prime itself for lobbying activities. The average voter, hardly able to comprehend his own income tax, stands by helplessly as the president, the Bureau of the Budget, and the Congress decide the tax laws. And the dominant influence determining the tax structure is that of big business, which has the resources both to understand all its implications and to take action in shaping it.

Then there is the matter of foreign policy. The government leads the citizenry to believe it has special expertise, which, if it could only be revealed, would support the official position against all critics. At the same time, the government hides the very information that would reveal its position to be indefensible. The mendacity of the government in the 1961 Bay of Pigs operation; the underhanded operations of the CIA in Iran, Indonesia, Guatemala, and other places in the 1950s; the withholding of vital information about the Tonkin Gulf events of 1964 are only a few examples of the way the average American becomes a victim of government deception.

Furthermore, the distribution of that information which the public does receive is a function of power and wealth. The government itself can color the citizen's understanding of events by its control of news at the source—the presidential press conference, news releases, the "leak" to the press, the White Papers, the teams of "truth experts" roving around the country at taxpayers' expense. As for private media, the nationwide networks and mass-circulation magazines and newspapers have the greatest access to the public mind. Against this onslaught of information controlled and screened through governmental and private agencies, critics of public policy have never succeeded in obtaining "equal time."

Universal suffrage, perceived as a threat by seventeenth-century monarchies, has been a useful device for control in the modern state —capitalist or socialist. In an article for the *American Political Science Review* on their 1967 study of voting on various issues in Louisiana in 1960, 1963, and 1964, the authors conclude that universal suffrage helps maintain loyalty to a regime and is no threat to property interests:

> . . . we have found that universal suffrage, i.e., the popular vote, inflicts no damage, even where the issues are most directly concerned with impact on propertied rights. . . . the "irresponsible" element of the population, the popular voters, can be just as responsible and restrained as the property voters. Decisions made by the popular vote have no dire consequences for the community in general or for the specific economic interests of the dominants in the society. If there is no need to fear the decisions made by a popular vote, as illustrated by our

data, then the advantages of universal suffrage measured in legitimacy for regimes and stability are doubly attractive.

In the 1950s, liberal political theorists, perhaps encouraged by the absence of protest to think all was well with most Americans, seemed to stress the stability of the system as a top priority in evaluating the American political mechanism. By the 1960s, the upsurge of blacks, welfare mothers, the "discovery" of poverty, the new awareness of waste, threw a different light on the political system. A younger political scientist, Jack Walker, responding to Dahl and others, differed with Dahl's emphasis on the value of a political system "for reinforcing agreement, encouraging moderation, and maintaining social peace." Walker writes:

> Political stability is indeed a precious commodity; I do not wish to create the impression that I reject its obvious importance. But I do think . . . that the time has come to direct our attention to the infinitely more difficult task of involving larger and larger numbers of people in the process of government.

How widely recognized was the failure of the American political system to fulfill the sanguine description of it as "democratic" is shown by the description of this system in 1970 by Princeton political scientist Duane Lockard. In his book *The Perverted Priorities of American Politics,* Lockard does not accept either the Mills "power elite" thesis or Dahl's pluralist thesis of "minorities rule." He is, however, closer to Mills. He thinks that while at the bottom of the system there is a dispersion of power along with the rule of small elites on top, *both* act to maintain inequality. He writes that

> . . . the concentrations of power and the dispersal both have an impact on policy making, for the elites use both their concentrated power and the dispersal of authority in the veto system to achieve their ends. . . .
>
> In Congress, for example, power is widely dispersed and toll gates are accordingly set up through which all legislation must pass. . . . Power, far from being structured, is variable, scattered. . . . But there is one constant in the power utilization process; the have-nots either cannot get in the bargaining room or they enter with meager resources. . . .

Lockard sums up his detailed study of the branches of American government as follows:

Thus, an historic bias against government action in general, a system of dispersed power in the legislature that inhibits or distorts policy making, an independent bureaucracy that often obfuscates and modifies policies, and a federal system that disperses power to the scattered states . . . all serve to constrain the effectuation of policies that would aid the have-nots.

The domestic politics of the postwar period bears out this failure of the electoral-representative system to represent adequately the underprivileged. Decisions made in Congress and the White House either enhanced or maintained the traditionally unjust distribution of wealth. The political parties were themselves undemocratic, from local clubhouse politics up to the national nominating conventions. Congress was dominated by a few small cliques. The Supreme Court made no decisions bold enough to make a difference in class-status-wealth alignments in the country. Elections became a periodic ritual, dominated by money and mass media, devoid of clear-cut issues, constricted by the limits of the two-party system and the information made available to the public.

The presidential election of 1968 was one more stark example of the lack of democracy in the American political system. It was basically no different from other election campaigns, but the intensity of national conflict over Vietnam and the race question made the inherent disabilities of the system more than usually visible. Almost in defiance of a public disaffected by Vietnam, as shown in public-opinion polls, for example, and in Johnson's retirement under antiwar pressure, both major parties nominated candidates who represented a continuation of the Johnson policies on the war: Hubert Humphrey and Richard Nixon. Johnson's election in 1964 on a peace platform, and his almost immediate escalation of the war, constituted an earlier manifestation of the emptiness of political promises and the inadequacy of public control over foreign policy. *Newsweek* magazine, hardly a radical critic of American democracy, was moved enough by the pre-1968 convention shenanigans to say: "The plain fact of the matter is that U.S. Presidential nominations are delivered not by the people, but by the party professionals." The nomination of Humphrey, whose unpopularity had been mirrored repeatedly in polls and primaries through the spring and summer of 1968, was not surprising, given the machinery by which delegates are selected to national political conventions, and the control exercised at a convention by a small coterie of party professionals in charge of the arrangements, the credentials, the gavel, and the microphone.

When young people—liberal, radical, disillusioned—gathered in the Chicago streets to protest the workings of the Democratic National Convention in what seemed a legitimate exercise of the First Amendment right to peaceable assembly, Mayor Richard Daley, a power at the convention, called out the police to club them, tear-gas them, disperse them, and arrest them. Bystanders were also indiscriminately beaten, and the police attacked newsmen and photographers, smashing their equipment. Behind the façade of democracy in the voting process, it was made clear in 1968, was political authoritarianism and the unrestrained power of the police.

On the eve of the 1968 Democratic convention it was quite apparent that radical dissent, despite the rhetoric of liberalism, was drawing Republicans and Democrats together. Daniel Moynihan, an assistant secretary of labor under Johnson who would soon take up an important post in the Nixon administration, spoke at that time to members of Americans for Democratic Action and asked that liberal Democrats seek a working partnership with conservatives. Professor Moynihan warned that war abroad and violence in the cities might soon be joined by terrorism, and therefore liberals must "see more clearly that their essential interest is in the stability of the social order, that given the present threats to that stability, it is necessary to seek out and make much more effective alliances with political conservatives who share that concern, and who recognize that unyielding rigidity is just as much a threat to the continuity of things as is an anarchic desire for change."

The president, whether liberal or conservative, Republican or Democrat, gravitated toward dead center: the foreign policy of "cold war," the domestic policy of tokenism in social reform. When John F. Kennedy presented his budget to the nation after his first year in office, Washington journalist James Reston—moderate, perceptive, realistic—wrote that the budget did not suggest any "sudden transformation of the home front." Kennedy, Reston said, aimed "to avoid alienating any major group that might wreck the major objectives of trade and economic expansion."

Kennedy was avoiding, Reston said, "a more ambitious frontal attack on the unemployment problem." Also:

He agreed to a tax break for business investment in plant expansion and modernization. He is not spoiling for a fight with the Southern conservatives over civil rights. He has been urging the unions to keep wage demands down so that prices can be competitive in the world markets and jobs increased. And he has been trying to reassure the business community that he does not want any cold war with them on the home front.

. . . this week in his news conference he refused to carry out his promise to bar discrimination in Government-insured housing, but talked instead of postponing this until there was a "national consensus" in its favor.

Politically, this approach is undoubtedly paying off for the President personally. He came into office just a year ago on the narrowest of election margins sounding like a liberal crusader. He is ending it like a calculating machine.

During these twelve months the President has moved over into the decisive middle ground of American politics. . . .

That Kennedy, the most eloquent of liberal postwar presidents, should seek the "decisive middle ground" was characteristic of American politics. On this middle ground, safe from any threat of dynamic, day-to-day mass participation in politics, the customary priorities of the American system stood firm.

4

Solving the Race Problem

American liberalism was presented with a puzzle in the postwar period. For years the liberal argument had been to the effect that yes, the United States had a race problem, but it also had enough democracy, enough goodwill to solve it, and Americans were going about the job of doing so. Why, then, suddenly in the mid-sixties, after twenty years of reform in race relations, including Supreme Court decisions, congressional legislation, and presidential position papers and executive orders, did the black population erupt in a series of riots and rebellions to the twin cries of "Freedom Now" and "Black Power"? A look at those years of reform might be helpful.

With the first postwar president, Harry Truman, there began the long chain of pronouncements that would make the promise of racial equality a national priority. The war itself, in mobilizing the nation to defeat the Nazi spokesmen for racial superiority, had produced much eloquent talk about freedom. But it was tacitly agreed that domestic racial problems would have to be postponed while the war was being waged. The prevailing sentiment was expressed by Negro Heavyweight Champion Joe Louis when he said: "America's got lots of problems, but Hitler won't fix them."

Truman took several steps toward solving these racial problems once the war was over. In December, 1946, he appointed a Committee on Civil Rights "to inquire into and to determine whether and in what respect current law-enforcement measures and the authority and means possessed by Federal, State, and local governments may be strengthened and improved to safeguard the civil rights of the people." A year later the committee issued its report, and it was quite blunt in ascribing the motives behind its recommendations. They were made, explained the committee, partly for moral reasons but mainly for political and economic reasons. "The Time Is Now," the committee said in urging immediate action on civil-rights legislation. The "moral reason" spoke of conscience. The "economic

reason" spoke of the financial costs of discrimination to the country
and said: "The United States can no longer afford this heavy drain
upon its human wealth, its national competence." As for the "international reason," the committee declared:

> Our position in the post-war world is so vital to the future
> that our smallest actions have far-reaching effects. . . . We can-
> not escape the fact that our civil rights record has been an issue
> in world politics. The world's press and radio are full of it. . . .
> Those with competing philosophies have stressed—and are
> shamelessly distorting—our shortcomings. . . . They have tried
> to prove our democracy an empty fraud, and our nation a con-
> sistent oppressor of underprivileged people. This may seem
> ludicrous to Americans, but it is sufficiently important to worry
> our friends. . . . The United States is not so strong, the final
> triumph of the democratic ideal is not so inevitable that we
> can ignore what the world thinks of us or our record.

The committee recommended the expansion of the civil-rights section of the Department of Justice and the establishment of a permanent Commission on Civil Rights. It also proposed congressional
legislation against lynching and voting discrimination, and recommended new laws on fair-employment practices and on the equitable
administration of justice. Truman then asked Congress to act on
the committee's report.

Congress did nothing. The whole sequence of events—from
Truman's declamations, to the report of the Committee on Civil
Rights, to the death of the program in Congress—illustrated the
limits of the orthodox American approach to social reform within
the confines of the liberal tradition. Perhaps the most important
fact about this customary approach to reform was that the impetus
for change from the aggrieved—in this case, the black population
—was present but not sufficiently strong to ensure firm action. Whatever pressure there was from the blacks—such as the scattered discontent among black war veterans and the legal arguments of the
National Association for the Advancement of Colored People—dis-
sipated itself by aligning with the political self-interest of the
American government. Speeches, investigatory committees, and
promises surged forth, but not much more.

The self-interest of dominant groups in society never has had the
motivating force sufficient to revolutionize social relations, espe-

cially when change might rebound against that self-interest. Such self-interest does generate speeches, promises, and token action; these do not bring about radical changes, only sufficient reforms to forestall rebellion. In July, 1948, stimulated in part by the pressure of potential black voters in key urban areas in a presidential election year, and by the expectation of the first peacetime conscription act, Truman issued an executive order asking that a policy of racial equality in the armed forces "be put into effect as rapidly as possible." He created a committee to implement this program, and gradual desegregation of the armed forces began. How gradual is suggested by the fact that twelve years later the armed forces had not been entirely desegregated, and certain reserve units and the National Guard were still segregated.

Was it an accident or was it legal propriety that for armed forces desegregation Truman issued an executive order, thereby skirting the necessity for congressional approval of such action, while for other forms of discrimination—in voting, in housing, in employment, in education—he merely appealed to Congress for legislation? Or was it that the most urgent of practical reasons—mainly, the need to build up the armed forces in the chilly atmosphere of a growing cold war, and to maintain black morale in these forces—operated here? Executive orders could have been issued just as well in the other areas of discrimination where Truman was asking Congress to act; the required legislation was already on the books, having been passed by Congress in the Reconstruction era following the Civil War. The Fourteenth and Fifteenth amendments, plus the civil-rights laws passed in 1866, 1870, and 1871, gave the president sufficient authority to begin doing away with discrimination in all areas of civil life. Neither Truman nor any president since the days of Ulysses S. Grant chose to do so. They preferred, when they gave any thought at all to discrimination, to seek specific congressional legislation, knowing well that Congress rarely acts swiftly on social injustices. Truman's message to Congress asked for legislation "prohibiting discrimination in interstate transportation facilities"; not only was this subject to executive action under the Fourteenth Amendment's prohibition against the denial of "equal protection of the laws," but specific legislation in 1887 already barred discrimination in interstate transportation.

The pattern for federal action in the postwar years was now set. The Supreme Court would make unprecedented decisions for racial equality. Congress would pass civil-rights laws in formidable number. The total effect was to give the impression abroad, and to whites at home unaware of the day-to-day lives of black people, that tumultuous changes were taking place in America's race relations. The reality, however, as the history of federal action through Presidents Eisenhower, Kennedy, Johnson, and Nixon testifies, was different.

The Fourteenth Amendment to the Constitution, adopted in 1868, seemed, on its face, to guarantee equal treatment to all citizens. It declared all persons born in the United States to be citizens; it then said that no state shall abridge the "privileges and immunities of citizens of the United States" or "deprive any person of life, liberty, or property without due process of law," and that all citizens are entitled to "equal protection of the laws." Nevertheless, in 1896, in *Plessy* v. *Ferguson,* the Supreme Court ruled that racial separation did not contravene the Fourteenth Amendment if public facilities for the races were "equal." The *Plessy* case, which established the "separate but equal" principle, was a southern transportation case in which Homer Adolph Plessy, a light-skinned Negro, was arrested after entering a railroad car reserved for whites. The Supreme Court, in a seven-to-one decision, upheld the Louisiana law requiring blacks and whites to ride separately; it was a decision that resulted in new Jim Crow laws throughout the South, and it was one which was not reversed for sixty years—until the Court ordered the Montgomery, Alabama, bus company to stop separating black and white passengers. The Montgomery bus decision overturned the doctrine of "separate but equal" transportation facilities for the races.

In the 1940s and early 1950s, the Supreme Court merely insisted that the "separate but equal" doctrine be enforced in graduate-school education for Negroes. For instance, where a state did not have a law school for blacks, the Court ruled it must admit a black applicant to a white law school. Not until 1954 did the Court tackle directly and comprehensively the principle of segregation in the public schools. That year a series of cases, brought by the NAACP and headed by *Brown* v. *Board of Education,* challenged the "separate but equal" doctrine as it applied to public educational facilities.

In the *Brown* case, ninety years after the war to end slavery and nine years after the war to end Hitlerism, the United States Supreme Court unanimously declared racial segregation in the public schools to be unconstitutional. The Court said that the separation of black schoolchildren "generates a feeling of inferiority as to their status in the community that may affect their hearts and minds in a way unlikely ever to be undone." It went on:

> We conclude that in the field of public education the doctrine of "separate but equal" has no place. Separate educational facilities are inherently unequal. Therefore, we hold that the plaintiffs and others similarly situated for whom the actions have been brought are, by reason of the segregation complained of, deprived of the equal protection of the laws guaranteed by the Fourteenth Amendment.

Supreme Court decisions, however, are not self-enforcing. Moreover, the year after the *Brown* decision, the Court retreated on the question of how soon segregation must end. It said that once school districts had made "a prompt and reasonable start toward full compliance" with the 1954 decision, the lower courts, which it charged with the responsibility of applying the desegregation decision, might "find that additional time is necessary." It urged lower courts to enter "such orders and decrees . . . as are necessary and proper to admit to public schools on a racially non-discriminatory basis with all deliberate speed the parties to these cases."

The Court's approach to the enforcement of the Constitution on the issue of segregation was unusual. It could hardly be imagined that the discovery of slavery in, say, a town in Nevada in 1954 would lead it to decide that though the Thirteenth Amendment outlawed slavery the town should be allowed to make a "prompt and reasonable start" toward its gradual elimination. Or that any violation of federal law by, say, a national syndicate for fraud through the mails would lead it to decide that the guilty parties must gradually desist from their activities. As black constitutional lawyer Loren Miller wrote with some bitterness in *The Petitioners:* "No American lawyer anywhere had ever supposed that the Supreme Court or any other organ of government could suspend the exercise of a peacetime constitutional right for a single day." By 1965, ten years after the "all deliberate speed" guideline of the Court, more than 75 per cent of the school districts in the South were still segregated.

The Supreme Court's decision on school desegregation met its first serious challenge in 1957 in Arkansas. Some progress toward desegregation had been made in the North and in the border states, but the South remained defiant. This defiance crystallized when Arkansas Governor Orville Faubus challenged a court order to begin gradual desegregation at Little Rock's Central High School by stationing the National Guard around the school to prevent nine Negro children from entering. The Courts forced him to remove the guard, but a mob of whites then gathered to take their place and stop the black children. A fifteen-year-old girl later told of her experience:

> Before I left home Mother called us into the living room. She said we should have a word of prayer. Then I caught the bus and got off a block from the school. I saw a large crowd of people standing across the street from the soldiers guarding Central. As I walked on, the crowd suddenly got very quiet. For a moment all I could hear was the shuffling of their feet. Then someone shouted, "Here she comes, get ready!" The crowd moved in closer and then began to follow me, calling me names. I still wasn't afraid. Just a little bit nervous. Then my knees started to shake all of a sudden and I wondered whether I could make it to the center entrance a block away. It was the longest block I ever walked in my whole life. . . .
> They moved closer and closer. Somebody started yelling, "Lynch her! Lynch her!" I tried to see a friendly face somewhere in the mob—someone who maybe would help. I looked into the face of an old woman, it seemed a kind face, but when I looked at her again, she spat on me.
> Then I looked down the block and saw a bench at the bus stop. I thought, "If I can only get there I will be safe. . . ." When I finally got there, I don't think I could have gone another step. I sat down and the mob crowded up and began shouting all over again. Someone hollered, "Drag her over to this tree! Let's take care of the nigger." Just then a white man sat down beside me, put his arm around me and patted my shoulder.

A handful of black students were finally admitted to Central High School, with soldiers, dispatched to Little Rock by President Eisenhower, protecting them for the rest of the year.

The general impression left on the world and on the nation by the Supreme Court decision in the *Brown* case, and by the use of federal troops to help enforce it, was that segregation was on its way out. The United States government had spoken through the Court, and resistance, such as that at Little Rock, could always be broken by firm presidential action. Eisenhower himself had enhanced the impression by stating, after sending troops to Little Rock: "Thus will be restored the image of America and of all its parts as one nation, indivisible, with liberty and justice for all." The general impression, however, was misleading. In some states—Virginia, North Carolina, Florida, and Tennessee, for example—there was only token integration. In 1961 not one school in South Carolina, Georgia, Alabama, Mississippi, or Louisiana had yet been integrated.

A similar sense of "progress" and optimism followed federal action on the voting rights of blacks. In 1944 the Supreme Court knocked out one of the obstacles to Negro voting in the South by declaring the "white primary" illegal. Until this decision, Democratic primary elections in the South, the important elections there since the Republican party was virtually nonexistent, were considered private activities restricted to whites. The Court ruled the primary election was really part of the state electoral machinery and therefore subject to the Fourteenth Amendment, which had been long interpreted to apply only to "public" discriminatory action and not to "private" discriminatory action.

Although the Court decision led to an increase in Negro voters in some southern urban areas, like Atlanta, in most of the South, especially in the rural Deep South, formidable obstacles to Negro voting remained. One was the poll tax, declared legal by the Supreme Court in the early twentieth century because it restricted voting for both whites and blacks who did not pay it; in practice, of course, blacks found it far more difficult to pay the penalty. Another obstacle was the literacy test, also constitutionally safe because it applied to both whites and blacks, though the test was administered exclusively by white registrars. In Mississippi the state constitution required that a prospective voter interpret a section of the constitution picked by the registrar. A favorite section given to Negroes to interpret was:

All lands comprising a single tract sold in pursuance of decree of court, or execution, shall be first offered in subdivisions
not exceeding one hundred and sixty acres, or one quarter section, and then offered as an entirety, and the price bid for the
latter shall control only when it shall exceed the aggregate of
the bids for the same in subdivisions as aforesaid; but the
chancery court, in cases before it, may decree otherwise if
deemed advisable to do so.

A favorite section given to white applicants was No. 30: "There
shall be no imprisonment for debt." When, on July 12, 1961, a
white man named John McMillan went to register, and was asked
to interpret that section, he wrote: "I think that a Neorger should
have 2 years in collage before voting because he don't understand."
McMillan passed and was registered. In New Orleans, according to
Justice Department records, one registrar wrote on a Negro's voting
application, as the reason for rejecting it: "Error in Spilling."

The poll tax and literacy tests were not the only means employed
by the white supremacists to disfranchise the Negro. Economic
pressure by employers against their black workers, tenant farmers,
and maids also kept blacks out of the voting booth. And finally, there
was always the persuasiveness of intimidation—violence and the
threat of violence against Negroes daring to register to vote. Thus, in
Mississippi at the height of Reconstruction, when federal troops enforced Negro rights in the South, 67 per cent of the Negro population were registered to vote, as compared with 55 per cent of the
white population; by 1955, the registration figure for Negroes was
down to 4 per cent while that of whites was 59 per cent.

A series of civil-rights laws was passed by Congress in the 1950s
and 1960s, spurred, it appeared, by the intense black protest of those
years: the Montgomery bus boycott, the sit-in movement, the Freedom Rides, the mass demonstrations in many southern cities. These
laws forbade voting discrimination against blacks, banned literacy
tests where a voter had a sixth-grade education, and enabled the
registering of voters by special federal officials where a pattern of
discrimination existed. In this same period, Congress and the states
passed the Twenty-Fourth Amendment to the Constitution outlaw-
ing the poll tax in federal elections, and the Supreme Court eliminated the poll tax in state elections on the ground that wealth as a

criterion for voting denied the "equal protection of the laws" clause of the Fourteenth Amendment.

The result of this legislative and judicial action was a dramatic increase in southern black voter registration, from one million (20 per cent of all eligible blacks) in 1952 to two million in 1964 (40 per cent) and three million in 1968 (60 per cent)—matching the 60 per cent registration figure for white voters. Further, more black legislators took office in the South—in state legislatures and in city councils. Also, a few blacks were elected sheriff and mayor of southern towns.

As late as January, 1966, however—half a year after Congress passed its strongest voting legislation to date, the Voting Rights Act of 1965—the following incident was reported in Tuskegee, Alabama, by black civil-rights worker Eldridge Burns:

> Wendy [Paris, a co-worker] and I said to the registrar, "Listen here, Doc. You got to register more people than one man every twenty minutes, you know. These people have been up here since eight o'clock, and you didn't start until ten-thirty." Then the registrar pulled out his little knife, which was red and yellow. "I'll take this knife," he said, "and cut your guts out. Spill your guts on this floor." Old Sammy came up and asked the man's name. The man said he gonna cut his guts out and call the sheriff on us.

Sammy was Sammy Younge, a worker for the Student Non-violent Coordinating Committee, who later that night, at a Texaco station where he argued over his right to use the "white" rest room, was shot to death by the attendant.

In housing, too, legislation, executive orders, and court decisions in the 1960s slowly created a legal basis for nondiscrimination. President Kennedy, who had criticized Eisenhower for failing to wipe out discrimination in housing, saying the president could do so with "a stroke of the pen," himself delayed using his pen for two years. When he at last did sign an order barring discrimination in housing, he exempted owner-occupants of one- and two-family houses, including those financed by the Federal Housing Authority and the Veterans Administration. He also failed to extend the order to all housing for which funds were provided by financial institutions under federal supervision—as suggested by the Civil Rights Commission several years earlier; only a fourth of new housing starts were therefore covered. In 1968 additional legislation on equal housing was passed, and the Supreme Court finally brought all housing sales and rentals under the protection of the Constitution. It ruled that all private transactions in housing which were discriminatory against Negroes violated the Thirteenth Amendment; such discrimination, said the Court, constituted "a relic of slavery." The decision brought back into use a statute made in 1866, and never enforced, giving all citizens "the same right . . . to make and enforce contracts . . . to inherit, purchase, lease, sell, hold, and convey real and personal property. . . ."

Conspicuously unprotected by Supreme Court action until 1964 was the right of blacks to use public facilities, such as hotels, restaurants, and theaters, that were exclusively available to whites. Back in 1883, the Supreme Court had ruled that the Fourteenth Amendment provision for "equal protection of the laws" applied only to the state governments' discrimination and not to that of private parties (innkeepers, restaurant owners). The 1964 Civil Rights Act forbade discrimination in "any place of public accommodation," not only where state action was involved, but where interstate commerce was affected, thus utilizing the commerce clause of the Constitution to bring virtually all places of public accommodation within the scope of the act. Almost immediately, the legislation was challenged by a motel owner in Atlanta, and the Supreme Court upheld the act's use of the interstate-commerce clause to bar discrimination.

Yet the new laws, the new court decisions, the new speeches delivered by the national political leaders on behalf of equal rights for the black man failed to solve the race problem, failed to still the growing anger in the nation's black community. How long could black forbearance last? In August, 1963, two hundred thousand black and white Americans gathered in Washington in an unprecedented outpouring of support for racial equality. The March on Washington was a protest against federal indifference to the black man's plight, and it was quickly and astutely embraced by President Kennedy and other national leaders; anger turned into amicability. Martin Luther King, Jr.'s, speech at that gathering, "I have a dream" —a magnificent oratorio—had just the right combination of poignancy, protest, and goodwill. When John Lewis, a much-arrested, much-beaten leader of SNCC, tried to introduce a stronger note of outrage, he was censored by the leaders of the march, who insisted he omit the sentence: "I want to know: which side is the federal government on?" Would rationality and peaceful protest be sufficient? The March on Washington came only three months after the nation had been treated to the spectacle of Birmingham police using clubs, fire hose, and police dogs on black demonstrators. And just eighteen days after the march, on September 15, a bomb exploded in the basement of a black church in Birmingham; four black girls attending a Sunday school class were killed.

Kennedy had praised the "deep fervor and quiet dignity" of the march, but in the light of events both before and after the march, the estimate of black militant Malcolm X was probably much closer to the Negro mood. Speaking in Detroit two months after the Birmingham bombing, Malcolm X said:

> The Negroes were out there in the streets. They were talking about how they were going to march on Washington. . . . That they were going to march on Washington, march on the Senate, march on the White House, march on the Congress, and tie it up, bring it to a halt, not let the government proceed. They even said they were going out to the airport and lay down on the runway and not let any airplanes land. I'm telling you what they said. That was revolution. That was revolution. That was the black revolution.
>
> It was the grass roots out there in the street. It scared the white man to death, scared the white power structure in Washington, D.C. to death; I was there. When they found out that this black steamroller was going to come down on the capital, they called in [Roy] Wilkins [NAACP leader], they called in Randolph, they called in these national Negro leaders that you respect and told them, "Call it off." Kennedy said, "Look you all are letting this thing go too far." And Old Tom said, "Boss, I can't stop it because I didn't start it." I'm telling you what they said. They said, "I'm not even in it, much less at the head of it." They said, "These Negroes are doing things on their own. They're running ahead of us." And that old shrewd fox, he said, "If you all aren't in it, I'll put you in it. I'll put you at the head of it. I'll endorse it. I'll welcome it. I'll help it. I'll join it."
>
> This is what they did with the march on Washington. They joined it. They didn't integrate it, they infiltrated it. They

joined it, became a part of it, took it over. And as they took it over, it lost its militancy. It ceased to be angry, it ceased to be hot, it ceased to be uncompromising. Why, it even ceased to be a march. It became a picnic, a circus. Nothing but a circus, with clowns and all. . . .

No, it was a sellout. It was a takeover. When James Baldwin came in from Paris, they wouldn't let him talk, because they couldn't make him go by the script. . . . They controlled it so tight, they told those Negroes what time to hit town, how to come, where to stop, what signs to carry, what song to sing, what speech they could make, and what speech they couldn't make, and then told them to get out of town by sundown. And every one of those Toms was out of town by sundown. Now I know you don't like my saying this. But I can back it up. It was a circus, a performance that beat anything Hollywood could ever do, the performance of the year. . . .

One year after the march, black anger simmered and boiled over in a number of cities. In precisely those years in which legislative activity on civil rights reached its peak—in 1964 and 1965—a series of urban riots and rebellions by blacks broke out in every sector of the country. They shook the nation so convulsively that it has still not settled down. In Jacksonville, the killing of a Negro woman, and a bomb threat against a Negro high school, led to students using rocks and Molotov cocktails. In Cleveland, the accidental crushing of a white minister sitting in the path of a bulldozer to protest discrimination against blacks in construction work produced violent reactions among blacks. In New York, the fatal shooting of a fifteen-year-old boy embroiled in a fight with an off-duty policeman led to days of looting and violence. Blacks also rioted in Rochester, in Jersey City, in Chicago, in Philadelphia. Still, these were small-scale disturbances. Lyndon Johnson was president, promising action for racial equality, and intoning the black rallying cry "We Shall Overcome!" In August, 1965, as Johnson signed into law the strong Voting Rights Act, and as if in direct comment on the faith of liberals in civil-rights legislation, the black population of Watts, a Los Angeles ghetto, rose up in the bloodiest urban violence since the Detroit race riot of 1943.

In almost all the urban riots, the precipitating incident was police action against a black man, woman, or child. In Watts, where relief rolls were growing, housing remained shoddy, and the police were never known for their neighborliness, it was the forcible arrest of a young Negro driver, the clubbing of a bystander, and the seizure of a young black woman erroneously accused of spitting on the police that touched off the uprising. National Guardsmen were called to quell the looting and the fire-bombing, and they and the police used firearms extensively. By the time it was over, thirty-four people had been killed, most of them black, hundreds had been injured, and nearly four thousand arrested. Some forty million dollars in property was destroyed. Robert Conot, a West Coast journalist, summed up the significance of the Watts riot in his book *Rivers of Blood, Years of Darkness:*

> The Los Angeles riot symbolized the end of the era of Negro passivity—passivity that took the form of the doctrine of non-violence, and the acceptance of white leadership in the civil rights struggle. In Los Angeles the Negro was going on record that he would no longer turn the other cheek. That, frustrated and goaded, he would strike back, whether the response of violence was an appropriate one or no.

More outbreaks occurred in the summer of 1966. In Chicago, rock-throwing, looting, and fire-bombing brought out the National Guard, and three Negroes were killed by stray bullets, one a thirteen-year-old boy, another a fourteen-year-old pregnant girl. In Cleveland, the National Guard was summoned, too; four Negroes were shot to death, two by law-enforcement officers, one by a white man firing from a car, the fourth by a group of whites.

In 1967, however, came the greatest wave of urban violence the nation had ever seen, with the worst riots ravaging Detroit and Newark. The National Advisory Commission on Civil Disorders, named later by Johnson to investigate the causes of the trouble and make recommendations, reported disorders that year in 128 cities; it described disorders in 39 of them as "major or serious."

All these disorders had a common history: long-standing grievances in the black ghetto based on poverty, unemployment, dilapidated housing; recurring instances of police brutality. In Newark two years earlier, for instance, a policeman had shot and killed an eighteen-year-old Negro boy, claiming the boy had assaulted another officer and was running away; after a hearing in which it was found that the policeman had not used excessive force, he remained on duty. In April, 1967, fifteen Negroes were arrested while picketing a grocery store that they claimed sold bad meat. In July, according to the report of the advisory commission, "a Negro cab driver was injured" during or after a traffic arrest; a crowd of blacks gathered, windows were broken, and looting began.

The language of the advisory commission's report in stating that "a Negro cab driver was injured" contrasted with the driver's own story. The driver, John Smith, had been stopped by two uniformed patrolmen, charged with tailgating and driving the wrong way on a one-way street. The police later claimed that Smith had used abusive language and punched them, and that they had to use "necessary force" to subdue him. Smith, at his bail hearing, put it this way:

> There was no resistance on my part. That was a cover story by the police. They caved in my ribs, busted a hernia, and put a hole in my head. . . . After I got into the precinct six or seven other officers along with the two who arrested me kicked and stomped me in the ribs and back. They then took me to a cell and put my head over the toilet bowl. While my head was over the toilet bowl, I was struck on the back of the head with a revolver. I was also being cursed while they were beating me. An arresting officer in the cell block said, "This baby is mine."

Before the Newark violence was over—and the National Guard was again sent to the scene—twenty-three persons were dead, twenty-one of them blacks. Before the Detroit riot was over, forty-three persons were dead, all but ten of them blacks. Most of the people killed in the nationwide disorders in 1967 were blacks, shot by police or National Guardsmen. A Senate committee which studied disturbances in sixty-seven cities reported 83 deaths and 1,897 injuries. About 10 per cent of those injured or killed were public officials, according to the advisory commission, and an "overwhelming majority of the civilians killed and injured were Negroes."

By 1965 the mood of bitterness and anger among blacks, always latent beneath the surface optimism of those in the civil-rights movement, was manifest. That was the year of the assassination of Malcolm X, just as he was emerging as a spokesman of the new militant nationalism. Shortly after Malcolm's death, a young black writer, Julius Lester, expressed the blacks' widespread disillusionment with liberalism in an essay entitled "The Angry Children of Malcolm X":

> Now it is over. America has had chance after chance to show that it really meant "that all men are endowed with certain inalienable rights." America has had precious chances in this decade to make it come true. Now it is over. The days of singing freedom songs and the days of combating bullets and billy clubs with Love. We Shall Overcome (and we have overcome our blindness) sounds old, out-dated, and can enter the pantheon of the greats along with the IWW songs and the union songs. . . . And as for Love? That's always been better done in bed than on the picket line and marches. Love is fragile and gentle and seeks a like response. They used to sing "I Love Everybody" as they ducked bricks and bottles. Now they sing
>
> > Too much love,
> > Too much love,
> > Nothing kills a nigger like
> > Too much love.

By 1965 not only was the mood of bitterness and anger among blacks apparent, it was also becoming clear that the conventional liberal response to racism was inadequate. When Lester declared an end to "the days of combating bullets and billy clubs with Love," he was referring to one element in the reality of race relations in the United States: that the black person could not depend on the government—whether liberal or conservative, Republican or Democrat—to protect him from physical assault or murder. The Supreme Court might make equalitarian rulings, the Congress might pass civil-rights laws, the president might make stirring speeches about the dignity of man, but the black man on the ghetto street or on the country road was still at the mercy of the white man—in uniform or out—and the power of the government was not available to protect him. The situation that obtained during slavery—the physical helplessness of the black before the white—was still being maintained in the post-slavery world. In the twentieth century—the "age of reform"—it had become an American tradition for "liberal reform" to mean meat-inspection laws, antitrust acts, and social security bills, but not to have reference to the situation of the black man and black woman.

The civil-rights movement illuminated the hypocrisy of the liberal promise. It made overt, and recorded on television for the world to see, an old daily fact of American life: that a black person who protested his condition, or moved one step out of line, would be arrested, or beaten, or inundated with water hoses, or killed, and the national government of the United States—the most powerful government in the world—would not act to save him.

In the sit-ins of 1960 and the Freedom Rides of 1961, hundreds of persons were arrested, most of them black students, for asserting their constitutional rights; yet the federal government did not interfere with those arrests. Indeed, in the Freedom Ride of May, 1961, Attorney General Robert Kennedy, instead of using the power of the federal government to protect the riders, asked the riders to desist in a "cooling-off period"—an executive branch version of the Supreme Court's suggestion that blacks' constitutional rights be granted "with all deliberate speed." Kennedy did send marshals into Alabama *after* riders had been beaten in Anniston and Birmingham. As for those who rode into Mississippi, the attorney general entrusted their safety to state officials in a compromise agreement under which they would be protected from beatings, but would be arrested on arriving at Jackson. That the federal government had the constitutional power to prevent those arrests was admitted by the man who was Kennedy's assistant in charge of civil rights at that time, Burke Marshall. Marshall argued, however, that this power should not be exercised because "the result would have been chaotic and more destructive of the federal system than what happened in Mississippi." He wrote later: "It would be possible to devise authority for the federal courts to enjoin such arrests. There is no constitutional or doctrinal difficulty involved. But the consequences would be to destroy the means by which Mississippi maintained order."

Marshall put it well. The federal government under the Kennedys, as before them and after them, refused to use its full constitutional power to protect blacks from official and unofficial beatings or arrest, in order not to detract from the ability of local police to maintain "order." That "order" has always been maintained at the expense of the black population in the South—and in the North, too, where local police have also been permitted to violate constitutional rights without federal interference. The refusal to invoke federal law and federal power to protect the rights of blacks has been the historic presidential liberal position on race in America since the compromise of 1877. In that year it was decided, in a deal between northern Republicans and southern Democrats, that the status quo (the subordinate position of the black man before the law—the wooing of white political power in the South) was to be maintained even at the cost of ignoring the Constitution, even at the cost of life and limb for the black.

Vigorous presidential gestures to enforce the Constitution with regard to blacks were made on occasion, such as Eisenhower's use of troops in Little Rock in 1957 and Kennedy's use of troops in 1962 to compel the registration of James Meredith at the University of Mississippi, the first black to enroll at "Ole Miss." But, in general, federal power was not available to stand between southern law and lawlessness and the black person. In Albany, Georgia, for instance, the constitutional rights of hundreds of black citizens were violated again and again in 1961 and 1962—a black lawyer was beaten by a sheriff, a pregnant black woman was kicked by a deputy sheriff and lost her child, a white civil-rights worker was beaten in jail—but the national government remained aloof. The only federal prosecution in Albany during the attorney generalship of Robert Kennedy was *against* civil-rights workers who had picketed a segregationist grocer.

The federal government ignored thousands of violations of civil rights by local law-enforcement officials in the early 1960s, despite the existence in the statute books of post-Civil War laws giving the national government the power to intercede, either by punitive action, or in a forceful preventive way, whenever the constitutional rights of citizens were violated. Among its legal recourses, the federal government could have made extensive use of Section 242, Title 18, of the U. S. Code, permitting criminal prosecution of any official who "willfully subjects any inhabitant of any State . . . to the deprivation of any rights, privileges, or immunities secured or protected by the Constitution or laws of the United States." In Selma, Alabama, in 1963, agents of the Federal Bureau of Investigation stood by and took notes as they watched black civil-rights workers beaten and unlawfully arrested. One Justice Department lawyer on the scene,

Richard Wasserstrom, frustrated over the FBI's (and his own) inaction at the time, later left the department to return to teaching the philosophy of law. In reviewing a book written by his former chief, Burke Marshall, in which Marshall defended the inaction of the federal government as necessary to maintain "the federal system," Wasserstrom suggested that the federal government's failure to act was not the result of the federal system, "but rather of a series of conscious decisions to reinterpret, redefine, and reconstruct the limits of justifiable federal action." Given the national government's long and persistent history of neglect in using its powers to protect the black person, that neglect could hardly be regarded as some temporary aberration from the real system, but rather as the system itself, the operating reality of liberal government in contradistinction to its rhetorical claims.

In 1964 there was further proof of this thesis. SNCC and other civil-rights groups planned a "Mississippi Summer," with a thousand young people, black and white, entering Mississippi to register black voters and run "Freedom Schools." It was clear, from the record, that they would be in danger of arrest, beatings, even murder—and that local law-enforcement officials would not protect them, and might even participate in the action against them. To impress the administration with this prospect of danger, and to request that the president send federal marshals into Mississippi to protect the civil-rights workers, a public hearing was held in Washington in early June, 1964. At that hearing, dozens of black Mississippians testified about police brutality as well as the lack of protection for life and limb; constitutional lawyers testified as to the statutory authority possessed by the federal government to respond to this request. Transcripts of the hearing were sent to President Johnson and Attorney General Kennedy. There was no response. Thirteen days later, three civil-rights workers—James Chaney, Michael Schwerner, and Andrew Goodman—were arrested in Philadelphia, Mississippi, released from jail late at night, and followed down the road by a group of men, including the deputy sheriff who had arrested them. The three youths were then taken into the woods and shot to death. The black youngster Chaney was beaten so ferociously with chains that a pathologist who later examined the body said he had seen such damage to a human body only in high-velocity airplane crashes.

Even after the murder of the three youths the federal government still refused to send men into Mississippi to protect the civil-rights workers from further harm. During the rest of the summer, unlawful arrests and beatings occurred repeatedly in Mississippi. J. Edgar Hoover, head of the FBI, claimed lack of jurisdiction. Robert Kennedy claimed there was no constitutional sanction for federal action —and was then soundly rebuked by a group of law-school professors who pointed, chapter and verse, to the statute books. Among the statutes they cited was Section 333, Title 10, which dates back to the administration of George Washington and which was strengthened after the Civil War. It reads:

> The President, by using the militia or the armed forces, or both, or by any other means, shall take such measures as he considers necessary to suppress, in a state, any insurrection, domestic violence, unlawful combination, or conspiracy, if it so hinders the execution of the laws of that State, and of the United States within the State, that any part or class of its people is deprived of a right, privilege, immunity, or protection named in the Constitution and secured by law, and the constituted authorities of that State are unable, or fail, or refuse to protect that right, privilege or immunity, or to give that protection. . . .

This statute, together with the Fourteenth Amendment, which prohibits the denial to any citizen of the "equal protection of the laws" and any state from depriving him of "life, liberty, or property without due process of law," has always provided the national government with ample power to uphold the rights of its citizens; it is a power, however, that it has rarely used.

When, in 1968, the president signed still another civil-rights act, questions arose concerning the reasons for its passage. Was it in response to the protests of those in the civil-rights movement against federal inaction in instances of violence against blacks? Or was it in response to the ghetto uprisings of blacks in the summer of 1967? The official description of the new law's purpose was: "To prescribe penalties for certain acts of violence or intimidation, and for other purposes."

Liberals had been complaining that the old Section 242, Title 18, of the U.S. Code was too weak to permit adequate federal action, though the real trouble was the lack of political will, not statutory inadequacies. Now a Section 245 was added to the code, applying criminal penalties to persons, "whether or not acting under color of law" (Section 242 specified "under color of law"), who interfered with the constitutional rights of others. It specifically listed the kinds of activities that could not be interfered with under this law: voting, participating in any federal or state program, going to public school, applying for employment, traveling on interstate transportation facilities, using public accommodations. It increased the penalties for such interference from the one-year imprisonment under Section 242 to ten years for bodily injury and life imprisonment for injury resulting in death. However, it also added the following:

> The provisions of this section shall not apply to acts or omissions on the part of law enforcement officers, members of the National Guard . . . or members of the Armed Forces of the United States, who are engaged in suppressing a riot or civil disturbance or restoring law and order during a riot or civil disturbance.

Thus, what Congress gave with one hand it took away with the other. Black people whose constitutional rights were being violated in the course of some "civil disturbance"—which might mean any demonstration or protest action—would still have no protection. More important, however, was the Section 2101, added to the act by Senator Strom Thurmond of South Carolina, and acceded to by virtually all the liberal members of Congress in order to increase the chances for passage of the bill. It was a typical maneuver in liberal politics: a bad provision is joined to a good provision as a "compromise"; the good provision then lies dormant while the bad provision is quickly enforced. Thurmond's Section 2101 said:

> Whoever travels in interstate or foreign commerce or uses any facility of interstate or foreign commerce, including, but not limited to, the mail, telegraph, telephone, radio, or television, with intent to incite a riot; or to organize, promote, encourage, participate in, or carry on a riot; or to commit any act of violence in furtherance of a riot; or to aid or abet any person in inciting or participating in or carrying on a riot or committing any act of violence in furtherance of a riot. . . . shall be fined not more than $10,000 or imprisoned not more than five years or both.

The act also defined a "riot" as meaning a public disturbance involving threats of violence or acts of violence by any person part of a group of three or more. The first person to be prosecuted under the new law was a young leader of the Student Non-violent Coordinating Committee, H. Rap Brown, who had made a militant, angry speech in Maryland, just before a racial disturbance there, and was therefore indicted for violating the Civil Rights Act of 1968.

Passage of the act came six days after the assassination of Martin Luther King and two months after another instance in which blacks failed to get "equal protection of the laws." In Orangeburg, South Carolina, students at South Carolina State College, a black college, had been turned away again and again by police from the only bowling alley in town; black co-eds had also been beaten by the police. In early February, 1968, a noisy night-time protest demonstration on the campus brought some 150 police and National Guardsmen to the scene. One policeman was struck by a flying object. Curse words also flew. As about 150 students moved along the campus in the direction of the police, the police opened fire. As reported by Jack Nelson and Jack Bass, two southern newspapermen, in their book *The Orangeburg Massacre:*

> The patrolmen's shotguns were loaded with deadly buckshot used to kill deer and other heavy game. . .
>
> Although some patrolmen later claimed the students were charging at them like a thundering herd, throwing bottles and bricks and other objects, the evidence was overwhelming that few objects were being thrown, that there was no shooting, and that the students were not running. . . .
>
> Suddenly a carbine fired. . . . Other witnesses later told of hearing . . . several shots fired into the air in rapid succession by a patrolman, apparently as an intended warning.
>
> Most of the students . . . turned to run. Some held up their hands and others dropped to the ground. Almost simultaneously a volley of shotgun blasts and the crack-crack-crack of a .38 caliber pistol caught them in a cross fire.
>
> [Policemen] Spell, Addy, and Taylor blasted away with shotguns from the students' left side. [Guardsman] Corporal Lanier opened up with a shotgun from the bushes on their right-front side. . . . All of the patrolmen were to later say they had not fired at any particular target, but had just shot into the crowd of students. . . .

> Henry Smith was in the first wave. . . . Smith caught the brunt of several shots from both sides, was spun around by the force, then shot again in the back.
>
> Samuel Hammond, eighteen, a stocky football player, was shot in the back. Delano Herman Middleton, seventeen, a high school student whose mother worked as a maid at the college, suffered seven wounds—three in the forearm, one in the hip, one in the thigh, one in the side of the chest, and one in the heart. . . .

Smith, Hammond, and Middleton died that night. Twenty-seven other students were wounded, most of them shot in the back or side. But the immediate message conveyed to the nation by the mass media blurred what had happened. As Nelson and Bass wrote in their study:

> No one had seen any students armed with guns, no firearms or spent cartridges were found on the campus after the shootings, and a bannister—not a bullet—had felled the only injured officer. A great preponderance of witnesses were to testify later that they heard no shooting from the campus for fifteen to thirty minutes prior to the time the patrolmen opened fire. Yet, on-the-scene press coverage, as well as the official version of what had happened, led the nation to believe that a gun battle had taken place.

This time, the civil-rights division of the Justice Department, supported vigorously by Attorney General Ramsey Clark, moved to prosecute the policemen who had done the shooting. When a federal grand jury failed to bring an indictment, the government initiated a trial through the information procedure. A local jury of ten whites and two blacks, however, exonerated the policemen.

What the Orangeburg affair seemed to show was that the labyrinths of racism in the United States are so complex that even if blacks manage to make their way through one obstacle, or two or three obstacles, more always await them on the path to justice. Even on those rare occasions when one sector of government acts on behalf of the black, other sectors move to thwart the action. In the Orangeburg case, not only the system of local justice, but the friendliness of the FBI toward the local police acted to protect the killers. Three FBI agents were eyewitnesses to the shootings that night, as they later admitted, but they did not inform the Justice Department of this fact, and an FBI report written two months later did not mention that FBI men were on the scene. Nelson and Bass concluded that "Orangeburg was an example of cases where aspects of the FBI's performance were little short of disgraceful."

In the two years following passage of the 1968 act, designed supposedly to protect blacks against "violence or intimidation," the press reported enough incidents of police action against blacks to indicate that the promise of the Fourteenth Amendment to protect the "life, liberty, or property" of the black citizen was still unmet. Either the federal government did not intercede when local police violated constitutional rights, or the judicial system failed to produce justice. For instance:

• Three Detroit policemen and a black private guard, charged with killing three black teen-agers at the Algiers Motel in Detroit during the 1967 riots in that city, were exonerated by juries of conspiring to violate the civil rights of citizens. A UPI dispatch noted that the defense conceded that the four men "separately made racial slurs, ripped the clothes off the prostitutes, beat the blacks, played 'death games' to frighten motel occupants to extract confessions about alleged snipers, and finally shot two youths—Fred Temple, 18 and Aubrey Pollard, 19."

• In Jackson, Mississippi, a local grand jury found "justified" an attack on the campus of Jackson State College, in May, 1970, in which the police laid down a 28-second barrage of gunfire that included shotguns, rifles, and a sub-machine gun. Four hundred bullets or pieces of buckshot struck the girls' dormitory, and two black students were killed. U.S. District Court Judge Harold Cox declared that students who engage in civil disorders "must expect to be injured or killed."

• In Boston, in April, 1970, a policeman shot and killed an unarmed black hospital patient in the Boston City Hospital, firing five shots after the black man snapped a towel at him. The chief judge of the municipal court of Boston exonerated the policeman.

• In Augusta, Georgia, in May, 1970, six Negroes were shot to death during looting and disorder in the city. The *New York Times* reported:

> A confidential police report indicates that at least five of the victims were killed by the police, reliable sources reported.

An eyewitness to one of the deaths said he had watched a
Negro policeman and his white partner fire nine shots into the
back of a man suspected of looting. They did not fire warning
shots or ask him to stop running, said Charles A. Reid, a 38-
year-old businessman. . . .

• In the urban disorders of spring, 1968, that followed the assassination of King, thirty-five of the thirty-nine killed were black.
• In April, 1970, when a twelve-man federal jury in Boston,
trying a civil suit for one hundred thousand dollars damages against
a policeman, found the policeman guilty of using "excessive force"
against two black soldiers from Fort Devens—one of them, hit with
the policeman's club, required twelve stitches in his scalp—the judge
awarded the servicemen three dollars.

The continued physical helplessness of the black in the face of
either official brutality in violating the Constitution or official lax-
ness in enforcing it was only the most obvious fact about a larger
truth. That truth was the general failure of the whole liberal parade
of court decisions, laws, and presidential declarations in affecting
the basic subordinate position of the black in the United States. It
was this failure that perhaps best explains the burst of black militancy after 1965.

The black voter learned, even as registration figures went up in
the South, even as Julian Bond, a SNCC leader, was elected to the
Georgia legislature, and Charles Evers, a local black NAACP official, was elected mayor of a small town in Mississippi, that such
victories did not change his basic subordination. Indeed, the experience of the North was being repeated; blacks had long voted in
Harlem and in the South Side of Chicago, and they still lived in
ghettos, they were still poor, still plagued by rats and disease, still
without power, still looked upon as inferior by the rest of the nation.

The black political leader learned, soon enough, that real power
in national politics remained in the hands of a small number of
powerful white politicians, North and South, and that at critical
points, the white liberal politicians, who made the greatest promises,
betrayed the black voter. In 1964, for example, when blacks from
Mississippi showed up at the Democratic National Convention in
Atlantic City and demanded proportional representation in their
state's delegation, "liberal" Democratic leaders, like Hubert Hum-

phrey, stood firm to keep the Mississippi delegation all white. In 1965, when blacks from Mississippi challenged the right of the five white representatives from that state to be admitted to the new Congress in view of the disfranchisement of the state's black population, which made up 45 per cent of the total, the Johnson administration and its congressional leaders once again used their parliamentary leadership to keep the Mississippi segregationist congressmen in their seats. In 1968 Negroes were 11 per cent of the national population; at the Democratic National Convention, the proportion of black delegates was 4 per cent; at the Republican National Convention, 2 per cent.

With the world hailing the Supreme Court's 1954 decision calling for school desegregation, the South followed to the letter the Court's 1955 ruling permitting "all deliberate speed." Leading white liberals were not forceful in demanding enforcement of the Constitution. Two years after the Supreme Court decision, Democrat Adlai Stevenson, a presidential candidate, told a Negro audience in Los Angeles that he would not use federal money or federal troops to enforce integration. "I think," he said, "that would be a great mistake. That is exactly what brought on the Civil War. It can't be done by troops, or bayonets. We must proceed gradually, not upsetting habits or traditions that are older than the Republic." The *New York Times* reported this speech, and the reaction of Stevenson's audience: "There was a murmur of protest in the crowd, and one tall Negro was heard to say: 'I think he is a phony.' "

Black youngsters knew, of course, that school segregation was not practiced in the South alone. Schools were also segregated by poverty and ghettoization in the North. As school desegregation in the South slowly increased toward 1970, it began to surpass in the degree of racial integration the racially distinct black ghetto schools and white suburban schools in the North. There was, to be sure, a problem beyond integration: if schools in general were inadequate, if they were bureaucratic, authoritarian, intellectually arid, a mechanical prototype of a larger culture of violence and competition, then blacks entering white schools were only gaining access to a sinking ship. Racial "progress" in school desegregation thus matched "progress" in voting, where blacks could now be admitted to all the inadequacies of the society at large.

Whatever the progress made in law by the passage of statutes calling for equality in housing and employment, the reality was different. The housing market was controlled by white real-estate men; decent housing depended on wealth; and the two dominant facts about blacks in America were that they were discriminated against and that they were poor. The job market was dependent on the vagaries of the American capitalist system, in which millions of Americans were always unemployed—with blacks, as always, disproportionately jobless. Those blacks who sought good-paying jobs as skilled workers faced the tight, white control of the craft unions. The 1964 Civil Rights Act might contain a fair-employment provision, but not one government contract was terminated with a company that discriminated against blacks.

In short, the liberal response to the "race problem" in the United States—that is, to the black uprisings, for black subordination was not a "problem" until blacks went wild in the streets—did not touch the heart of the matter. The heart of the matter was not the lack of laws, or lack of words, or lack of promises. It was insufficient economic resources, the absence of real, direct political power, and, surrounding those hard needs—something more subtle and yet enormous—the psychology of racism that inhabited the minds of whites, the acceptance of white superiority so deeply in every aspect of American society that black children might grow up believing it.

The convulsions of the 1967 urban upheavals led the National Advisory Commission on Civil Disorders to lay bare some of these realities. The commission concluded:

> White racism is essentially responsible for the explosive mixture which has been accumulating in our cities since the end of World War II. Among the ingredients of this mixture are:
> Pervasive discrimination and segregation in employment, education, and housing . . . growing concentrations of impoverished Negroes in our major cities, creating a growing crisis of deteriorating facilities and services and unmet human needs.
> The black ghettos where segregation and poverty converge on the young to destroy opportunity and enforce failure.

The report also said:

> The frustrations of powerlessness have led some Negroes to the conviction that there is no effective alternative to violence

as a means of achieving redress of grievances, and of "moving the system." These frustrations are reflected in alienation and hostility toward the institutions of law and government and the white society which controls them, and in the reach toward racial consciousness and solidarity reflected in the slogan "Black Power."

A new mood has sprung up among Negroes, particularly the young, in which self-esteem and enhanced racial pride are replacing apathy and submission to the "system."

The failure of the American political system and the failure of its economic system for the black person can only be described in the most personal terms by the victims themselves. Kenneth Clark, in his book *Dark Ghetto,* recorded the statements of people in Harlem:

A thirty-year-old male drug addict:
You know the average young person out here don't have a job, man, they don't have anything to do. They don't have any alternative, you know, but to go out there and try to make a living for themselves. Like when you come down to the Tombs down there, they're down there for robbing and breaking in. They want to know why you did it and where you live, but you have to live. You go down to the employment agency, and you can't get a job. They have you waiting all day, but you can't get a job. They don't have a job for you. Yet you have to live. I'm ready to do anything anyone else is ready to do— because I want to live.

A thirty-eight-year-old man:
No one with a mop can expect respect from a banker, or an attorney, or men who create jobs, and all you have is a mop. Are you crazy? Whoever heard of integration between a mop and a banker?

A thirty-three-year-old man:
The white cops, they have a damn sadistic nature. They are really a sadistic type of people and we, I mean me, myself, we don't need them here in Harlem. We don't need them! They don't do the neighborhood any good. They deteriorate the neighborhood. They start violence, that's right. A bunch of us could be playing some music, or dancing, which we have as an outlet for ourselves. We can't dance in the house, we don't have clubs or things like that. So we're out on the sidewalk, right on the sidewalk; we might feel like dancing, or one might want to

play something on his horn. Right away here come a cop.
"You're disturbing the peace!"

A woman:
I have been uncomfortable being a Negro. I came from the
South—Kentucky, on the Ohio River line—and I have had
white people spit on me in my Sunday suit.

In the 1960s, the anger of the black not only exploded in the
streets; it also expressed itself in art and literature—in the furious
poetry of LeRoi Jones; in the prose of Eldridge Cleaver, writing in
Soul on Ice; in the speeches of Malcolm X; in the new open, defiant
talk of blacks to one another all over the nation. James Baldwin said
it in 1962 in *The Fire Next Time:*

This past, the Negro's past, of rope, fire, torture, castra-
tion, infanticide, rape; death and humiliation; fear by day and
night, fear as deep as the marrow of the bone; doubt that he
was worthy of life, since everyone around him denied it; sorrow
for his women, for his kinfolk, for his children, who needed his
protection, and whom he could not protect; rage, hatred, and
murder, hatred for white men so deep that it often turned
against him and his own, and made all love, all trust, all joy
impossible—this past, this endless struggle to achieve and reveal and confirm a human identity, human authority, yet contains, for all its horror, something very beautiful. I do not mean
to be sentimental about suffering—enough is certainly as good
as a feast—but people who cannot suffer can never grow up,
can never discover who they are. That man who is forced each
day to snatch his manhood, his identity, out of the fire of
human cruelty that rages to destroy it knows, if he survives his
effort, and even if he does not survive it, something about himself and human life that no school on earth—and indeed, no
church—can teach. He achieves his own authority, and that is
unshakable.

As the seventies began, it was plain that the working creed of
liberalism, like its rhetoric, was inadequate to deal with the depth
of black-white relations in the United States. That working creed
emphasized the "progress" represented by formal laws, token gifts
and appointments, procedural rituals such as voting. It ignored the
root problem of poverty, the layer upon layer of racism in the psychology of the American people, the impassable void that separated

the black man and black woman from political power. The liberal system's defense of this "progress" was elaborate. Was it not true that the black was overcoming one obstacle after another—chattel slavery, legal segregation, voting restrictions of a dozen kinds?

Yet, was not the goal of real equality, of stature as a human being, always so far away as to be barely visible? By 1970 this was just beginning to be understood, and with it one great lesson: that the premise of liberal reform, that "someone," the white reformer, would solve the problems of the black man, was false. Now, especially among the young black people, the most essential element of a real democracy had begun to take hold—that an oppressed people can depend on no one but themselves to move that long distance, past all defenses, to genuine dignity.

5

Justice

When all other elements of the liberal vocabulary are exhausted—when the best of wars reveals viciousness, when "world responsibility" shows rapacity, when parliamentary democracy is shaped by the dollar sign and racial "progress" involves patronization—one last bulwark of American liberalism always stands firm: constitutional rights. Free speech, free press, free assembly, due process of law—these are presumed to be the unique qualities of American society that mark its superiority over all other systems. It is the thesis of this chapter, however, that this last bulwark of American liberalism is like the other elements of the liberal creed: impressive in theory, weak in reality.

True, many Americans would probably concede that constitutional rights are, on occasion, violated, as in the anti-Red, antiforeign raids of Attorney General A. Mitchell Palmer after World War I, and in the witch-hunts of Senator Joseph R. McCarthy in the 1950s. But these, they would add, were momentary aberrations, followed by a return to "normalcy." In the conventional analysis of the postwar years, the shrinking of rights in the McCarthy era was followed by a magnification of American liberty.

Without question, the nation did begin in the sixties to scorn McCarthyism, and the Supreme Court did expand procedural rights. But as the needle of civil liberties moved back from the fluctuations of the McCarthy years to its normal position, it again pointed to a persistent historical reality: the judicial system of the United States was still biased against the poor, the radical, the peculiar. Freedom of expression and due process remained pleasant myths. The policeman's club and the potency of the dollar continued to restrict constitutional rights so effectively that those of wealth and power in America could maintain their wealth and their power. McCarthy was repudiated. But just as World War II defeated the Fascists, but not the Fascist cult of violence, just as the New Deal ended the Depression, but not economic injustice, just as the Supreme Court ended legal segregation, but not the reality of racism, so did liberalism in postwar America defeat McCarthy, but not what he stood for.

American liberal capitalism has a remarkable protective mechanism that thus far has saved it from its own extravagances. This mechanism corrects the excesses of its normal behavior, but not that behavior itself. Historian Richard Drinnon, in a remarkable essay, describes what is considered excessive and what is considered normal in American behavior patterns. In 1955 the forces of government moved swiftly against a young man named Farmer. He had invaded the faculty office at the University of California and fired away with a shotgun, killing a graduate student and disfiguring a professor. Farmer did this, he insisted, as an act against communism and Communists; he was declared schizophrenic and put away. In exactly the same period, Drinnon points out, the United States government, in order to "contain communism," was building up a stockpile of thermonuclear weapons capable of killing hundreds of millions of people. Farmer, with a shotgun, was considered insane. The heads of government, with hydrogen bombs, were considered sane.

Joseph McCarthy was a minor judge in Wisconsin who built up a spurious record in World War II, and was elected to the Senate in 1946, the first year of the Republican party's postwar ascendancy. He had already shown signs of that imaginative fabrication and ruthlessness that were to characterize his later political conduct. As a judge, he had destroyed part of a trial transcript, and was criticized by the Wisconsin Supreme Court for "highly improper" behavior. As a candidate, he had made much of his war record; he had been a behind-the-lines marine intelligence officer, but he began labeling himself a "tail gunner."

Early in 1950 McCarthy took hold of the Communist issue. It was a time when cold war anti-communism was especially intense: the Communists had just taken power in China, and the American press was full of stories of espionage and subversion. Alger Hiss, a former State Department official who had earlier stood accused of spying in sensational testimony before the House Un-American Activities Committee (HUAC), had been convicted of perjury, and the eleven top leaders of the Communist party had been sentenced on charges of conspiring to teach and advocate the overthrow of the government by force and violence.

McCarthy launched his first assault early in 1950. On February 9, speaking before the Women's Republican Club in Wheeling, West Virginia, McCarthy referred to Communists in the State Department and declared: "One thing to remember in discussing the Communists in our Government is that we are not dealing with spies who get 30 pieces of silver to steal the blueprint of a new weapon. We are dealing with a far more sinister type of activity because it permits the enemy to guide and shape our policy." Two weeks earlier, Congressman Richard Nixon, a member of the HUAC, had told the House of Representatives: "The great lesson which should be learned from the Alger Hiss case is that we are not just dealing with espionage agents who get 30 pieces of silver to obtain the blueprint of a new weapon . . . but this is a far more sinister type of activity, because it permits the enemy to guide and shape our policy."

According to reporters from the *Wheeling Intelligencer* and radio station WWVA in Wheeling, McCarthy then held up some papers and shouted: "I have here in my hand a list of 205—a list of names that were made known to the Secretary of State as being members of the Communist Party and who nevertheless are still working and shaping policy in the State Department." The next day, in a speech in Salt Lake City, McCarthy claimed that he had a list of 57 names. Shortly afterward, McCarthy appeared on the floor of the Senate with photostatic copies of about a hundred dossiers drawn from State Department loyalty files. The dossiers were three years old, and most of the people were no longer with the department, but McCarthy read from them anyway, inventing, adding, and changing data from the material as he went along. For instance, he changed the description "liberal" to "communistically inclined" in one case and "active fellow traveler" to "active Communist" in another; "considerable derogatory information" became "conclusive evidence of . . . Communist activity" and "inclined towards communism" he read as "he was a Communist."

Responding to McCarthy's charges, the Senate passed a resolution asking the Senate Foreign Relations Committee to investigate. A subcommittee headed by Senator Millard Tydings of Maryland undertook the task, and in the course of the investigation, McCarthy told reporters that Owen Lattimore, a well-known scholar on the Far East, was the "top Russian espionage agent" in the United States. Later, McCarthy changed this description to "the principal architect of our Far Eastern policy." At one point he said: "I believe you can ask almost any school child who the architect of our Far Eastern policy is, and he will say, 'Owen Lattimore.'" McCarthy also attacked a number of State Department officials on vague charges that he could not prove. In one case he referred to an administrator in Truman's Point Four foreign-aid program, a supplement to the Marshall Plan, as a man with "a mission to communize the world"; McCarthy said he based his statement on quotes from a book the man had written. Under questioning, McCarthy told the Tydings committee that he did not know the name of the book, but would look it up.

McCarthy, nevertheless, overcame with public accusations what he could not prove in private. He talked of "egg-sucking phoney liberals" and "prancing mimics of the Moscow party line," and he turned his attack to important government figures, like Secretary of State Dean Acheson and Philip Jessup, whom he called "dilettante diplomats" who "cringed" in the face of communism. He also referred to General Marshall, who preceded Acheson as secretary of state, as a "pathetic thing" who was "completely unfit" for high office.

The Tydings committee's final report accused McCarthy of "a fraud and a hoax" upon the Senate and the country, and charged him with deliberately lying. The Senate adopted the report on a straight party vote, Democrats for it, Republicans against it. But it was only a brief setback for McCarthy. The fact was that he was garnering support from many quarters—from key Republicans like Senator Robert Taft and the chairman of the Republican National Committee to veterans groups and certain women's organizations. Passage in September, 1950, of the McCarran Internal Security Act, which Truman described as "a long step toward totalitarianism," was not only a response to the onset of the Korean War, but added proof that McCarthy was not out of step with the times. He continued his "lists" of State Department subversives, and he continued to attack

Marshall and Jessup on the ground that they, among others, had permitted the Communists to take over China. More immediately, he took after Senator Tydings himself. Tydings was up for re-election that November, and McCarthy's office helped forge a photograph of the senator talking pleasantly with a leader of the Communist party. Tydings lost the election.

McCarthy was chairman of the Permanent Investigations Subcommittee of the Senate's Committee on Government Operations, and the subcommittee majority members were among his ardent supporters: Everett Dirksen of Illinois, Karl Mundt of South Dakota, Charles Potter of Michigan. In 1953, as the Korean War was winding down, he began a series of investigations into communism in various parts of the government, with seventeen of the investigations reaching the point of public hearings. He again investigated the State Department, this time probing into its information program, including the Voice of America, and the overseas information libraries, which included books by people McCarthy considered subversives or Communists. As Robert Griffith writes in his book *The Politics of Fear,* the "State Department, like some wounded prehistoric animal, aroused itself first in puzzlement and then in panic. Between February and June there was a steady stream of directives and counterdirectives on book policy in library centers across the world. Books were removed, replaced, and even, in some instances, burned."

In the spring of 1954, McCarthy began the hearings that were to culminate in his downfall—the "Army-McCarthy hearings" in which he investigated supposed subversives in the Army and Defense Department. He made much of a dentist drafted into the Army who had been a member of the American Labor Party in New York, and he denounced a general for discharging the dentist instead of court-martialing him, saying that General Ralph Zwicker was "not fit to wear that uniform" and did not have "the brains of a five-year-old." For one month the nation watched the hearings on television. And as McCarthy became more and more vituperative, he made more and more enemies among high-ranking Republicans as well as Democrats. In December, 1954, the Senate, by an overwhelming vote, passed a motion of censure against him: "Resolved. That the conduct of the Senator from Wisconsin, Mr. McCarthy, is unbecoming a Member of the United States Senate, is contrary to senatorial traditions, and tends to bring the Senate into disrepute, and such conduct is hereby condemned."

McCarthy, who then sank into obscurity and died three years later, had gone too far. He was set aside not because he represented a different national policy than that espoused by the nation's leadership, but because he carried that policy of anti-communism at home and abroad to the point where it became ridiculous. He pressed his attacks beyond liberals and radicals to high members of the Establishment. He embarrassed the Senate, the Army, the State Department, the White House, and much of the mass media by extending their basic beliefs to the point where they could be discredited. He became a danger to his own ideological colleagues. The reactions of national leaders to McCarthy himself, as well as the structure of national policy both before and after McCarthy's tumultuous appearance on the scene, show that the senator was not an anachronism. Griffith's comment is apt:

> "McCarthyism" has been dismissed by some as a passing aberration, a chimera of mid-century politics. It was not. It was a natural expression of America's political culture and a logical though extreme product of its political machinery. What came to be called "McCarthyism" was grounded in a set of attitudes, assumptions, and judgments with deep roots in American history.

It was not the values of McCarthy that were challenged by the nation's political leaders, but his clumsy tactics, his lack of caution, his failure to lend credibility and probity to anti-communism. The censure resolution was not based on McCarthy's brand of anti-communism, but on much less substantive issues: his refusal to appear before the Subcommittee on Privileges and Elections in 1952, and his abuse of General Zwicker at the hearings.

One of the key elements in the working liberal creed in the United States is a flimsy pragmatism in which temporary objectives are achieved at the minimum cost to the nation's institutions, in which battles are fought on the least important points. In this way, support is broad and hostility is minimized, since there is little of substance to be hostile about. The result is to gain "victories" without disturbing the basic values of the citizenry; the immediate representation of an evil is knocked down, leaving the evil itself intact. As Griffith points out:

> The men who had fought [McCarthy] were neither idealistic nor especially courageous. They made no impassioned pleas against "McCarthyism" or in defense of civil liberties. They did not even attack McCarthy himself, but rather his lieutenants. Nevertheless, they fought a politically wise inner battle over procedures and appointments which had the net effect of blocking the Wisconsin senator at almost every point.

Lyndon Johnson, for example, moved efficiently as Senate Minority Leader to pass the censure resolution on McCarthy, but also to keep it within narrow bounds of unbecoming conduct. "Lyndon Johnson and others are literally demanding that we refrain from rocking the boat," one Washington worker for censure wrote. He was a liberal, and though critical of Johnson, he endorsed his basic tactic: "I hate to see the entire issue decided on as narrow a base as the . . . report [on censure] establishes, but I am pretty well convinced that the size of the vote is more important than the arguments that are made."

John F. Kennedy was also cautious in his opposition to McCarthy. He voted against him at key points, but he never spoke out openly against him. Kennedy was hospitalized at the time of the censure motion on McCarthy, and he never did reveal how he would have voted had he been present. But they were not far apart as the passion over communism mounted. McCarthy's attribution of the Communist victory in China to American scholars on the Far East was only a more furious version of what Kennedy—and other leading liberals and conservatives—had said earlier. In January, 1949, Kennedy had spoken before the House of Representatives as follows:

> Mr. Speaker, over this weekend we have learned the extent of the disaster that has befallen China and the United States. The responsibility for the failure of our foreign policy in the Far East rests squarely with the White House and the Department of State.
>
> The continued insistence that aid would not be forthcoming unless a coalition government with the Communists was formed, was a crippling blow to the National Government.
>
> So concerned were our diplomats and their advisers, the Lattimores and the Fairbanks [Professor John F. Fairbank of

Harvard], with the imperfection of the democratic system in China after 20 years of war and the tales of corruption in high places that they lost sight of our tremendous stake in a non-Communist China. . . .

This House must now assume the responsibility of preventing the onrushing tide of Communism from engulfing all of Asia.

The working pragmatism of the liberal creed, proposing shrewdness and caution at the expense of bold criticism, was never better illustrated than in the battle of 1950 over the McCarran Internal Security Act. The legislation, which proposed an intricate system of registration procedures for organizations labeled "Communist-action" or "Communist-front," troubled the liberal members of Congress. But instead of attacking it head on, a number of them, led by Paul Douglas, Harley Kilgore, Humphrey, and Herbert Lehman, proposed a substitute measure. They wanted detention centers set up for suspected subversives who, upon the declaration of an "internal security emergency" by the president, would be held without trial. A White House aide called it, with more blunt honesty than the liberal senators chose to muster, the "concentration-camp bill." Lehman's legislative assistant thought the bill "very bad" and probably unconstitutional, but nonetheless advised Lehman that it would "certainly impress the public with the fact that you are determined to act against communists." The liberals failed, however, even in their own limited objective; the detention-camp bill was voted down as a substitute, and voted in as an addition to the McCarran Act.

Fighting McCarthy without fighting McCarthyism became the strategy of the liberals. While they professed to be upset with the Wisconsin senator's methods, they subscribed eagerly to his doctrines. Maurice Rosenblatt, member of the National Committee for an Effective Congress, organized in 1948 to help liberals in congressional campaigns, suggested in 1953 that since there was bound to be antisubversive legislation, the liberals might draft a "good bill" of their own, rather than accept one by the "totalitarians." Amidst the wave of anti-Communist legislation in 1954, Humphrey amended a bill proposing the registration of "Communist-infiltrated" groups to make it even stronger; he wanted to outlaw the Communist party and strip from it any rights or privileges held by other political parties or organizations. Said Humphrey: "I do not intend to be a half patriot. I will not be lukewarm. . . . Either Senators are for recognizing the Communist Party for what it is, or they will continue to trip over the niceties of legal technicalities and details." Wayne Morse, Democratic liberal from Oregon and cosponsor of the Humphrey amendment, said: "In the Senate there is no division of opinion among liberals, conservatives and those in between when it comes to our united insistence that as a Senate we will fight the growth of the Communist conspiracy."

Whatever resolutions of censure might be passed, the liberals of the nation were in the grip of the anti-Communist fever, before, during, and after the McCarthy years. Harry Truman disliked McCarthy, but early in his presidency, in March, 1947, he established a federal loyalty program—an action foreshadowed by the wartime orders of Franklin D. Roosevelt —to scrutinize the political affiliations and activities of federal employees. From that point on, several million Americans who worked for the government were less free in their speech, their actions, and their associations. Under Truman's program, loyalty boards were created and the Civil Service Commission set up a master index on all persons who had been investigated since 1939.

Truman's Executive Order 9835 also required the Department of Justice to prepare a list of organizations it determined to be "totalitarian, fascist, communist or subversive, or as having adopted a policy of advocating or approving the commission of acts of force or violence to deny others their rights under the Constitution of the United States, or as seeking to alter the form of government of the United States by unconstitutional means." Not only membership in, affiliation with, but also "sympathetic association" with any organization on the attorney general's list was to be considered in determining disloyalty. That list grew longer and longer. By 1954, stretching into the hundreds, it included, besides the Communist party, the Socialist Youth League, the Ku Klux Klan, the Chopin Cultural Center, the Cervantes Fraternal Society, the Committee for the Negro in the Arts, the Committee for the Protection of the Bill of Rights, the League of American Writers, the Nature Friends of America, People's Drama, Inc., the Washington Bookshop Association, and the Yugoslav Seaman's Club.

While the machinery of Congress was working to censure Mc-

Carthy, for procedural irregularities and personal insults, the machinery of the judicial system was preparing to put to death Julius and Ethel Rosenberg, in vindication of the very values McCarthy stood for. McCarthy used anti-Communist emotionalism to do damage to individual lives—but he went beyond accepted practices. The nation itself was perfectly willing to use anti-Communist emotionalism against life and liberty, but it insisted on the proper procedures. And so, with all the proprieties of due process, the Rosenbergs were executed, having been convicted of conspiring to commit espionage by passing atomic secrets to the Soviet Union.

The period of the Rosenberg case—they were arrested in the summer of 1950 and executed in the summer of 1953—coincided with a period of especially great excitement. The Korean War had just begun, and the Russians had recently exploded their first atomic bomb. Atomic energy was mysterious, almost supernatural; anything connected with it was frightening. The idea that other nations might also possess the bomb—particularly Communist countries— terrified an American population clinging to the notion that only the United States could be trusted with such dangerous weapons. When, after World War II, Japanese scientists developed cyclotrons to further biological and medical research, the United States ordered them destroyed, and what had taken twelve years to build was dismantled in five days.

The evidence against the Rosenbergs was supplied almost entirely by a few witnesses who had already confessed to being spies, and were either in prison or under indictment. The testimony of David Greenglass, Ethel Rosenberg's brother, was crucial in sending his sister and brother-in-law to the death chamber. Greenglass, a machinist, worked at the Manhattan Project's Los Alamos laboratory in 1944 and early 1945 on part of the apparatus necessary to detonate the atomic bomb. He testified that Julius Rosenberg had asked him to get information from the New Mexico site for the Russians, and that he had made sketches from memory for Rosenberg of experiments with lenses to be used for detonation. Rosenberg, he said, had also given him half a Jello box top and told him that in Los Alamos someone would approach him with a matching half, to whom he could give more information. He testified that in June, 1945, in Albuquerque, a man named Harry Gold showed up with the other half of the box top, saying: "Julius sent me." Gold then went off with sketches of lenses and descriptions of experiments that Greenglass prepared from memory.

Gold, who at the time of the Rosenberg trial was serving a thirty-year sentence after confessing that he had passed secrets to the Russians, came out of jail into court to corroborate Greenglass's testimony. He had never met either of the Rosenbergs, but he said that a Soviet embassy official named Yakovlev had given him half a Jello box top and told him to contact Greenglass with instructions to say "I come from Julius." Gold said he then took the sketches and descriptions and turned them over to the Russian official. Greenglass and his wife testified that Ethel Rosenberg had typed up the information Greenglass gave to Julius. In addition, Elizabeth Bentley, a professional informer on communism, testified that in 1942 her husband, a leading Communist, had received a phone call from one "Julius."

Whether or not the Rosenbergs did participate in the transmittal of information to the Russians will probably never be known for certain. Only the Greenglasses—who were themselves in jeopardy of the law—gave direct testimony of their involvement. The Rosenbergs denied their guilt to the end; they stubbornly rejected any deals with the government, which kept offering to commute their death sentence in return for confessions of guilt. Two weeks before their execution, James Bennett, director of the Bureau of Prisons, visited them with a final plea for a confession which would save their lives. They refused, and went to their deaths, leaving two boys, four and eight, in the custody of the world that had let them die.

Even if the Rosenbergs had done what the Greenglasses claimed, only a country obsessed by fear of communism could have magnified their deed into a crime so terrible as to deserve death. The espionage statute set a maximum sentence of twenty years, except that in wartime the sentence could be either thirty years or death. At the time of the alleged espionage, 1944 and 1945, the United States was at war, but with Germany, not Russia. Russia at that time was America's ally, and, indeed, was playing the major military role in destroying the German war machine. In the postwar anti-Soviet fervor, however, the Fascist enemy was forgotten. The atmosphere of the trial was such that the United States appeared to be at war with Soviet Russia.

The cold-war psychology of the time made it easier for the nation to accept the idea that Greenglass, graduate of a technical high school, who had tried to go further in science but had flunked eight out of the eight courses he took at the Brooklyn Polytechnic Institute, could from memory make sketches that would transmit the "secret" of "the atom bomb." On the stand, Greenglass, questioned by Roy Cohn, an assistant to the prosecuting attorney, and later an assistant to McCarthy, said he had told Julius Rosenberg that he had a "pretty good description of the atom bomb." Cohn asked: "The atom bomb itself?" And Greenglass replied. "That's right." However, the lens mold Greenglass had supposedly drawn from memory related not to the bomb itself, but to one of many possible ways in which the bomb might be detonated, not a great secret to any determined team of engineers.

A number of atomic scientists have agreed on two important points in connection with the Rosenberg case: that Greenglass could not have produced any important information out of his head, and, even more important, that the Soviet Union had no urgent need of information on the atomic bomb. The *Scientific American* pointed out at the time that "without quantitative data and other necessary accompanying technical information, the Greenglass bomb was not much of a secret. The principle of 'implosion' by means of a shaped charge has often been suggested in speculation on a possible mechanism for detonation of the atomic bomb." After the trial, but before the executions, a report on Soviet espionage by the Joint Congressional Committee on Atomic Energy pointed to the relative unimportance of Greenglass's information. Nine months after the executions, James Beckerley, director of the Atomic Energy Commission's classification office, said it was time the United States stopped "kidding" itself about atomic "secrets." The *New York Times* reported a speech he made to a group of industrialists:

> The atom bomb and the hydrogen bomb were not stolen from us by spies, Dr. Beckerley emphasized. Espionage played a minor role in the attainment of successful weapons by the Soviets. . . .
> Atom bombs and hydrogen bombs are not matters that can be stolen and transmitted in the form of information, Dr. Beckerley said, in emphasizing the relative unimportance of spying in nuclear physics.

There was no "secret" to the atom bomb. The Russians knew its principles; they had the resources, both material and mental, to produce it. It was only a matter of time and persistence. When the Americans produced their bombs in 1945, scientists predicted that the Russians, on their own, could probably produce a bomb in four years. And it was precisely four years later, in 1949, that the Russians did explode their first atomic bomb.

But the nation was in no mood to consider these points, and the American judicial machinery, despite its look of detachment, can usually be counted on to reflect the prevailing national mood. Irving Saypol, the chief prosecutor, opened the trial by telling the jury he would show that the Rosenbergs stole "the one weapon that might hold the key to the survival of this nation and means the peace of the world, the atomic bomb." When Saypol summed up his case to the jury, he said: "We don't know all the details . . . but we know that these conspirators stole the most important scientific secrets ever known to mankind from this country and delivered them to the Soviet Union. . . . No defendants ever stood before the bar of American justice less deserving of sympathy than these three."

The third defendant was Morton Sobell, a friend of the Rosenbergs, who was also charged with conspiracy. The one witness produced by the government to testify that Sobell spied for the Russians was his old friend Max Elitcher. Elitcher, facing possible prosecution for perjury after denying membership in the Communist party on a loyalty-oath form, had then talked with the FBI. He testified that he drove Sobell one night in 1948 to the vicinity of the Rosenbergs' home, that Sobell took a 35-millimeter film can from the car, went out for a while, and returned without the can; Elitcher said he did not know the can's contents. The case against Sobell was so weak that Sobell's lawyer did not bother to call any witnesses and rested his case on the paucity of evidence against his client. But Sobell was found guilty along with the Rosenbergs and sentenced to thirty years in prison. (He was released in 1969.)

Julius Rosenberg refused during his trial to testify about his possible membership in the Communist party. Judge Irving Kaufman told the jury his refusal did not prove his guilt, but that it might be considered by the jury in connection with his intent. When the guilty verdict was returned, Kaufman told the jury: "My own opinion is that your verdict is a correct verdict. . . . The thought that citizens of our country would lend themselves to the destruction of their own country by the most destructive weapons known to man is so shocking that I can't find words to describe this loathsome offense." Prosecutor Saypol, before the sentencing, told the court:

> It would be delusion indeed to believe that the war in Korea is anything but a war inspired by Russia. . . . These defendants gave their allegiance to forces . . . allied to the real enemy in that fight. . . . The secrets they sought and secured were of immeasurable importance and significance. How could the life of a single individual engaged in such treasonable activities be weighed against the life of a single American soldier fighting in a distant land?

Kaufman then sentenced the Rosenbergs to death.

Throughout 1952 and the first half of 1953, legal moves were made to stop the execution. But the court of appeals, avoiding a reconsideration of the facts and limiting itself to questions of law, refused to overturn the verdict. The Supreme Court, also confining itself to legal and procedural questions, declined to review the case, with only Justice Hugo Black dissenting. President Truman, and then President Eisenhower, denied the Rosenbergs executive clemency. The persistent attorney for the Rosenbergs kept going up the judicial ladder, trying Kaufman, the court of appeals, the Supreme Court. All refused to give a new trial or stay the execution. A last-minute plea to Justice William O. Douglas, on June 17, 1953, brought a stay as the Court left Washington for the summer, but the other Justices were then flown back from all over the country and Douglas's stay was overturned. And so the Rosenbergs died.

Few Americans stood up against the anti-Communist furies of that period to plead for the Rosenbergs. Much more of a protest came from Europeans; Picasso drew a sketch of Ethel and Julius Rosenberg sitting in electric chairs, side by side, holding hands. But in the United States, liberal newspapers and magazines were cool. Only the left-wing *National Guardian* challenged the court and printed a series of articles calling the trial into question. The American Civil Liberties Union found no grounds to intervene. The liberal periodical *Commentary,* itself long-obsessed with anti-communism, joined the pile-up on the Rosenbergs with an especially vitriolic attack. The Jewishness of the Rosenbergs embarrassed some liberal Jews, who rushed to disavow them.

The Rosenberg case was a particularly dramatic episode in that long anti-Communist crusade after World War II, which claimed many victims besides those two who died: hundreds of men and women who went to prison, thousands who lost their jobs or were blacklisted in their professions, and, most important, millions who were frightened into silence.

One of the principal governmental instruments for maintaining anti-Communist passions in the postwar period was the Committee on Un-American Activities of the House of Representatives. While liberals might criticize—and sometimes bitterly—its tactics and objectives, the House Un-American Activities Committee continued to function year after year, and was granted increasing sums of money by overwhelming votes of both houses of Congress. The United States Supreme Court overrode one or another action by the HUAC, but all through the postwar years, and even at the peak of the Court's liberalism, under Chief Justice Earl Warren in the 1960s, it failed to declare the committee unconstitutional. Working very much inside the liberal tradition, the Court decided civil-liberties cases before it on the narrowest of grounds, enabling the committee to continue its work.

The committee was founded on a temporary basis, in 1938. With fascism in power in Italy and Germany, and communism firm in Soviet Russia, there was at first some doubt about the main concern of the committee. By 1945, when the committee was made permanent, the Fascist powers had been defeated in war, the Soviet Union was one of the victors, and the direction of the committee was already apparent. The campaign to make it permanent was conducted by Congressman John Rankin of Mississippi, who spoke on the floor of the House as follows: "These alien-minded communistic enemies of Christianity, and their stooges, are trying to get control of the press of the country. Many of our great daily newspapers have now taken over the radio. Listen to their lying broadcasts in broken English...."

Charged by Congress with investigating "the diffusion within the United States of subversive and Un-American propaganda," the House Un-American Activities Committee was never able to give a satisfactory definition of the term "Un-American propaganda." One of its chairmen said he understood it meant "any activity that strikes at the basic concept of our Republic." Under that cloud of ambiguity, the committee carried on its investigations, summoned hundreds of witnesses to the stand to testify about their political affiliations and beliefs, called dozens of informers to testify about the witnesses, and then cited witnesses for "contempt of Congress" when they refused to answer questions about political beliefs or affiliations.

One of the committee's most colorful sorties was its "communism in Hollywood" investigation in 1947. It brought to the stand such "experts" on communism as Lela Rogers, mother of the actress Ginger Rogers, and Adolphe Menjou, the actor. Even before the committee took its testimony, one of its members, John McDowell of Pennsylvania, had said that Mrs. Rogers "has become, in my opinion, one of the outstanding experts on communism in the United States." A preliminary report by the committee had already told of Communists in Hollywood who "employed subtle techniques in pictures glorifying the Communist system and degrading our own system of Government and Institutions." Now came testimony to corroborate Congressman McDowell's opinion and the report:

> [ROBERT E.] STRIPLING (*for the committee*): Mrs. Rogers . . . as your daughter's manager, so to speak, have you and your daughter ever objected to or turned down scripts because you felt that there were lines in there for her to speak which you felt were un-American or Communist propaganda?
> MRS. ROGERS: Yes sir. We turned down *Sister Carrie*, by Theodore Dreiser.

Menjou, whom McDowell had called "one of the greatest patriots I ever met," was asked by the committee how he identified Communists. He replied: "A Communist is anyone who attends any meeting at which Paul Robeson appears—and applauds." Robeson, a concert singer and actor, was a supporter of the Soviet Union and of the American Communist Party. Gary Cooper was another star witness:

> COOPER: I have turned down quite a few scripts because I thought they were tinged with Communist ideas.
> STRIPLING: Can you name any of those scripts? . . .

COOPER: I don't think I could, because most of the scripts I
read at night.

Ten Hollywood writers and producers who refused to testify before the committee on their political ideas and connections were
cited for contempt, convicted, and sent to prison. Their appeal was
not accepted by the Supreme Court. And through the years that
followed, the Court refused to accept the First Amendment, guaranteeing freedom of speech, press, and assembly, as grounds for refusing to testify before the HUAC.

In 1959, in the contempt of Congress case of a Vassar College
mathematics instructor, Lloyd Barenblatt, Justices Black, Douglas,
and Warren wrote a dissenting opinion in which they declared: "The
First Amendment says in no equivocal language that Congress shall
pass no law abridging freedom of speech, press, assembly or petition.
The activities of this Committee [HUAC], authorized by Congress,
do precisely that, through exposure, obloquy and public scorn." The
majority of the Court, however, pointed out that its reversal of contempt citations in previous cases, on narrow procedural grounds,
did not mean it would destroy the substance of the work of the House
Committee on Un-American Activities.

The Supreme Court, in the Barenblatt case, invoked the "balancing principle": the resolution of First Amendment rights "always
involves a balancing by the courts of the competing private and
public interests at stake in the particular circumstances shown." It
was a convenient principle, because if the right of free speech was
merely a private interest, how could it outweigh the enormous public
interest of a state beset by subversion and possible external attack?
In 1968, in *United States* v. *O'Brien,* the Court upheld the conviction of David O'Brien for burning his draft card. O'Brien said his act
was one of symbolic speech, protesting against the Vietnam War.
The Court, in an opinion written by one of its liberal members, Abe
Fortas, held that the government's right to keep its Selective Service
records straight superseded O'Brien's right to free speech. It was the
balancing principle again, with the government's thumb on the scale.

In the Barenblatt decision, the Court made clear the influence of
the cold war. It was extremely important for the HUAC to get an
answer from the Vassar instructor on whether he had been a member
of the Communist party:

To suggest that because the Communist Party may also sponsor peaceable political reforms the constitutional issues before us should now be judged as if that Party were just an ordinary political party from the standpoint of national security, is to ask this Court to blind itself to world affairs which have determined the whole course of our national policy since the close of World War II. . . .

We conclude that the balance between the individual and the governmental interests here at stake must be struck in favor of the latter, and that therefore the provisions of the First Amendment have not been offended.

The anti-Communist feeling generated by the loyalty hearings for government employees and the work of the House Un-American Activities Committee reached absurd lengths—but it did not seem absurd at that time; it was a pervasive feeling. One man in the naval reserve was refused a commission because he continued "closely to associate" with a former Communist; the former Communist was his mother. On November 20, 1954, the *Washington Post* reported that "a young music teacher turned piano dealer was refused a license here last week to sell second-hand pianos because he had pleaded the Fifth Amendment before the House Un-American Activities Committee."

Fantasies about a Communist take-over of the United States government were graphically illustrated in 1957 by Congressman Francis E. Walter of Pennsylvania, then HUAC chairman. Walter estimated that there were two hundred thousand Communists in the United States, though the FBI, never known to minimize Communist strength, put the number at about twenty thousand. Said Walter: "Anyone who thinks that Communism in the U.S. is no longer a threat, constitutes a serious menace. They should consider that at the moment on American soil are the equivalent of twenty combat divisions of enemy troops engaged in propaganda, espionage, subversion and loyal only to the Soviet Union."

A constitutional challenge to the existence of the House Un-American Activities Committee was made in 1968 by three Chicagoans, including heart surgeon Dr. Jeremiah Stamler, who had refused to answer the committee's questions and who then asked the courts to abolish it as a breach of the First Amendment. A three-judge court of appeals in Chicago ruled against them, two to one, with Judge Julius Hoffman writing the opinion. In November, 1968, the Supreme Court—at its most "liberal," with Warren, Thurgood Marshall, William J. Brennan, Jr., and Abe Fortas among the majority—refused to consider the plea; it upheld the appeals court without comment. Two years later, though the High Court was still unable to find the HUAC's activities repugnant to the First Amendment, the committee had begun to look both foolish and dangerous to many Americans. Congress, therefore, changed its name to the Internal Security Committee, and its work continued.

It has long been a favorite belief of Americans that whatever may be wrong with the United States, with its foreign policy or its economics or its treatment of the blacks, the right of free speech—protected by the Constitution and upheld by the Supreme Court—is one mighty pillar of liberty that they all possess. Yet it was not until 1925 that the Court even recognized that the First Amendment applied in any way to state infringements of free speech—and these were the most numerous. In wartime—World War I being the prime example—the Court protected the government from criticism and formulated rules, including the doctrine of "clear and present danger," that sounded libertarian on paper but in practice put those who criticized the war in prison. The most liberal members of the Court, Oliver Wendell Holmes and Louis Brandeis, participated in this wartime curtailment of First Amendment rights. After World War II, the Court wove an even thicker web of legal humbug: freedom of speech on paper, restrictions of rights for radicals and dissenters. President Truman was presumably a liberal, but when his appointees dominated the Supreme Court—Chief Justice Fred M. Vinson was a political crony—it was at its worst. The Court affirmed the constitutionality of the Smith Act, which made it a crime to conspire to teach or advocate the overthrow of the government by force and violence, to conspire to publish material advocating overthrow, or join organizations with such intent. It effectively crippled the Communist party by sending its leaders to jail. Altogether 141 were indicted, and 29 served terms, but the threat of jail for the rest played its part in breaking up the party.

Subsequent court decisions slightly modified the Vinson decision of 1951 on the Smith Act, so that by 1961 the Court was saying that a person had to be an "active and knowing" member of the Communist party to be jailed under the act. By the 1960s, the Communist party was a ragged remnant, heavily infiltrated by FBI agents. Yet anti-communism was still so rampant, and liberals still so much in the forefront of that sentiment, that when World War II veteran Robert Thompson, a Communist leader convicted under the Smith Act, was to be buried in Arlington National Cemetery, the government objected. Thompson was a holder of the Distinguished Service Cross for combat heroism in the Pacific theater, but Attorney General Nicholas Katzenbach, in the administration of Lyndon Johnson, found a rule supported by what the *New York Times* called "an intricate seven-page legal memorandum," under which he could bar Thompson's burial in Arlington.

Had the anti-Communist hysteria of the McCarthy period disappeared with McCarthy himself? Or had McCarthy only illuminated a persistent feature of American society? Evidence for the latter can be adduced from two 1968 news items. In one, the *New York Times* reported that the Communist party candidate for president that year would not get Secret Service protection, although a law had been passed after the assassination of Senator Robert Kennedy that presidential candidates must be protected by the government. "A department spokesman said it could be assumed that the advisory commission created by the new law regarding protection for candidates had not felt that the Communist Party was entitled to protection under the law." The other item pertained to a letter sent by an assistant attorney general in Arizona, Philip M. Haggerty, to the Communist party, informing it that Arizona law "flatly prohibits official representation" for Communists on the ballot in that state. Haggerty added: "The subversive nature of your organization is even more clearly designated by the fact that you do not even include your zip code on your letter."

In World War I, many Americans critical of the war had been convicted under the Sedition Act of 1918. The act was to be in force only in wartime, and therefore by 1921 it was considered inoperative. But when in 1950 President Truman declared a state of "national emergency"—which was still in effect by 1972—all wartime statutes became operative, including the thirty-two-year-old Sedition Act. And it was a liberal attorney general, Robert Kennedy, who asked Congress to extend the jurisdiction of the act to statements made overseas; among other penalties, the act provided up to twenty years in prison for statements attempting to "obstruct recruitment" in the armed forces. The House passed the amendment overwhelmingly, but it died in the Senate. Kennedy's performance was not reassuring to those with faith in liberal politicians' support to free speech.

Freedom of speech in the United States is not as secure as the words of the First Amendment would imply: "Congress shall make no law . . . abridging the freedom of speech, or of the press; or the right of the people peaceably to assemble, and to petition the Government for a redress of grievances." These words are the rhetoric of American liberalism. Liberalism's operating creed, however, declares that freedom of speech shall be limited, depending on circumstances, and depending on who is exercising that freedom. Any American can stand on a soapbox in the street and speak his mind, the liberal credo says. But in 1949, a Syracuse University student, Irving Feiner, got up on a wooden box in Syracuse and denounced President Truman, the American Legion, the mayor, and other local political officials; he said that "colored people don't have equal rights, and they should rise up in arms and fight for them." A man in the crowd told police if they did not take "that son of a bitch" off the box, he would. Feiner was advised several times by a policeman to stop talking, but he refused; he was then taken off the box, arrested for "disorderly conduct," and convicted. When the appeal finally got to the Supreme Court, Chief Justice Vinson, for the majority, termed the arrest within "the bounds of proper state police action." Black, for three dissenting justices, called the conviction "a mockery of the free speech guarantees of the Constitution." The basic premise of the Feiner decision—that police officials can exercise their discretion without violating the First Amendment—has never been overturned by the Court.

Even if the Court should become a staunch supporter of free speech in the streets, how much meaning would its endorsement have so long as the police have the physical power to arrest anyone whose speech disturbs them? The arrested person might eventually get a reversal by the courts—if he is willing to spend some time in jail, tens of thousands of dollars in legal fees, and several years waiting for his case to come before the Supreme Court. In other words, the protection of the Constitution is a distant one; the immediate power over free speech is with those who possess club and gun on the spot where exercise of the freedom is being sought.

The power of police over constitutional rights is perhaps more apparent in their actions against those choosing to exercise the right of a free press, a right that is not so hedged by Supreme Court rulings as the free speech doctrine. On the right to a free press—specifically, the right to distribute leaflets in public places—the Supreme Court has been clear. A string of decisions affirms the right of persons to distribute leaflets, without permits, even if anonymous, even if distributed in semiprivate places like company towns, government housing projects, shopping centers, or from door to door. Yet the power of local police can effectively nullify these decisions. In Lynn, Massachusetts, in 1970, for instance, police arrested several young people for distributing antiwar leaflets in front of a high school. Ultimately, the Supreme Court might have protected the distributors; immediately, their right to distribute was revoked by police power.

The liberal claim of free expression in the United States has a more serious flaw than police power over constitutional rights. In the mass society of postwar America, with its complex and expensive forms of communication, the right of free speech has had a strong economic component. It is reasonable to ask not only do you have free speech? but also how *much* do you have? how loud is your voice? how many people can you reach? A man's right to free expression has been limited by his wealth and power. A radical can use a soapbox and reach a hundred people in the park. Someone else can rent a loudspeaker system and reach several thousand people. A corporation can buy prime time on television and reach ten million people in one evening. A critic of the president would have to strain to buy a moment of television time, but the president can command all the major television channels, and the ears of fifty million people, any time he chooses. The dissenters can publish their little magazines and newspapers. But whoever owns *Time* or *Newsweek* or *McCall's* or the *Reader's Digest* or the *Los Angeles Times* has enormous advantages in freedom of expression.

Other realities intrude on the theoretical right to free expres-

sion. Certain situations are constricting. Whether in office or factory or university, there is the fear that saying the wrong thing
may result in being fired. In that abstract, large place called
"America," men are free to talk; but in the actual chambers of
"America," where they live, work, and study, there is likely to be
more tyranny than democracy. In the classroom, the teacher dominates; on the job, the employer dominates; in the home it is the
parent who dominates; in the courtroom, it is the judge.

The firing of a young Boston schoolteacher, Jonathan Kozol, is an
example of how an employer controls speech. Kozol, author of the
award-winning *Death at an Early Age,* a book about the Boston
school system, once read to pupils a poem by Langston Hughes,
"Ballad of the Landlord." The following stanzas suggest its
thrust:

> Landlord, landlord,
> My roof has sprung a leak.
> Don't you 'member I told you about it
> Way last week? . . .
>
> Ten bucks you say I owe you?
> Ten bucks you say is due?
> Well, that's ten bucks more'n I'll pay you
> Till you fix this house up new. . . .
>
> Police! Police!
> Come and get this man!
> He's trying to ruin the government
> and overturn the land! . . .
>
> Precinct Station.
> Iron cell.
> Headlines in press:
>
> MAN THREATENS LANDLORD
> TENANT HELD NO BAIL
> JUDGE GIVES NEGRO 90 DAYS IN COUNTY JAIL

Kozol was fired from his teaching job by the school committee, which
said in its report: "It has been established as a fact that Mr. Kozol
taught the poem, 'Ballad of the Landlord,' to his class and later
distributed mimeographed copies of it to his pupils for home
memorization."

Certain classes of Americans do not have even the restricted constitutional rights of the ordinary citizen. Inmates in jails are deprived of the right of free expression and communication—their visitors are limited, their mail is censored, their books are controlled, their writing is regulated. Men in the armed forces—and these numbered more than three million in 1970—also live under special restrictions.

In 1970 John Dippel, a member of army intelligence on Okinawa and opposed to the war in Vietnam, was arrested with two fellow soldiers for distributing leaflets critical of the American military presence on Okinawa. They were released, but warned that leaflet distribution was illegal. The army regulation allowed distribution, except for material considered by a post commander to be "a clear danger" to discipline, loyalty, and morale. Dippel decided to test his right to free speech by requesting the right to distribute, without comment, a passage from the Declaration of Independence. He chose the passage starting "We hold these truths to be self-evident." Dippel then went through a bewildering maze of requirements and regulations, denials and blockages. Permission finally came from the Pentagon itself. The Declaration of Independence could be distributed if it took place on one certain day, within a four-hour time span, in two specified areas, and only by the person asking permission, without editorial comment, and unaccompanied by any other material. At one point in the process of trying to obtain permission, an army major, who was also an assistant judge advocate and a Yale Law School alumnus, and who recommended that distribution be denied, told him: "To be painfully blunt, the Declaration of Independence is a subversive document."

Ultimately, the right of free expression can only be secured by a citizenry determined to protect it. When that right is consistently abridged, the abridgment gains legitimacy, and citizens begin to think that this is as it should be. Thus, a circle is created, in which restrictive action and public opinion reinforce each other. The circle rests solidly on the hypocrisy of liberalism, in which obeisance is given to general rights but not to specific ones. A test of public opinion by several scholars in the sixties disclosed that 81 per cent of those polled believed "nobody has a right to tell another person what he should or should not read," but 51 per cent agreed that "a book that contains wrong political views cannot be a good book and does not deserve to be published"; 82 per cent believed that

Wide World Photos

Demonstrators in Cambridge, Maryland, 1964, blocked by National Guardsmen with fixed bayonets. About one hundred fifty strong, they had marched a mile and a half through the city and were stopped by the Guard as they tried to enter the downtown area.

Wide World Photos

"A white Freedom Rider, James Zwerg, was beaten again and again, refusing to defend himself. They then turned to the blacks. . . ." (Page 206)

Wide World Photos

Victims of a napalm bombing attack. In 1972, as U.S. ground forces were gradually being withdrawn from Vietnam, American bombing of Indochina continued on a ferocious scale.

Refugee and her child in Indochina. One result of the war was that close to one-third of the population of South Vietnam—about five million men, women, and children—had to flee their ancestral homes. What was being torn apart in Vietnam was an entire culture, an ancient web of custom and human relations.

Wide World Photos

Dresden, Germany, February, 1945, after Allied bombers set fire to the city, leaving more than one hundred thousand dead. The bombing of villages, towns, and cities, condemned when Hitler did it, became official American policy during World War II, and later in Korea and Vietnam.

United Press International Photo

Wide World Photos

Malcolm X: ". . . when you stay radical long enough, and get enough people to be like you, you'll get your freedom."

Freedom Riders' bus set afire by mob outside Anniston, Alabama, May, 1961.

Wide World Photos

United Press International Photo

"I suspect that all the crimes committed by all the jailed criminals do not equal in total social damage that of the crimes committed against them," wrote psychiatrist Karl Menninger in *The Crime of Punishment*. In the early 1970s prison revolts against intolerable conditions grew, and were treated, as shown here, with police clubs or, as in Attica, New York, by a massacre of inmates and their hostages.

Wide World Photos

Supporters of the Women's Liberation Movement, protesting at the Republican National Convention in Miami in the summer of 1972.

Kent State University, Ohio, May 4, 1970, when four students were shot to death by National Guardsmen who were breaking up a student demonstration against the American invasion of Cambodia. Here, a fifteen-year-old girl kneels over the body of one of the dead students.

Copyright:
Tarentum, Pa. Valley News Dispatch

Wide World Photos

"Our apologies, good friends, for the fracture of good order, the burning of paper instead of children, the angering of the orderlies in the front parlor of the charnel house. We could not, so help us God, do otherwise. For we are sick at heart, our hearts give us no rest for thinking of the Land of Burning Children." From a meditation of Daniel Berrigan, shown here with his brother Philip, left, as they and other members of the Catonsville Nine burned draft records to protest the Vietnam War.

Veterans of the war in Vietnam, marching in protest against their own country's policy of continuing that war. In Washington, D. C., in 1971, veterans publicly threw away their medals to dramatize their feelings about the war.

Courtesy of Audrey Schirmer

United Press International Photo

Poverty— in the capital of the richest nation in the world.

"people who hate our way of life should still have a chance to be heard," but 57 per cent said that "freedom does not give anyone the right to teach foreign ideas in our schools."

The First Amendment also grants the right "peaceably to assemble, and to petition the Government for a redress of grievances." Of all constitutional rights, this freedom is the most fragile, interpreted with the greatest ambiguity by the courts, and—most important—violated again and again by the police. Furthermore, the right to assemble is perhaps the most vital because, politically speaking, it becomes an issue when the power of the citizenry is needed to oppose governmental abuse. Freedom of speech and press can be tolerated by the Establishment so long as they do not lead to organized movements that represent threats to the status quo. Such movements require joint action. To resist authority, to build and sustain power for political change, freedom of assembly is probably the most critical of all rights.

The Supreme Court has left this right beset with uncertainty. It was not until 1937—at the end of that long period of obstreperous, necessary assembly, from the railroad strikes of 1877 to the sitdown strikes of 1936 and 1937—that the constitutional right of free assembly was held to apply also to *state* restrictions—which were the most common ones. And in that same year, ruling on the sitdown strikes, the Court declared that any assembly that turned to *action,* such as workers occupying factories to dramatize and strengthen their demands, was not to be tolerated.

The Supreme Court decisions of the 1960s—in cases developing mostly out of the civil-rights movement—were confusing about when peaceable assembly would be tolerated and when it would not. In a 1963 case (*Edwards* v. *South Carolina*), the Court overturned breach-of-peace convictions for 187 Negro students who demonstrated on the statehouse grounds. The students had been well-behaved, had sung "The Star-Spangled Banner" and clapped their hands, but they had refused to leave the grounds when told to do so by the police. Three years later, another group of 32 Negro students had their convictions for trespass upheld by the Court (*Adderley* v. *Florida*), which ruled that an assembly near a jail could not be tolerated, even if peaceful. Justice Douglas spoke for the dissenting minority, which included Fortas, Brennan, and Warren:

The jailhouse, like an executive mansion, a legislative chamber, a courthouse, or the state house itself, is one of the seats of government, whether it be the Tower of London, the Bastille, or a small county jail. And when it houses political prisoners or those who many think are unjustly held, it is an obvious center for protest. The right to petition for the redress of grievances has an ancient history and is not limited to writing a letter or sending a telegram to a congressman; it is not confined to appearing before the local city council or writing letters to the President or Governor or Mayor. Conventional methods of petitioning may be, and often have been, shut off to large groups of our citizens. Legislators may turn deaf ears; formal complaints may be routed endlessly through a bureaucratic maze; courts may let the wheels of justice grind very slowly. Those who do not control television and radio, those who cannot afford to advertise in newspapers or circulate elaborate pamphlets may have only a more limited type of access to public officials. Their methods should not be condemned as tactics of obstruction and harassment as long as the assembly and petition are peaceable, as these were.

Douglas's was a powerful plea, but it lost. Other Supreme Court decisions were more favorable. A demonstration across the street from a courthouse in Louisiana was deemed legitimate in a 1965 decision (*Cox* v. *Louisiana*). In the same year, a civil-rights leader who refused to move on when requested by a policeman had his conviction overturned (*Shuttlesworth* v. *Birmingham*), the Court ruling that a person's right to stand on the street should not depend on "the whim" of a police officer.

Yet the very uncertainty of how strongly the courts will protect the individual's rights is a deterrent to the free exercise of those rights. How could a group, noting the Supreme Court's tolerance of an assembly near a courthouse, know that their arrest for assembling near a jailhouse would be approved? How great an effect did the confusion resulting from these two decisions have on others who might wish to exercise their freedom of assembly? Could the favorable decision in the *Edwards* case, which was based on the fact that surrounding whites were not strongly perturbed by the demonstration, change if onlookers got unruly? How could demonstrators possibly predict the effect of their assembly on other people? What if demonstrators did not, as in the *Edwards* case, sing "The Star-

Spangled Banner" but "The Internationale"? Uncertainty about which actions will be protected by the courts, and which will not, is itself intimidating, in the same way that a helpless prisoner, subjected to alternating acts of cruelty and kindness, is terrorized more effectively than a person who knows what he faces.

There are still other problems in the exercise of constitutional rights within the American system of justice. Money and time, for example, are both required in extraordinary amounts to take a case all the way up to the Supreme Court. It has been estimated that between $25,000 and $40,000 and between two to four years are needed in the process. Even then the Court, which hears less than 5 per cent of the cases presented to it, may decide not to review it. Another problem is that Supreme Court decisions are uniquely applicable to the particular case under consideration, so that each subsequent case can always be considered different in some detail, and therefore deserving of a different decision. A third major problem is that the immediate decision on whether a person has exercised a constitutional right or should go to jail is made by local courts, which may have neither the knowledge, the will, nor the desire to apply Supreme Court decisions.

In the spring of 1963, the Supreme Court overturned the conviction of six Negro boys in Savannah, Georgia, for a breach of the peace because they were playing basketball in a white park and refused to obey a police order to leave. Chief Justice Warren said their refusal to obey the police was justified because the police order was unconstitutional and invalid. Two months later several young black people were arrested in Greenville, Mississippi, for breach of the peace after a protest against segregation. It was as if the Supreme Court decision in the Savannah case did not exist, for the Greenville Municipal Court found them guilty.

To protest this conviction, fifty black people met in front of the courthouse where they were addressed by Charles MacLaurin, a field secretary for the Student Non-violent Coordinating Committee, who criticized the conviction and urged that blacks register to vote in order to deal with such injustices. Told to move on by a Greenville police officer, MacLaurin, believing that his freedom to speak was being violated, continued to speak. He was arrested, charged with disturbing the peace and resisting arrest, and found guilty in

Greenville Municipal Court. An appeal to the county court failed, and he was sentenced to 180 days in jail. The sentence was upheld by the Washington County Circuit Court, and later by the Mississippi Supreme Court. The case was then appealed to the Supreme Court of the United States. Four Supreme Court judges must agree to accept a case for review; only three judges voted to hear Mac-Laurin's case, and so it was turned down. MacLaurin was ordered to start his jail term—almost four years from the time of the arrest.

The limitations on the constitutional freedom of assembly depend not only on the vagaries of the American court system but on police reaction. In the civil-rights demonstrations of the early 1960s, thousands of protesters were arrested for assembling peaceably; they were unprotected by the Constitution, which, in effect, was at the mercy of the local police. And the federal government, charged with defending the constitutional rights of citizens against local police officials, made no move to defend the freedom of assembly.

In Albany, Georgia, seven hundred persons were arrested in 1961 and 1962 for walking down the street together to protest racial discrimination. Several hundred more were arrested for picketing, assembling in public parks, marching to the City Hall, praying at the City Hall, praying at the public library. It didn't matter what the Constitution or the Supreme Court said; their freedom was foreclosed by the local chief of police, and they lost it at the moment when they wanted it. In Birmingham, in 1963, thousands were arrested for assembling on the streets for the specific purpose mentioned in the Constitution, "to petition the government for a redress of grievances." In Selma two years later, marchers were attacked and clubbed mercilessly by state troopers.

What was revealed about the reality of the right of peaceable assembly during the civil-rights movement of the early sixties became even more apparent during the antiwar demonstrations of the late sixties. Again and again, police and National Guardsmen attacked, usually with clubs and tear gas, sometimes with guns, assemblies of people gathered to voice a protest. Sometimes the police could point to acts of provocation from a crowd—insults or rocks thrown—but the magnitude of the police reaction was far beyond the level of provocation. The use in America of provocations by individuals in a large mass as an excuse to club, gas, or shoot anyone in the vicinity has had its equivalent abroad in the wiping out of a Vietnamese village by United States armed forces because several shots came from somewhere inside it.

The violence that occurred on the streets of Chicago during the 1968 Democratic National Convention was termed a "police riot" by a committee that investigated the disorder. The Walker Report to the National Commission on the Causes and Prevention of Violence declared:

> During the week of the Democratic National Convention, the Chicago police were the targets of mounting provocation by both word and act. It took the form of obscene epithets, and of rocks, sticks, bathroom tiles and even human feces hurled at police by demonstrators. Some of these acts had been planned; others were spontaneous or were themselves provoked by police action. Furthermore, the police had been put on edge by widely published threats of attempts to disrupt both the city and the Convention.
>
> That was the nature of the provocation. The nature of the response was unrestrained and indiscriminate police violence on many occasions, particularly at night.
>
> That violence was made all the more shocking by the fact that it was often inflicted upon persons who had broken no law, disobeyed no order, made no threat. These included peaceful demonstrators, onlookers, and large numbers of residents who were simply passing through, or happened to live in, the areas where confrontations were occurring.

This summary gives only the mildest picture of that series of bloody beatings and forays by police that are described in the body of the report, and it must be remembered that the Walker Study Team was headed by a prominent businessman and lawyer, conservative in background, Daniel Walker, who utilized the accounts of more than three thousand eyewitnesses and participants in the Chicago events. The Walker Report cites some examples of police violence:

> A priest who was in the crowd says he saw a "boy about fourteen or fifteen, white, standing on top of an automobile yelling something which was unidentifiable. Suddenly a policeman pulled him down from the car and beat him to the ground by striking him three or four times with a nightstick. Other police joined in. . . .
>
> A well-dressed woman saw this incident and spoke angrily to a nearby police captain. As she spoke, another policeman

came up from behind her and sprayed something in her face with an aerosol can. He then clubbed her to the ground. He and two other policemen then dragged her along the ground to the same paddy wagon and threw her in. . . .

"A wave of police charged down Jackson," another witness relates. Fleeing demonstrators were beaten indiscriminately. . . . Two men lay in pools of blood, their heads severely cut by clubs.

Another report—*The Politics of Protest*—was made to the National Commission on the Causes and Prevention of Violence by sociologist Jerome Skolnick. Skolnick also called the commission's attention to the widespread occurrence of police violence against peaceful assemblies of people:

For example, in March, 1968, in New York's Grand Central Station, while demonstrators engaged in typical Yippie tactics (non-violent, but shouting, and playacting), police suddenly appeared and without giving the crowd any real chance to disperse, indiscriminately attacked and clubbed demonstrators. A similar outburst occurred a month later in Washington Square, and, of course, the police violence that spring at Columbia [University] . . . is by now a matter of common knowledge. The dispersal of a march of thousands to Century City in Los Angeles during the summer of 1967 is also a case in point. There, as reported in *Day of Protest, Night of Violence,* a report prepared by the American Civil Liberties Union of Southern California, dispersal was accompanied by similar police clubbing and beating of demonstrators, children, and invalids.

One of the most shocking examples of official violence against assemblies of citizens came in May, 1970, as students on the campus of Kent State University in Ohio protested the invasion of Cambodia ordered by the Nixon administration. National Guardsmen had been sent to the campus the day before, after students had burned down Kent's ROTC building. Facing a noisy but unarmed crowd, the guard fired into it, killing four students. An FBI investigation of the killings was summarized by Senator Stephen Young of Ohio, on October 13, 1970, in a speech to the Senate: "Most of the National Guardsmen who did fire their weapons do not specifically claim that they fired because their lives were in danger. Rather, they generally state in their narrative that they fired after they heard others fire. We have reason to believe that the claim by the National Guard that their lives were endangered by the students was fabricated subsequent to the event." An Ohio grand jury exonerated the National Guardsmen; instead, it indicted twenty-five students on various charges.

One year after the tragedy at Kent, in May, 1971, nearly thirteen thousand people were arrested on the streets of the nation's capital. They had come to Washington to protest the war in Indochina— many of them to commit acts of nonviolent civil disobedience. But only a few of them were actually arrested for committing such acts as blocking traffic. Most of them were arrested for simply being on the streets, alone or in groups. One young man was arrested because he was walking down the street; he wore long hair and jeans, and this was the basis of many arrests at that time. This writer, who stopped to inquire why the arresting officer was beating that young man around the legs with his club, was also arrested. A young man who stopped to take a photo of the scene was arrested. Two young people who stopped to listen were arrested. And six other people nearby who were walking down the street singing "America the Beautiful" were arrested.

Of what use was it to these thousands of people that the Supreme Court in 1960, in *Thompson* v. *Louisville,* had ruled that a policeman could not arrest a Negro standing peacefully in a café for refusing to move on when told? The Court had said that Thompson was arrested under a vagrancy statute, not for *doing* something, but for *being* something. Yet as Professor Milton Konvitz points out, "Prosecutions such as these, based on a crime of status or condition rather than acts . . . are disposed of unceremoniously by the thousands in American city and police courts, and there is no outcry over them. . . ."

It is standard in courses and books on constitutional law to quote with satisfaction, as proof of the steady expansion of constitutional liberties in recent years, the 1939 Supreme Court decision in *Hague* v. *the CIO.* The case came before the Court after Frank Hague, the mayor of Jersey City, had interfered with people assembling in a labor organizing drive. The Court's words in that case have often stirred pride in the American system of justice:

Wherever the title of streets and parks may rest, they have immemorially been held in trust for the use of the public and, time out of mind, have been used for purposes of assembly, communicating thoughts between citizens, and discussing public questions.

Of what use was this decision to those nineteen pacifists who were walking through Griffin, Georgia, in 1961, with placards announcing their "Quebec-Washington-Guantanamo" march for peace, and, while distributing leaflets, were arrested by police? When they went limp in protest against what they considered an illegal arrest, they were tortured with cattle prods on their arms, legs, and genitals. Of what use was this decision ten years later during those sweeping arrests in Washington, D.C., when thousands upon thousands were locked behind fences and bars, their right of assembly, their right to petition for a redress of grievances a matter of rhetoric?

In May, 1970, the Supreme Court, with only Douglas dissenting, upheld the power of mayors to prohibit public gatherings during times of urban unrest. The mayor of Philadelphia had banned outdoor gatherings of twelve or more persons. The *New York Times* reported:

> The ban lasted five days, during which three peaceful assemblies were broken up by the police and more than 100 persons were arrested. . . .
> The three meetings that were broken up consisted of a group of civil rights advocates who went to the home of Representative William A. Barrett to petition for the enactment of the proposed Civil Rights Act of 1968; an assembly of about 100 persons who planted a tree as a symbol of peace, and a group of about 250 students who met on the University of Pennsylvania campus to protest the ban on assemblies.
> The appeal pointed out that, while the tree-planting group was being dispersed, a crowd of 10,000 people were attending ceremonies nearby for the recommissioning of the battleship New Jersey. It also noted that the group at Mr. Barrett's home had stood quietly for some time with only 11 persons present. They were undisturbed by the police until a 12th person arrived and arrests were made.
> In a brief order, the Court dismissed the appeal "for want of a substantial Federal question."

Perhaps the most realistic statement on the constitutional right of free assembly is that made by the constitutional scholar E. S. Corwin. Corwin, after telling how since the thirties the Supreme Court has held the right of peaceable assembly "cognate to those of free speech and free press and is equally fundamental," comments: "Even so, the right is not unlimited. Under the common law any assemblage was unlawful which aroused the apprehensions of 'men of firm and rational minds with families and property here.' "

The customary emphasis of American liberalism on the freedoms described in the Constitution and prescribed by the courts simply does not square with the realities of contradictory court decisions, of judicial ambiguities, of the power of lower courts to ignore High Court decisions, of the power of the police to abrogate all constitutional rights and court rulings, of the privileges of property and wealth. The working creed of liberalism, acted out in the courts and in the streets, has told far more.

The civil liberties guaranteed in the Fourth, Fifth, Sixth, and Eighth amendments have also not remained inviolate. Have stop-and-frisk laws or wiretapping or wholesale arrests confirmed "the right of the people to be secure . . . against unreasonable searches and seizures" as the Fourth Amendment declares? Is the Fifth Amendment's statement that no person shall "be deprived of life, liberty, or property without due process of law" a right of the rich and a delusion of the poor? How long do the poor languish in America's jails in flagrant violation of the Sixth Amendment's injunction that "the accused shall enjoy the right to a speedy and public trial"? To what extent do the poor have the "assistance of counsel" as this amendment stipulates? Is America guilty of inflicting "cruel and unusual punishments" on those it jails, despite the prohibition specified in the Eighth Amendment? How many rights, how many laws, how many provisions of the United States Constitution has the United States government violated for the sake of "law and order"?

An atmosphere of self-congratulation has surrounded the accumulating decisions by the Supreme Court expanding the right of counsel in criminal cases. In 1963 civil libertarians acclaimed the Supreme Court's decision in the *Gideon* case. In *Gideon* v. *Wainwright* the Court decided that, henceforth, state and local courts must provide counsel for indigent defendants in felony cases; prior to the decision, counsel had to be appointed only where the death penalty was involved. Any pride over "progress" should have been accompanied by the question: Why did it take so long? Not until 1932—140 years after the Bill of Rights was adopted—was the Sixth Amendment's right of counsel in criminal cases applied to state proceedings, where by far the largest number of trials take place. In 1963 the right, as stated in the Constitution, was finally applied to all *felony* cases. The Court's decision, however, did not apply to misdemeanor cases, which may also involve jail sentences of several years.

The *Gideon* decision was, theoretically at least, a much-needed extension of the right of counsel to the poor in all serious criminal cases. Yet in too many instances the counsel have been appointed by the court—and most appointees have not been so much interested in defending their poor clients as in getting the matter settled. In one East Coast city in 1970, court-appointed attorneys spent an average of seven minutes with their clients from the time they were appointed to the case to the time they appeared before the judge to have the defendant plead—in most cases—guilty. The prevailing advice given by court-appointed attorneys is to plead guilty, usually to a lesser charge. Most court-appointed attorneys are familiar courthouse figures, political friends of the judge and prosecuting attorney alike, and they work out an arrangement under which the prosecutor will accept a guilty plea to a lesser charge, an arrangement that has been termed "bargain justice" or "negotiated justice." The attorney does the legwork, exercises his power of persuasion on the defendant, and all concerned can then mark the case "closed."

Many defendants who insist on their innocence are induced to plead guilty simply because they are told that if they plead not guilty and are convicted by a jury their sentence will be much heavier. The persuasive argument used here is that defendants run the risk of additional punishment for insisting on too much due process of law when the courts and lawyers are already very busy. George Jackson, author of *Soledad Brother,* pleaded his innocence to a charge of robbing a filling-station operator of seventy dollars, but was persuaded by his court-appointed attorney to change his plea to guilty. He then received, at eighteen, a one-year-to-life indeterminate sentence. Instead of being released in 1961 at the end of one year, he spent the next ten years in prison. Each year he was turned down for release by the parole board for not being a submissive, apologetic prisoner. On August 21, 1971, Jackson was shot to death by prison guards at San Quentin.

The *Gideon* decision was followed a year later by the Supreme Court's extension of the right of counsel to the police station in the *Escobedo* case, and, in 1966, in *Miranda* v. *Arizona,* the Court declared that police officers must inform persons they arrest of their right to counsel and of their right to remain silent during interrogation. The *Escobedo* ruling was made to deter forced confessions without benefit of counsel. But two years after it was made, the *New York Times* reported:

> Many of the nation's top prosecutors conceded Tuesday that law enforcement had not suffered from a controversial confession ruling made by the United States Supreme Court in 1964.
>
> The clear consensus at the 60th annual meeting of the National Association of Attorneys General was that the Supreme Court's ruling in *Escobedo v. Illinois* had had little or no effect on the obtaining of confessions.

As for the *Miranda* decision, a study of arrest situations in Washington, D.C., in 1968 by the Institute of Criminal Law and Procedure at Georgetown University found that its real effect was not great. Most policemen did not follow the *Miranda* ruling, and almost as many suspects were interrogated and confessed before they saw a lawyer as they did prior to the *Miranda* decision. Professor John Kaplan of the Stanford University Law School commented in 1970 that "the Court's decisions on the rights of suspects have in fact had very little effect in handcuffing the police." He wrote: "As far as we can tell, the major impact of its decisions has been to permit our society to maintain a higher level—at least on the books—of adherence to constitutional rights while at the same time suffering relatively little practical inconvenience. . . ."

Money is still crucial in determining the quality of justice received in the American court system. It determines whether the defendant gets a harried court-appointed counsel, or an experienced attorney who can leisurely use time and resources to develop his case. It determines whether the defendant will be freed on bail, or must remain in jail until the time of his trial—a period that might last two years. In his book *Ransom,* a study of the bail system in the United States, Ronald Goldfarb noted that in 1963 about 1.5 million defendants went to jail—before any verdict had been delivered in their case—because they did not have money for bail (or to pay bondsmen to put up their bail; the bond business amounts to a quarter of a billion dollars a year). One New York judge in 1970 estimated that persons charged with a felony who cannot make bail spend an average of nine months in jail before trial, hardly a following of the Sixth Amendment's stipulation that all are entitled to a "speedy and public trial." The well-to-do are not affected by the Eighth Amendment's provision that "excessive bail shall not be required." Simply put, the rich are released on bail, the poor go to jail. Rich offenders get all sorts of help from experienced counselors, doctors, and psychiatrists; the poor get sentenced. Professor Richard Korn, a Berkeley criminologist, has pointed out that "a wholly private and unofficial system of correctional treatment has long been available to the violent scions of the socially fortunate. . . . The scandal lies in the fact that such alternatives are denied to the poor, through nothing more deliberate than the incidental fact of their inferior economic position."

For some Americans, the distance between the words of the Bill of Rights and the reality of American life are beyond theory and practice. They are the several hundred thousand people who at any one time are locked up in city jails, county jails, state prisons, and federal penitentiaries—in cells, dungeons, and isolation boxes—all over the country. For them constitutional rights do not exist. They have no freedom of speech, or press, or assembly. They live in a totalitarian state where every moment of their time, all aspects of their lives, are controlled by the prison authorities.

At its best, liberal America has worked to ameliorate prison conditions, to reduce sentences, to lower bail, to replace capital punishment by life imprisonment, to introduce better visiting privileges, television sets, and recreation programs into the prisons. But virtually no one in high public position has called for an end to the system of punishment, has challenged the idea that the proper response to a hurtful act is to hurt the person who committed the act. By 1970 constitutional lawyers were arguing before the Supreme

Court that the death penalty constituted "cruel and unusual punishment" and therefore violated the Eighth Amendment. But there was no loud call from any quarter to end the "usual" punishment, no argument that jails—which deprive freedom on its basic level—are inherently cruel and should be eliminated.

Presumably, this has been the century of reform in America. But if a society's state of civilization can be judged by its prisons, as Dostoevski said, then the state of prisons in America is one more vivid example of the failure of liberal reform to effect significant changes in the United States. In 1956 convicts at the Buford Rock Quarry Prison in Georgia, who had been struck, cursed, and shot at because they lingered at an outdoor latrine, and who had been subjected to continuous brutality, finally could take it no more. They did not know how to communicate with the outside world except by a desperate act. Forty of them sat down near a rock wall, and used their ten-pound iron hammers to break their own legs and call attention to their plight.

In March, 1971, Stephen Clapp, a staff writer for the Public Information Center in Washington, D.C., wrote regarding a survey of American prisons: "Most of the nation's 187 state prisons are so lawless that they are more productive of crime than of its cure." Nine months later, corroboration of Clapp's statement came from a federal judge in Virginia, who cited instances of brutality in that state's prison system: one prisoner was chained to cell bars for fourteen hours, then left naked in his small cell for seventeen days; another was forced to spend 266 days in solitary confinement; a third died in solitary after screaming in vain for medical attention for one week.

The general policy of the courts regarding the prison system has been hands-off. In 1966, as an example, a federal court was asked to do something about a prisoner who was placed naked in solitary confinement, in forty-degree temperature, without blankets and mattress for twenty-seven hours, denied a bath for sixteen days. The court, in Maryland, concluded that even if true the allegations were not exceptional enough to override the principle that prison discipline should be left to prison officials. In May, 1970, came a rare decision, one by Judge Constance Motley in the federal district court of New York, enjoining prison officials from continuing the solitary confinement of a prisoner they had punished because he had prepared and tried to mail legal papers for a codefendant in his case. Her decision was overruled.

In the late 1960s and early 1970s, prison revolts grew in number and seriousness throughout the nation. A *New York Times* dispatch on October 3, 1970, reported:

> The revolt of city prisoners demanding speedier trials, lower bail and improved prison conditions spread yesterday from a Queens jail to the Manhattan House of Detention, where 18 hostages were seized. . . .
>
> Yesterday there were more than 1400 prisoners in the Tombs, which was built for 932. Last August prisoners there revolted against overcrowded conditions, purported brutality by guards, and long detention before court appearances.

In September, 1971, inmates at New York's state prison in Attica rose up in protest against conditions there. They took over part of the prison, and held thirty-eight guards and prison workers as hostages. After four days of unsuccessful negotiations, state police moved in with tear gas and machine guns, killing ten hostages and thirty inmates.

The events at Attica were not a bizarre departure from the American system of penological justice. They were a particularly savage example of how that system operates every single day—in which certain Americans, among the enormous number guilty of crimes, are singled out, put in cages, and treated like beasts whose lives can be snuffed out legally. The prisoner is a permanent hostage of the law, and his life can be taken without his assailant facing the risk of being brought before any bar of justice. Attica was a lightning flash that illumined the ordinary workings of the American prison system as Vietnam illumined the ordinary workings of American foreign policy. "I suspect," psychiatrist Karl Menninger has said, "that all the crimes committed by all the jailed criminals do not equal in total social damage that of the crimes committed against them." It is a sign of how much progress was made in postwar America that his statement was as true in 1971 as in 1945, or, for that matter, in 1871 or 1845.

To any person in prison, one conclusion from the history of the past decade must be especially ironic and bitter: that the greatest violator of the law, the greatest violator of the Bill of Rights, is the United States government. Beyond all other inequality before the law—between blacks and whites, poor and rich, radical and conservative, odd and orthodox—is the inequality between the private citizen and the government. The government makes the law, and enforces the law, which the citizen is expected to obey. But that same government has the job of deciding who is and who is not to be prosecuted. How can a government claim that all its citizens are equal before the law when those who hold government posts have the power to decide what constitutes a crime and to declare publicly who is a "defendant"?

In the late sixties, this disturbing thought about the impunity of the government in violating the law became widespread because of the American military intervention in Vietnam. Respected lawyers pointed out that by its unilateral action, by sending—on presidential orders only—half a million troops to South Vietnam, by bombing and shelling villages and hamlets in Indochina, by forcibly removing villagers from their homes (five million South Vietnamese had become refugees by 1970), by destroying rice crops and foliage with poisonous chemicals, by supervising the torture of prisoners of war, the United States was violating the Hague Convention of 1907, the Geneva Convention of 1949, and the Nuremberg principles unanimously affirmed by the General Assembly of the United Nations. It was in violation of the Kellogg-Briand Pact, the SEATO treaty, and the United Nations Charter. It was also in violation of its own Constitution, which gives the war-making power to Congress.

The United States had applied certain principles—along with its allies in World War II—to the trial of Nazi war criminals at Nuremberg. Allied Control Law 10, of 1945, declared as criminal: "Initiation of invasion of other countries. . . . Atrocities or offenses against persons or property . . . including but not limited to murder, ill-treatment or deportation . . . of civilian population from occupied territory, . . . ill-treatment of prisoners of war, . . . wanton destruction of cities, towns or villages. . . ." All these criminal acts describe those committed by the United States in Vietnam, and a generation that still remembered World War II and the Nuremberg trials could not easily dismiss the connection. Professor Richard A. Falk of Princeton University, an authority on international law, has written:

"It is unusual for a group of international lawyers to go on record to the effect that their own government is waging a war in violation of international law." It was also unusual that in 1971 a number of returning veterans of the Vietnam War not only graphically reported the atrocities they had seen or participated in, but proceeded to repudiate the war. As for the question of the constitutionality of the American war in Southeast Asia, the Supreme Court, despite requests by Justices Douglas and Potter Stewart, has refused to consider the issue.

Another instance of the government's violating the law with impunity occurred in Boston in May, 1971, when policemen assaulted nonviolent demonstrators who were sitting on the sidewalk around the federal building. The demonstrators were charged with disorderly conduct, but no policeman was charged with assault. Several policemen beat and stomped on one of the arrested demonstrators right outside the courtroom of the chief justice of the municipal court, Elijah Adlow, who ignored the cries of the prisoners and went on with the case before him.

One much-neglected flaw in the rhetorical concept of "equal justice before the law" is the invulnerability of local governments and local officials to the claims of citizens. During the 1960s:

· A man was run over in Atlanta, Georgia, by a pickup truck owned by the city and operated by one of its employees. He had the right of way, and he sued the city. His claim was denied by the Georgia courts, the judge saying: "In the negligent performance of its governmental duties a municipal corporation is not liable in damages to one who is injured while the municipality is engaged in the performance of such duties."

· In Fayetteville, North Carolina, a child fell into an open ditch and drowned. Several residents had previously complained to the city that water accumulation in the ditch was creating a danger. The judge barred a suit by the child's family against the city, saying that in establishing a free sewage system for the public benefit, the city was "exercising its police power for the public good . . . and . . . a city in the performance of its police regulations cannot commit a wrong."

· A patient in a San Francisco hospital died when technicians were negligent in the way they gave her a blood transfusion. When her family sued the city, the judge declared: "Respondent operates this hospital in a governmental capacity and is not liable for the injury of a patient caused by the negligent acts of an employee of respondent." Ronald Goldfarb, citing these instances, comments:

In each of these three cases the courts were propounding what is now the general rule in most American jurisdictions: state and local governments are immune from responsibility to citizens for the misconducts of their employees. This bizarre notion, so out of keeping with modern American concepts about the role and duties of government, is rooted in the ancient fiction that "the king can do no wrong." It is a monarchial privilege which, basing responsibility on status, should have no place in our society. Nonetheless, this doctrine of sovereign immunity has slipped into American law and has remained the majority rule.

It is a federal crime to tamper with the mails, but who is to prosecute this crime if it is committed by the government? In 1970, the Post Office Department quietly issued regulations authorizing the opening and reading of all mail from overseas. The *St. Louis Post-Dispatch,* which broke the story, said: "The new regulations would permit the opening of first-class mail without any showing of probable cause, any search warrant or anything beyond the belief of a postal clerk that the mail should be opened and inspected." A Post Office Department spokesman said that the regulation was needed chiefly to stop the flow of "hard-core pornography" from overseas. But the implication was that it could also be used for other purposes. The regulation exempted mail sent to ambassadors and high government officials; presumably they could not be affected by hard-core pornography.

No attorney general of the postwar years made firmer declarations about the need to respect "law and order" than President Nixon's appointee, John N. Mitchell. Yet the Justice Department under Mitchell declared in 1970 that it would not prosecute those fund-raising committees that failed to comply with federal reporting laws during the 1968 presidential campaign. The department explained that the laws were ineffective, and had never been enforced, which was true; it was also true that twenty of the twenty-one committees charged with violating the law were Nixon-Agnew committees.

Another striking example of the government's violation of its own laws has been the history of wiretapping. Section 605 of the Federal Communications Act of 1934 prohibits the interception and the divulgence of telephone and telegraph messages, as well as the "use" of such intercepted messages. Yet the Federal Bureau of Investigation has conducted thousands of wiretaps, asserting that (1) tapping itself is legal so long as the contents of what is tapped are not divulged, and (2) the disclosure of tapped information by one government employee to another government employee does not constitute divulgence. No FBI agent was ever prosecuted under the 1934 law.

In 1937 the Supreme Court ruled (*Nardone* v. *United States*) that federal agents could not tap wires and that wiretap evidence could not be used in court. In 1957 it affirmed (*Benanti* v. *United States*) that wiretap evidence gathered by *state* officials also could not be used in federal court. Not until 1967 (*Berger* v. *New York*) did it say that electronic surveillance of conversations—where no wires were physically tapped—was subject to the same restrictions as wiretapping. The government, to put it another way, still broke the law but did not bring the fruits of its law-breaking into court. Would this kind of justice be applied to a private citizen? Would he be allowed to steal, so long as he then did not try to deposit the stolen money in a bank?

It did not seem to matter what the law said, or what the Supreme Court said. Government agencies, especially the FBI, violated the law repeatedly in their wiretapping activities, and furthermore, lied about doing so, both in court and out of court. For example, Supreme Court Justice Byron White, in the midst of his opinion in the *Butenko* case (1969), noted that the government admitted in one of its briefs "that Alderisio's conversations had been overheard by unlawful electronic eavesdropping."

Alan Westin, in his book *Privacy and Freedom,* a study of the invasion of privacy in America, tells how, after the *Nardone* decision against wiretapping, "federal agents simply ignored the judicial rulings and continued wiretapping, secure in the knowledge that, while the Supreme Court declared the law, the Attorney General enforced it." Referring to the trial of Judith Coplon, a Barnard College graduate and Justice Department "political analyst" who was charged with stealing classified documents in order to turn them over to a Russian engineer at the UN, Westin says:

> The Judith Coplon case made wiretapping a matter of national attention in 1948, when it was revealed that F.B.I. agents had not only tapped her home and office telephones, but were also monitoring the calls between Miss Coplon and her attorneys during her trial for passing government information. In reversing her conviction because of these wiretaps, Judge Sylvester Ryan reminded the Justice Department that wiretapping by the F.B.I. remained "unlawful and prohibited" despite the Attorney General's authorizations of these interceptions.

In 1965 a Senate Judiciary subcommittee heard testimony about illegal wiretapping by the government. Officers of the Internal Revenue Service admitted that phones not only of suspects but of their own agents were tapped. J. Edgar Hoover had often said that the FBI did not tap wires except for national security, but testimony before the Senate subcommittee showed that special lines were constantly being run by the Southwestern Bell Telephone Company into FBI headquarters to facilitate wiretapping of suspected gamblers. Martin Luther King, for several years before his murder in 1968, had his phones tapped by the FBI. The disclosure came in June, 1969, when an FBI agent testified in court that he was in charge of telephone surveillance of King until May, 1965, and that it went on after that date. The FBI conceded that it engaged in wiretapping the phones of both King, and Elijah Muhammad, the Black Muslim leader.

With the phrase "law and order" gaining wide political potency, Congress legalized wiretapping and electronic surveillance in the Omnibus Crime Control and Safe Streets Act of 1968. The act simply made legitimate what was going on anyway. By way of safeguards, it required a court order for surveillance, and listed only certain crimes for which the order could be used. But the list was quite long, and the order was good for thirty days, renewable indefinitely. As Joseph L. Rauh, noted Washington attorney and political leader, said after the bill passed: "The restrictions are hogwash. The court order for a tap or bug is meaningless. A judge can't weigh all the evidence. And it will be easy to shop for a sympathetic judge." Moreover, the act contained escape clauses. One section permitted "any investigative or law-enforcement officer," where "an emergency situation exists with respect to conspiratorial activities threatening the national security interest," to proceed with wiretapping or electronic surveillance without a court order, for forty-eight hours, before applying for an order. This took the use of wiretapping beyond that specified in the 1967 decisions in the *Berger* case and the *Katz* case, where the Court said surveillance could only take place after the issuance of a court order in which the place, time, persons, and the conversations to be intercepted were specified.

Though the 1968 legislation allowed vast opportunities for surveillance, the government nevertheless continued to act outside the law. In June, 1969, the government admitted that immediately after the 1968 act passed, it tapped the wires of David Dellinger and three other defendants in the "Chicago Conspiracy" trial that followed the disorders at the 1968 Democratic National Convention—without a court order and without observing the law's requirement that a court order be obtained within forty-eight hours of surveillance. The following year, at a trial of White Panther radicals, the government admitted again it had tapped outside the provisions of the 1968 act. The Justice Department argued that the executive branch had an inherent right, based on the president's power to defend the nation against those "seeking to attack and subvert the Government by unlawful means," to eavesdrop without court supervision and despite the Fourth Amendment.

The United States Court of Appeals for the Sixth Circuit rejected the Justice Department argument, saying there was not "one written phrase" in the Constitution or statutes to support Attorney General Mitchell's contention. Mitchell, however, was defending the American liberal tradition, not in its rhetoric as expressed in the Constitution, but in its behavior. Victor Navasky, a *New York Times* editor who has made a study of the Justice Department under Robert Kennedy, notes:

> President Franklin D. Roosevelt wiretapped in the name of "grave matters involving the defense of the nation," "sabotage," "subversive activities." Harry Truman wiretapped in the name of "domestic security." The Kennedys talked about

"national security" but ended up tapping Dr. Martin Luther
King. The difference is that, although for at least 30 years
Attorneys General have been authorizing F.B.I. wiretaps in the
national security area without getting court warrants, they confined their rationales to internal memoranda. Mr. Mitchell is
the first Attorney General to admit in court what every Attorney General since Robert Jackson, at least, has admitted out
of court about the government wiretapping without a court
order.

In view of the relative unimportance of statutes or court decisions
against the overwhelming police power of the government, it is perhaps worth only passing mention that in 1971 the Supreme Court
(*U.S.* v. *White*) said it was all right, without a warrant or any other
statutory requirement, for an informer to record the conversation of
someone he was talking with through a secret electronic device. This
was too much even for such a conservative member of the court as
John Harlan, who, in his dissenting opinion, spoke of:

> ... the expectation of the ordinary citizen, who has never en-
> gaged in illegal conduct in his life, that he may carry on his
> private discourse freely, openly, and spontaneously without
> measuring his every word against the connotations it might
> carry when instantaneously heard by others unknown to him
> and unfamiliar with his situation or analyzed in a cold, formal
> record played ... years after the conversation.

Constitutional rights on the local level are in the hands of the
police; on the national level they are in the hands of the FBI and
the Department of Justice. Elected executives and legislators come
and go, but the police remain as a powerful force before whom
elected officials are often subservient. This has been especially true
of the FBI, not only because of the long tenure of J. Edgar Hoover
as chief of that bureau, but because a secret police, in any society,
causes tremors among even the highest officials.

For years, the FBI has collected information on American
citizens, which it keeps in secret dossiers, from various sources,
verified or unverified, and from various informants, known or anonymous. FBI files have been used in the scrutiny of the "loyalty" of
government employees, and in the 1950s, a study of this screening
practice reproduced excerpts from the transcripts of some of the
loyalty proceedings. In one case an employee was confronted with

the following: "Information has been received that you expressed to others that you were opposed to the institution of marriage, which is one of the tenets of the Communist Party." In another case, "derogatory information" was brought out about an employee, who was then questioned about it, as follows: "We have a confidential informant who says he visited your house and listened in your apartment for three hours to a recorded opera entitled 'The Cradle Will Rock.' He explained that this opera followed along the lines of a downtrodden laboring man and the evils of the capitalist system." In yet another case, information was placed in an employee's file that she had written a letter to the Red Cross questioning the segregation of blood by race in Red Cross blood banks. As late as 1970, the FBI was still accumulating information about the political beliefs of citizens. After the Kent State University shootings of early 1970, students reported that FBI men asked them questions about a sociology professor, such as: "Did he advocate any radical views?" "Did he advocate the overthrow of the mass communications system of the United States?" They also asked whether an English professor "ever spoke against the government."

Through the postwar period, the FBI developed into an ever more powerful bureaucratic institution, with secret agents, secret informants, a huge budget, impunity before the law, and great powers of intimidation over its own agents and private citizens. In 1970 an agent wrote a paper for a class, in which he was critical of the FBI and Hoover: "Internal discipline within the bureau is swift and harsh. . . . Yes, a 'personality cult' does extend through the echelons of management in the FBI. . . . adulation of the director in some form or other provides the main catalyst in the process of 'administrative advancement'. . . . We are not simply rooted in tradition. We are stuck in it up to our eye-balls." He was dismissed from his FBI job. That same year, a new headquarters for the FBI was under construction, the most expensive government building in history, costing one hundred million dollars. As for Hoover, each year the FBI bought for him a new bullet-proof limousine, which by 1971 cost thirty thousand dollars.

One of the more important facts about the FBI, beyond its institutionalized power, was the way in which it spread, by means of an exceptional public-relations effort, its cult of punishment and

violence through the population. Hoover was one of the strongest
advocates of capital punishment in the United States, of more severe
jail sentences, of the use of deadly weapons by police forces. The
difference between a humanist's approach to violence and the FBI's
was brought out in 1969, when a young ex-marine who had served
in Vietnam hijacked a commercial airliner to Rome. The plane
first had to refuel, and the FBI wanted to use that opportunity to
shoot the boy and get the plane back. As the pilot, Donald J. Cooper,
Jr., later reported:

> The Rome police put the F.B.I. to shame. The F.B.I. just
> thought they were playing Wyatt Earp and wanted to engage
> in a shoot-out with a supposed criminal and bring him to jus-
> tice. They would have wound up unnecessarily killing this boy,
> and, probably, completely destroying a seven million dollar
> airplane and wounding or endangering the lives of four crew
> members.

One further point needs to be stressed in addition to what has
already been said in this chapter on the difference between constitutional rights on paper and real rights on the streets, in courts,
schools, places of employment, prisons, barracks. The traditional
institutions that maintain wealth and power for a relative few in the
United States are supported by the system of beliefs held by the
majority. This common system includes: (1) a belief in a double
standard of violence, with violence impermissible for private citizens but approved when committed by officers of the law; a survey
in 1971, sampling opinions of American males, found that 85 per
cent thought of looting as violence, while only 35 per cent thought
of the shooting of looters by police as violence; (2) a belief in punishment to body and soul as the proper response to crimes against
property; (3) a belief that freedom of expression should be limited
in whatever the state defines as an "emergency"; and, most important, (4) a belief in the sacredness of man-made law.

This adoration of law is an essential part of the education and
training of citizens in the modern state, and it is common both to
the totalitarian states of this century and to those that consider
themselves "liberal" and "democratic," including the United States.
"Law and order" is the guiding principle for all powerful nation-
states, whether Hitler's Germany, Stalin's Russia, or Kennedy's,

Johnson's, and Nixon's America. Deification of law has been based, in the United States as in other nations, on certain powerfully nurtured, and thus widely held, notions.

With the civil-rights movements and antiwar movements of the postwar period, however, with the widespread experiences of many Americans with jails and the judicial system, new notions about law and justice have begun to appear:

• That in its haste to declare the blessings of modern civilization, America has exaggerated the benefits of what the liberals of modern nation-states call "the rule of the law." For the "rule of law" merely codifies, standardizes, and legitimizes all the basic injustices of pre-modern times—the maldistribution of wealth, the tyrannical abuse of power, the widespread use of violence, the authoritarian control over private human relationships and even over the mind itself.

• That the grossest injustices stem not from the violations of the law, but from the workings of the law. For the illegal abuses of individuals are insignificant compared with those committed by business corporations for profit and government representatives for power. Thus, the greatest corruption is not in deviance from the established rules, but in adhering to those rules.

• That what we call "the law" is a complex body of statements, some of which defend human rights, some of which violate them, but all of which Americans are expected to revere.

• That those who hold governmental power do *not* revere the law in this undifferentiated way; they choose which laws to enforce and which laws not to enforce; which laws to violate and which not to violate; which laws to make and which laws not to make.

• That in the workings of the judicial system, money is the single most important factor, and that justice is distributed in a liberal capitalist society as money is, with everyone having a theoretically equal right to it, but with some citizens having a great deal and some having very little.

• That the judicial system itself is not neutral, but is a branch of government and represents the interests of government, not of the governed.

• That the exterior dignity and quiet of the courts and the judicial process conceal the social reality just outside the courtroom doors: the fierce day-to-day economic struggle to keep alive; the violence of the social order. The prisoner leaves the decorous atmosphere of the court and its game of due process, goes through a door, and is immediately part of another world where brutality and fear rule, and human feelings are of little account.

The slowly growing recognition of these facts by even a small part of the American population was a sign of something new developing in the nation in the sixties—a movement of resistance, creating hope for change.

6

Bunker Hill: Beginnings

Several hundred veterans of the war, bedraggled, bearded, in remnants of their uniforms, were camping on Bunker Hill, in defiance of local regulations. These were not farmers, fresh from Concord and Lexington, resisting the tyranny of England across the ocean. These were veterans of another war, nearly two centuries later, anxious about the tyranny at home, angry about the brutal use of American power abroad.

They were veterans back from Vietnam who, on May 30, 1971 (Memorial Day weekend), were protesting the continuation of the war in Southeast Asia. But more than that, they were part of a great, loose, tangled movement in postwar America—of men and women, white and black, of all ages and backgrounds—that was trying, against overwhelming odds, to change the institutions, the human relations, the ways of thinking that had marked American society for so long.

The World War II armies of the capitalist and Communist worlds united to destroy the Nazi and Fascist military machines. But they did not destroy the values represented by fascism—racism, nationalism, militarism, bureaucracy, secret police, the violence of war abroad and the repression of freedoms at home, the supremacy of *things* over the individual. In the postwar years, the disparity between the promises and the reality of these societies, both capitalist and socialist, became distressingly clear. Their wealth and power had never been greater—their failure in human terms never more stark.

Yet something remarkable did begin to develop in those same postwar years, especially in the United States. A broad, heterogeneous movement started to take form. Disorganized, troubled, unsure of itself, vague about its vision of the good society, puzzled about the means of building that society, the movement, nevertheless, was alive and in motion as the seventies began.

America has had reform movements and even radical movements in its past, but never anything quite like this one, where in one decade, protests against racism, against war, against domination by males, reverberated one against the other, to produce a widespread feeling that the traditional liberal solutions were not enough. Fundamental changes were needed, it came to be thought, not just in America's political and economic institutions, but in its sexual and personal and work relationships, in the way in which Americans thought about themselves and about one another.

Beyond sheer political questions, more and more evidence began to appear of a fundamental unease deep within the culture of the nation. People began boldly to question the very assumptions they had grown up with and had been taught to believe—that America was a God-given place. Two women of different backgrounds expressed this questioning in their own ways. One was a professional writer, Joan Didion:

> The center was not holding. . . .
> It was not a country in open revolution. It was not a country under enemy siege. It was the United States of America in the cold late spring of 1967, and the market was steady and the G.N.P. high and a great many articulate people seemed to have a sense of high social purpose and it might have been a spring of brave hope and national promise, but it was not, and more and more people had the uneasy apprehension that it was not. All that seemed clear was that at some point we had aborted ourselves and butchered the job.

The other was a young mother, whose job was tending a counter in a cheap department store. She felt her own life stunted; she had just experienced the death of an old woman close to her, who had spent her last days in one of those macabre city hospitals, those department stores of death, rotting away, uncared for until the end. One day in 1970, amidst counters piled with shoddy merchandise, in a sea of price tags, she scrawled her feelings on a piece of brown wrapping paper:

> I feel so damn angry Lord, so angry! I hate the thought that fills my mind—that sight before me! It was cruel, the cruelest of all things I've seen—man is so awful cruel in his damn modern plastic ways. Look! Look! All around—too modern, too plastic!

In the ten years that followed World War II, America was relatively calm. Neither the Korean War, nor McCarthyism, nor the continued humiliation of blacks, nor the increasing diversion of the country's wealth to the nuclear arms race aroused any widespread movement of opposition. Amidst the general complacency, based on middle-class prosperity, on lower-class fatalism, on agreement that communism was the great enemy, and on faith in the two-party system, only a few flurries of dissent were visible.

After World War II, a small number of veterans, just out of the services, formed a new organization to counter the superpatriotic conservatism of the American Legion and the Veterans of Foreign Wars. This was the American Veterans Committee; its slogan was "Citizens First, Veterans Second," its program called for more housing, price control, civil rights for Negroes, a de-emphasis on armaments. It was energetic and contentious, but it never attracted large numbers of veterans, was torn by political squabbles, and dwindled away after a few years of intense activity.

In opposition to the bipartisan politics of the cold war, Henry A. Wallace ran for president in 1948 as a Progressive. Wallace had been vice president for one term under Roosevelt, and he now tried to represent Rooseveltian social reform and a less bellicose foreign policy. This third-party movement failed of mass support, Wallace polling barely a million votes as Truman scored an upset victory over Thomas E. Dewey, the Republican candidate.

There was a small, agonized reaction to the development of atomic weapons. John Hersey's book *Hiroshima* brought to the American public's attention in 1946 the horror of the destruction and the suffering, from blast, fire, and radioactive fallout, among Japanese men, women, and children. But Hersey's reportorial account was not translated into any significant movement to stop the atomic arms race. Indeed, when J. Robert Oppenheimer, who had endorsed the dropping of the atom (fission) bomb on Hiroshima, spoke out against the development of the far more deadly hydrogen (fusion) bomb, it strengthened suspicion that he was untrustworthy and led to the withdrawal, in 1954, of his security clearance for government work.

Tiny clusters of courageous men and women did protest the development of nuclear bombs, but no mass protests materialized. A few groups took sailing boats out into the Pacific where bombs were being tested. Albert Bigelow, a navy skipper during World War II, had been horrified by the devastation of Hiroshima, and later was host for several months to two Japanese who had been disfigured in the bombing. In early 1958, as he prepared to sail his boat into the testing area, he reflected on their visit:

> . . . when they were bombed in 1945, the two girls in our home were nine and thirteen years old. What earthly thing could they have done to give some semblance of what we call justice to the ordeal inflicted upon them and hundreds like them? What possible good could come out of human action— war—which bore such fruits? Is it not utter blasphemy to think that there is anything moral or Christian about such behavior?

He and his crew were arrested when they attempted to set sail. Other pacifists registered their opposition to nuclear testing and the arms race by committing civil disobedience. But here, too, mass support was lacking. The pacifists remained a small, determined band.

Against McCarthyism, also, acts of resistance occurred on occasion. Some went to jail for refusing to speak before the congressional committees; others picketed and demonstrated. Against racial segregation, isolated challenges were made. But they did not rouse large numbers of Negroes; nor did they affect the white population. In fact, no protest activity—against war, against segregation, against the stockpiling of atomic weapons, against the All-American profit motive, against governmental duplicity and secrecy, against the violation of the individual's constitutional rights—had much of an impact on the American conscience.

At the end of 1955, however, came the event that may be considered the starting point of the period of resistance and rebellion in postwar America—the bus boycott by Negroes in Montgomery, Alabama. Mrs. Rosa Parks, a 43-year-old seamstress, was arrested for sitting in the "white" section of a bus. She explained later why she refused to obey the Montgomery law providing for segregation on city buses:

> Well, in the first place, I had been working all day on the job. I was quite tired after spending a full day working. I handle and work on clothing that white people wear. That didn't come

in my mind but this is what I wanted to know: when and how would we ever determine our rights as human beings? . . . It just happened that the driver made a demand and I just didn't feel like obeying his demand. He called a policeman and I was arrested and placed in jail, later released on a $100 bond and brought to trial on December 5th. This was the first date that the Negroes of Montgomery set to not ride the bus and from December to this date [March, 1956] they are still staying off the bus in large numbers, almost 100%. . . . Montgomery today is nothing at all like it was as you knew it last year. . . .

The black population of Montgomery responded overwhelmingly to a plea by its leaders to boycott city buses. Car pools were organized to take Negroes to work, but most of them walked. The city then indicted a hundred boycott leaders, sending many to jail. White segregationists turned to violence, and bombs exploded in four Negro churches. A shotgun blast was fired through the front door of the home of Dr. Martin Luther King, Jr., the twenty-seven-year-old Atlanta-born minister who was one of the leaders of the boycott. His home was bombed. But the blacks held out, and in November, 1956, the Supreme Court outlawed segregation on local bus lines as unconstitutional.

In Montgomery the nation saw a preview of the style and mood of the mass protest movement that would sweep the South in the next ten years—the emotional church meetings, the Christian hymns, the references to lost American ideals, the commitment to nonviolence, and as strong a commitment to struggle and sacrifice. A *New York Times* reporter, Wayne Phillips, described one of the mass meetings in Montgomery where King spoke:

> One after the other, indicted Negro leaders took the rostrum in a crowded Baptist church tonight to urge their followers to shun the city's buses and "walk with God."
> More than two thousand Negroes filled the church from basement to balcony and overflowed into the street. They chanted and sang; they shouted and prayed; they collapsed in the aisles and they sweltered in an eighty-five degree heat. They pledged themselves again and again to "passive resistance." Under this banner they have carried on for eighty days a stubborn boycott of the city's buses. . . .
> Reverend Martin Luther King, Jr., head of the Montgomery Improvement Association, which has directed the boycott, told

the gathering that the protest was not against a single incident but over things that "go deep down into the archives of history."

"We have known humiliation, we have known abusive language, we have been plunged into the abyss of oppression," he told them. "And we decided to raise up only with the weapon of protest. It is one of the greatest glories of America that we have the right of protest."

"If we are arrested every day, if we are exploited every day, if we are trampled over every day, don't ever let anyone pull you so low as to hate them. We must use the weapon of love. We must have compassion and understanding for those who hate us. We must realize so many people are taught to hate us that they are not totally responsible for their hate. But we stand in life at midnight, we are always on the threshold of a new dawn."

In the years following the Montgomery boycott, blacks slowly built up their determination to end segregation, to do away with their long humiliation, to do something on their own toward solving the race problem. And, as always, there were enough reminders of white supremacy in America to build their anger. In October, 1958, two North Carolina black boys, David Simpson, seven, and Hanover Thompson, nine, were arrested because they had been playing "house" with white children, one of whom sat on young Thompson's lap and kissed him on the cheek. The girl's mother, on hearing about the kiss, became hysterical, called the police, and the two boys were arrested and thrown into the county jail on charges of rape. The parents of the two boys were not notified of their sons' whereabouts for several days. The local judge held a quick hearing, and sentenced the boys to fourteen years in the reformatory. The "Kissing Case" became an international scandal; President Eisenhower finally intervened, and the governor released the children a few months later.

In Monroe, North Carolina, a year earlier, black anger at white supremacists did not remain "passive." When an armed motorcade of the Ku Klux Klan came to attack the home of Dr. Albert E. Perry, vice president of the local NAACP, members of the chapter, armed with guns, chased the motorcade away. (At about the same time, a KKK raid on an Indian community in North Carolina was repelled by Indians firing rifles.) Robert Williams, an NAACP leader in Monroe, probably spoke for many Negroes when he said in 1959, in response to the beating of a pregnant Negro woman by a white man, that Negroes should use arms in self-defense where the government would not protect them.

In early 1960 came a new movement in the upsurge of blacks efforts to obtain equal rights: the sit-in. On February 1, 1960, four college freshmen in Greensboro, North Carolina, sat down at the Woolworth's lunch counter downtown, where Negroes were not expected to sit. They were refused service. The lunch counter was closed for the day, and they went home. But they came back the next morning, and in the next two weeks, sit-ins spread to fifteen cities in five southern states. A seventeen-year-old sophomore at Spelman College in Atlanta, Ruby Doris Smith, heard about the Greensboro sit-in and ran home that evening to see it on television:

> I began to think right away about it happening in Atlanta, but I wasn't ready to act on my own. When the student committee was formed in the Atlanta University Center, I told my older sister, who was on the Student Council at Morris Brown College, to put me on the list. And when two hundred students were selected for the first demonstration, I was among them. I went through the food line in the restaurant at the State Capitol with six other students, but when we got to the cashier, she wouldn't take our money. She ran upstairs to get the Governor. The Lieutenant Governor came down and told us to leave. We didn't and went to the county jail.

In the next twelve months, more than fifty thousand people, mostly black, some white, participated in one kind of demonstration or another in a hundred cities, and more than thirty-six hundred of them were put in jail. The sit-in, nevertheless, was a successful movement as many public lunch counters in the South began serving Negroes. Even the Woolworth counter in downtown Greensboro was opened to blacks before 1960 ended.

Black students who had taken part in the sit-ins gathered in Raleigh a few months after the initial sit-in at Greensboro to form the Student Non-violent Coordinating Committee (SNCC), with the help of a veteran of the freedom struggle, Ella Baker, a black woman working with the Southern Christian Leadership Confer-

ence. The SCLC had been created by King and others after the
Montgomery bus boycott in order to carry on the work for equal
rights on a national scale. SNCC became the militant arm of the
civil-rights movement for the next four years. Its working force
consisted of black students, and a few whites, who left college to
become full-time organizers of civil-rights actions in southern black
communities. Living on subsistence salaries—ten dollars a week—
sent by the small SNCC headquarters office in Atlanta, these "field
secretaries" moved into southwest Georgia, Alabama, and Mississippi and built up grass-roots movements of local people on the
basis of voting and other constitutional rights. They were beaten,
jailed, and hounded, but they did a remarkable job along decentral-
ized, nonbureaucratic lines, combining the dedication of revolutionaries with a concern for immediate problems that attracted
local Negroes to their side.

One year after Greensboro, a new action toward gaining equal
rights for the Negro was begun, the "Freedom Rides," sponsored
by the newly formed Congress of Racial Equality (CORE). They
were aimed at desegregating buses and bus terminals. Two buses
made up the first Freedom Ride; with blacks and whites riding together, they left Washington, D.C., on May 4 headed for New
Orleans. They never got there. In South Carolina, the riders were
beaten. In Alabama, one of the two buses on which they rode was
set afire. When the second bus arrived, the Freedom Riders were
attacked with fists and iron bars. The police, in the words of a report
by a research organization in Atlanta, the Southern Regional Council, were "either inactive, not present, or strangely late on arrival."
The Ride was stalled in Birmingham as the bus drivers refused to
go further.

Young militants of SNCC then initiated a new Freedom Ride
from Nashville to Birmingham. Before they started on their journey, two SNCC people called the Department of Justice; Ruby
Doris Smith told of the phone calls: "Both of them asked the federal government to give protection to the Freedom Riders on the
rest of their journey. And in both cases the Justice Department said
no, they couldn't protect anyone, but if something happened, they
would investigate. You know how they do. . . ." In Birmingham,
the SNCC Freedom Riders were arrested, spent a night in jail, were

taken to the Tennessee border by police, made their way back to Birmingham, took a bus to Montgomery, and there were attacked by a group of whites, with fists and clubs. A white Freedom Rider, James Zwerg, was beaten again and again, refusing to defend himself. They then turned to the blacks, Ruby Doris Smith recalled:

> Someone yelled: "They're about to get away!" Then they started beating everyone. I saw John Lewis beaten, blood coming out of his mouth. People were running from all over. Every one of the fellows was hit. Some of them tried to take refuge in the Post Office, but they were turned out. . . . We saw some of the fellows on the ground, John Lewis lying there, blood streaming from his head.

Several days later, now joined by a group of CORE people, they resumed their trip from Montgomery to Jackson, where they were again arrested and beaten. They spent about two months in the Hinds County jail and in Parchman Penitentiary.

The experience of arrest and jail was undoubtedly a crucial force in affecting the sensibilities of tens of thousands of people involved in the movements of the sixties. Jail changed people. In jail, people learned suffering and cooperation. They also acquired a disrespect for the whole system of American justice, and developed the spirit to resist. Stokely Carmichael, one of the Freedom Ride prisoners in Parchman, talked later of those days:

> I'll never forget this Sheriff Tyson—he used to wear those big boots. He'd say, "You goddam smart nigger, why you always trying to be so uppity for? I'm going to see to it that you don't ever get out of this place." They decided to take our mattresses because we were singing. . . . So they dragged Hank Thomas out and he hung on to his mattress and they took him and it and dropped him with a loud klunk on his back. . . . And then they put the wristbreakers on Freddy Leonard, which makes you twist around and around in a snake-like motion, and Tyson said, "Oh you want to hit me, don't you" and Freddy just looked up at him meekly and said, "No I just want you to break my arm." And Sheriff Tyson was shaken visibly and he told the trusty, "Put him back." I hung on to the mattress and said, "I think we have a right to them and I think you're unjust." And he said, "I don't want to hear all that shit, nigger," and started to put on the wristbreakers. I wouldn't move and started to sing "I'm Gonna Tell God How You Treat Me" and

everybody started to sing it and by this time Tyson was really to pieces. He called to the trusties, "Get him in there!" and he went out the door and slammed it, and left everybody else with their mattresses. . . .

Out of jail, the SNCC people went to work all over the South. Some of them ended up in Albany, and there in December, 1961, came the first mass uprising of black people since the Montgomery bus boycott, the beginning of several years of such uprisings in southern cities. Of twenty-two thousand black people in Albany, more than one thousand went to jail in a series of protest marches against segregation in that city.

In Birmingham, in 1963, many thousands of Negroes moved into the streets, facing police clubs, tear gas, dogs, and high-powered hoses. And in the Birmingham of Police Commissioner Eugene ("Bull") Connor, it was more apparent than ever that the young Negro was a leading participant in the struggle for change. As Bayard Rustin, civil-rights leader, wrote:

> It was the loss of all fear that produced the moment of truth in Birmingham: children as young as six paraded calmly when dogs, fire hoses and police billies were used against them. Women were knocked to the ground and beaten mercilessly. Thousands of teen-agers stood by at churches throughout the whole country, waiting their turn to face the clubs of Bull Connor's police, who are known to be among the most brutal in the nation. Property was bombed. Day after day the brutality and arrests went on. And always, in the churches, hundreds of well-disciplined children eagerly awaited their turns.

Other cities in the South had their demonstrations and mass arrests. And in Mississippi in 1964, all the forces of the civil-rights movement—the militants of SNCC, CORE, and the SCLC, and the more moderate elements of the NAACP—joined forces, aided by almost a thousand white students from the North, to register blacks to vote, to run Freedom Schools, to organize campaigns for desegregation. But violence continued. The national government was not responsive enough, national politicians had other priorities, and by 1965 the disillusionment with both nonviolent tactics and the established political system was strong.

Then came the mass uprisings in the urban ghettos of the North, in 1964, 1965, 1966, 1967, 1968. And "Black Power," the voice of Malcolm X, the mood of rebellion, not just against southern segregation but against the American system of racism, seen now to permeate the entire culture, its institutions, its thought, its day-to-day behavior, its most liberal manifestations.

The new black mood expressed itself in many ways, and with a special militancy among the young. In the black colleges of the late sixties, there was a surface calm contrasting with the earlier excitement of the sit-ins, but underneath that exterior, in the attitudes of black students, dwelt an anger with the American system, more widespread, more profound, more portentous than the feeling of the early 1960s. And the young were influencing their elders, or perhaps acting out what their elders, under more constraint, found difficult to do. Jerome Skolnick, in his study of black activism for the National Commission on the Causes and Prevention of Violence, wrote:

> The available evidence suggests that we are presently witnessing the rise of a generation of black activists, enjoying wide support from their communities and relatives, committed to the principles of local community control and cultural autonomy, and disenchanted with techniques of peaceful protest associated with the civil rights movement of the 1950's.

What was happening was not the abandonment of nonviolence as an ultimate principle; the new mood still did not lend itself to aggressive violence, and little of it was committed by blacks. Black activism was, rather, an acceptance of self-defense against attack, and a readiness to turn to violence if it should ever become tactically feasible and if no alternatives remained. More significant, blacks now saw neither political reforms—civil-rights laws, executive orders, court decisions—nor well-publicized privileges for a few well-placed blacks as sufficient. The shift in emphasis was from changing laws to changing the relations of power and wealth in the society. To accomplish this goal would require a revolution in the way blacks, as well as whites, *thought* and *felt* about their racial identities.

For the first time in postwar America, a break was taking place in the liberal tradition, a tradition in which racial equality was either promised in words or granted on paper, but without the needed radical changes in the society's economic and political institutions, without the necessary changes in the value structure of the culture. The slogan "Black Power" meant that equality could not be *given,* but had to be *taken* by a powerful, organized black community. The slogan "black is beautiful" meant that blackness and the Negro heritage were no longer to be seen as deficiencies, but as sources of pride; that oppression was a shame for the oppressor, not the victim; that strength and courage and all the noble qualities of the human race came not from superiority on an artificial social scale, but from the will to fight back, whatever the individual's social position was.

The ideological variations among the representatives of black militancy were not as important as the fact that they expressed, whatever their different tactics, the new feeling among blacks. The Black Muslims brought a burst of support from many Negroes not because of faith in the Koran or in Elijah Muhammad or in the specific doctrines of Islam, but because of the Muslim insistence on pride, on independence, and on discipline. Whether Malcolm X was a Muslim or an ex-Muslim was not as relevant as what he stood for —a fierce rejection of the old liberal idea of waiting for the powers to bestow gifts. The Black Panther ascendancy in the late 1960s was similarly based on this new readiness, more than on political doctrine as expressed by Panthers like Eldridge Cleaver, Bobby Seale, and Huey Newton.

A black man testifying before the National Advisory Commission on Civil Disorders investigating the urban uprisings said:

> You can't go through any community without seeing black youth with Huey P. Newton buttons and "Free Huey." Many of them who have no connection with the Panthers officially wear the Panther uniform. We all groove on Huey. No two ways about it. We dig him. And I use that rhetoric because that's the way it is. Not for any exotic reasons.

Malcolm X was assassinated while on a public platform in New York in February, 1965, under mysterious circumstances. After his death, Malcolm's influence became greater than ever. Hundreds of thousands of people—white and black—read his *Autobiography,* which showed the gradual growth in radical consciousness in a black man of ordinary background, growing up in an environment of poverty, theft, prostitution, and drug addiction, becoming a rebel against the society that produced that environment. Speaking at the Hotel Theresa in late 1964 to a group of black students from Mississippi, Malcolm said:

> You'll get freedom by letting your enemy know that you'll do anything to get your freedom; then you'll get it. It's the only way you'll get it. When you get that kind of attitude, they'll label you as a 'crazy Negro,' or they'll call you a 'crazy nigger' —they don't say Negro. Or they'll call you an extremist or a subversive, or seditious, or a red or a radical. But when you stay radical long enough and get enough people to be like you, you'll get your freedom.

Ossie Davis, another spokesman for the new militancy in black culture, said at Malcolm X's funeral: "Malcolm, as you can see, was refreshing excitement. He scared hell out of the rest of us, bred as we are to caution, to hypocrisy in the presence of white folks, to the smile that never fades." Davis pointed to the break from the liberal tradition of patronization that Malcolm represented:

> Protocol and common sense require that Negroes stand back and let the white man speak up for us, defend us, and lead us from behind the scene in our fight. This is the essence of Negro politics. But Malcolm said to hell with that! Get up off your knees and fight your own battles. That's the way to win back your self-respect. That's the way to make the white man respect you.

Black and white have always been morally intertwined in American history, even when physically separated, even when playing out the roles of subordinate and superior. The new black consciousness of the sixties, the activism, the militancy, the radicalism, could not leave untouched the sensibilities of whites, many of whom were moved, some easily, some through great inner turbulence, to rethink their attitudes and their behavior. Conflict shakes up old ways, it hastens reorientations, and the race conflicts of this postwar period were intense. Just how many whites began to recognize the inadequacy of the old liberal behavior toward Negroes—the emphasis on laws, on gifts, on words—was not easy to determine. The process of rethinking, however, was under way.

Probably the most direct impact of the black revolt was on white students. Student activism was not new in American society. But the quality of student protest was now different. There was not as solid a core of organized left-wing students as in the thirties, when the American Student Union was strong and the Communist party influenced many on campus. The new student radicalism cut deeper: it was looser, more spontaneous, less tied to a creed or party, more suspicious of all national governments, whether socialist or capitalist. It began, especially as the Vietnam War escalated, to develop a base among the millions in college, and to reach down into the high schools.

The closest thing to an organized radical group in the colleges was the Students for a Democratic Society; it started as a small organization at state universities in the Midwest, grew influential as the result of student uprisings on different campuses from 1964 to 1968, and then fell apart in factional disputes. In 1964 members of the SDS, meeting in Port Huron, Michigan, drew up a remarkable statement that voiced the feelings of betrayal among students:

> When we were kids the United States was the wealthiest and strongest country in the world; the only one with the atom bomb, the least scarred by modern war, an initiator of the United Nations that we thought would distribute Western influence throughout the world. Freedom and equality for each individual, government of, by, and for the people—these American values we found good, principles by which we could live as men. Many of us began maturing in complacency.
>
> As we grew, however, our comfort was penetrated by events too troubling to dismiss. First, the permeating and victimizing fact of human degradation, symbolized by the Southern struggle against racial bigotry, compelled most of us from silence to activism. Second, the enclosing fact of the Cold War, symbolized by the presence of the Bomb, brought awareness that we ourselves, and our friends, and millions of abstract "others" we knew more directly because of our common peril, might die at any time.

The Port Huron Statement spoke of the paradoxes in America: the promise of equality, and the facts of Negro life; the proclaimed peaceful intent of the United States, and its militarization in the cold war; the ability of modern technology to make a better world, and the waste of its skills in destructive and useless ways; the poverty of most of the world, and the affluence of the middle and upper classes in America. The statement decried the absence of a passionate pursuit of a new world in the stale bureaucracy of the university, challenged the adequacy of the "old socialism" and the "old liberalism," and expressed dissatisfaction with what was called "democracy" in America, with decision-making by national leaders raised to prominence by hierarchical political parties. It called for "participatory democracy," asking "that the individual share in those social decisions determining the quality and direction of his life, that society be organized to encourage independence in men and provide the media for their common participation."

Not many students of the millions who attended colleges and universities in the sixties read the Port Huron Statement. Thousands upon thousands of them, however, signified by their actions that they adhered to its point of view, its critique of American and world society, its insistence on a more human way of living. Its ideas can be said to form the common denominator of the student upsurges from one end of the nation to the other, from Berkeley in California in 1964 to Columbia University in New York in 1968. The precipitating issue varied: at Berkeley it was free speech, at Columbia it was the university's treatment of Harlem tenants; at other schools it was the failure of the administration to admit more black students, to sever government contracts or drop the ROTC program, to allow students to have a vote in university affairs.

When the Urban Research Corporation did a survey of student protest—for the first six months of 1969 only, and for only 232 of the nation's 2,000 institutions of higher education—it found that at least 215,000 students had participated in campus protests, that 3,652 had been arrested, that 956 had been suspended or expelled. The FBI estimated that in the 1969-1970 school year 1,785 student demonstrations took place, including the occupation of 313 buildings. On the basis of the Urban Research survey for part of 1969 and the FBI figures for late 1969 and early 1970, it is reasonable to estimate that between 1964 and 1970, as the war in Vietnam escalated and as police began to use their clubs on peace marchers, several million young people participated in demonstrations, that the number arrested reached into the tens of thousands, and the number of expelled or suspended into the thousands. In one way or another, a sizable minority of the nation's college students had engaged actively in protesting against the authority of either the university or the American government.

One Columbia University student, James Kunen, a crew man who turned to politics in the course of the 1968 events, wrote that the rebellion there had been set in motion by "the Biggies":

> The Biggies are a small group of men. Little else about them is known. They are probably old. They possess wealth surpassing the bounds of imagination. . . . In the councils of the Biggies one might hear decisions that one thought no one could make. Buy Uruguay. Sell Bolivia. Hold India. Pollute New York. The decisions are of incomprehensible variety, but they have in common the fact that they are swiftly implemented and invariably soak the Little Man. . . .
>
> The Biggies lie. They shout up and down that Vitalis has V7, but they don't say what V7 is. They say that Arrid stops wetness, but they don't explain why wetness should be stopped. (I can think of a lot of things that qualify for stoppage way ahead of wetness.) They lie about little things like that, and big things like Vietnam, the ghetto, Democracy. . . .

He went on to explain the action at Columbia:

> As I write this and as you read it people are dying. So you see it isn't really a topic for suburban conversation or magazine articles. It's something that must be dealt with. That's what's happening at Columbia, not a revolution but a counterattack. We are fighting to recapture a school from business and war and rededicate it to learning and life. Right now nobody controls Columbia, but if we get it, we will never give it back. And there are 5 million college students in the country watching us. And a lot of them have just had it with the Biggies.

Of course, the student rebels at Columbia had to give the university back. They occupied buildings for a week. Then the police came, in force, swinging their clubs. It was a bloody scene, in which 150 students and 10 faculty members were injured, and 711 arrested.

What happened to the thinking, the values, the estimate of American democracy and culture, among those students who encountered "the Biggies," who put their bodies into demonstrations, who were beaten, who went to jail? There is enough evidence to indicate that when so many people engage power directly, struggle against it, suffer for it, tumultuous changes take place in the heads of the participants. Another student at Columbia described such a change in himself:

> In other words, both Sissy and I were fairly unsure about our involvement. But, of course, the bust changed everything. That was the clincher for us. It wasn't simply the cops, the beatings, the blood, all the running and the panic. Seeing how the cops acted was one thing, something I hadn't really known about before. But the thing that really affected me was the simple fact that this was how [Grayson] Kirk [university president] and the Trustees and [Mayor John] Lindsay had chosen to deal with us, that this was how they'd chosen to respond to the demands of everyone, of the students, the Harlem community, the involved faculty—everyone, me included. That's what really changed my thinking, because it made me realize that it was true, everything the radicals had been saying about the way the system works in this country, about how power is used when the demands for change reach a certain level.

The spread of discontent through elite universities and small state colleges, North and South, was remarkable. A *New York Times* dispatch of November 3, 1969, spoke of the change in the *Harvard Crimson:* "In 1954, the *Crimson* had editorials against two law students who were members of the Communist party. Two weeks ago, it editorially supported the National Liberation Front, the political arm of the Vietcong." Students demonstrated at the black Bowie State College in Maryland, and Oklahoma City University called off a student convocation because of picketing against the guest of honor, Senator Allen J. Ellender of Louisiana. At Florida State University in Tallahassee, students staged a ten-day sleep-in; at the University of Iowa, student demonstrators soaked the steps of the Memorial Union building in their own blood to protest the presence of marine recruiters.

In the spring of 1970 came the American invasion of Cambodia. A demonstration at Kent State University in Ohio against the invasion led to the murder of four students by the National Guard on May 4. Students at 400 colleges and universities went on strike in protest. It was the first general student strike in the history of the nation, and virtually every major institution of higher education was affected. One student at Boston University said:

On May 4, I permanently and of necessity suspended my work in all courses. . . . This had nothing to do with a conscious "decision" but rather was part of an instinctive response to the events in Indochina and Ohio. As is true of many students, I simply lost the capability for the detached and abstract reflection which is academic thought. . . .

The grotesque implications of last week's events, I'm afraid, make any non-political activity seem trite and meaningless, and to continue to give the necessary attention to my papers and other formal commitments, I think I would have to be totally insensitive or perhaps simply insane. I see a useless absurdity in turning in an essay on Marx's Theory of "Estranged Labor" or work in three other humanities courses when logic and already-frail order are collapsing all around, and matters of ultimate importance—literally of life and death—are demanding some sort of personal action.

Commencement ceremonies after the Kent State killings were not like any the nation had seen before. Two news dispatches in the *Boston Globe* reported:

Almost the entire graduating class at Tufts University boycotted commencement yesterday in favor of the students' own ceremonies to be held on the Medford campus today. . . .
"I think the general feeling was that this was insignificant," Senior Class President Richard Giachetti explained.

And from Amherst, Massachusetts:

The 100th Commencement of the University of Massachusetts yesterday was a protest, a call for peace.
The roll of the funeral drum set the beat for 2600 young men and women marching "in fear, in despair and in frustration."
Red fists of protest, white peace symbols, and blue doves were stenciled on black academic gowns, and nearly every other senior wore an armband representing a plea for peace.

Undoubtedly, most students were politically inactive most of the time during the late sixties. Even among the active ones, there were strong strains of either escapism or cynicism. One student, who had read of the struggles of the radical Emma Goldman at the turn of the century, wrote, in a paper:

There is a feeling now that people are "getting together," that more people than ever are coming around to at least a semi-radical attitude. It is reassuring and something one wants to believe. It seems strange that in 1913, the same sentiment should be said by Mabel Dodge—"the new spirit was abroad and swept us all together"; everywhere "barriers were down and people reached each other who had never been in touch before." Does every radical movement have a false sense of security, of progress, of hope?

There were measurable results obtained from the student-protest movement. The admission of black students rose sharply in many places, and black-studies programs were initiated; ROTC programs were canceled in more than forty colleges and universities; curricular changes were made to adapt to contemporary problems; students were given more of a say in the operation of universities. But its crucial effect was that students learned about the nature of the society, the nature of education, the advantages of protest and resistance, and the power of the apparently powerless.

In the late sixties this learning process also began to take place in high schools, and even in junior high schools. High-school students staged demonstrations and protest rallies, insisted on the right to dress as they wanted and to wear their hair as they wished, criticized their teachers, sought to be free from the regimentation so common to the school system, argued they had a right not to pledge allegiance to the flag or sing the national anthem. In 1968 and 1969, more than five hundred underground newspapers were established in the nation's high schools. They carried articles against the tracking system, in which youngsters from poor families tended to be segregated into programs funneling them into technical schools rather than colleges; they protested against school censorship, questioned the system of grades and examinations, opposed the draft, criticized the presence of ROTC recruiters at their schools, demanded the removal of police and plainclothesmen from the corridors and grounds, asked for more democracy in the classroom and in the school system.

A Wisconsin high-school student was suspended for questioning, during a pep rally, the importance of athletics. Two Minneapolis students were suspended for participating in antiwar activities. In Des Moines, three students were suspended for wearing black armbands to protest the Vietnam War. In Wellesley, Massachusetts, the high-school production of a LeRoi Jones play, *The Slave,* in which a white girl and black man embrace and in which plain language is spoken, led to a public meeting at which residents vented their outrage at the showing of the play to high-school students. The editor of the school paper, a football player and an A-student, said to the audience:

> I think one of the things that is affecting you the most is the word "fuck"!
> Well, the first time I heard the word "fuck," I was five years old and that was right here in Wellesley. In fact, I know some people in Wellesley who cannot say a sentence without using the word "fuck."

People in the audience shouted "Get him out!" "Arrest him!" "Stop him!" A policeman jumped up on the stage and arrested the boy. A fellow student later commented on the incident: "Here was America right before our eyes. This is what America really is."

The sixties was an angry decade. The most powerful protest movement of all was against the war in Vietnam, starting with a handful of Americans in 1964, and involving millions by 1971. The war exposed, as nothing else had in American history, the great gap between political rhetoric and national behavior. The war tested the elements of the liberal creed, and they were found wanting by large numbers of Americans. The implications of the war reached far beyond foreign policy, into the fundamental character of American political institutions, American culture, American values.

Antiwar movements had sprung up before in American history—indeed, in every war, but especially in the Mexican War, the Spanish-American War, and World War I. Yet never did an antiwar movement touch so many Americans, never did one take on such intensity, with so many demonstrations, as did the one against the Vietnam War. National polls—Gallup and Harris—showed a steady rise in the late sixties in the number of Americans who wanted the United States to withdraw from Vietnam, a number that by 1970 reached a majority. In cities where the issue of American intervention in Vietnam was put on the ballot, a clear change in opinion was registered from 1967, when, for instance, in Dearborn, Michigan, 41 per cent of the voters called for immediate withdrawal from Vietnam, to 1970, when in several cities on the West Coast and in Madison,

Wisconsin, from half to two-thirds of the voters called for immediate total withdrawal or withdrawal within the year. At the same time, the polls also showed that most Americans did not believe what the government was telling them about the situation in Vietnam.

In part, the dimension of this antiwar movement was due to the special brutality of the Vietnam War—the use of napalm against women and children, the bombing of villages and hamlets, the forcible removal of millions of Vietnamese from their homes, the use of chemicals to ruin the forests and soil of Vietnam, the spoliation of an ancient culture by the intrusion of five hundred thousand American troops and one hundred fifty billion American dollars, in defiance of international and national laws and in support of a succession of strong-arm regimes in Saigon. In part, it was due to the astounding disparity between the two adversaries: the world's most powerful nation raining shells and bombs on one of the least powerful, the kind of bullying that had shocked Americans when Germany invaded Czechoslovakia and when Russia invaded Finland.

When, in early 1965, the United States began the sustained and systematic bombing of North Vietnam, on the pretext that the North Vietnamese had attacked two American destroyers in the Gulf of Tonkin, groups of several hundred people gathered in protest here and there throughout the country. On Moratorium Day, four years later, two million Americans across the nation participated in antiwar demonstrations; the size of the outpouring was unprecedented in American history.

It was not surprising that blacks in the United States—fresh from their encounters with the government, disillusioned with the liberal performance as contrasted with the liberal promise—should look with distaste on the Vietnam War. In August, 1964, when the Gulf of Tonkin incidents were allegedly taking place, funeral services were being held in Philadelphia, Mississippi, for James Chaney, the black civil-rights worker who, with two young white men, had been murdered by a gang of whites, while the federal government claimed lack of protective jurisdiction. The contrast was stark. LBJ SAYS "SHOOT TO KILL" IN GULF OF TONKIN, read the headline in the Jackson, Mississippi, newspaper; while the United States was ready for aggressive military action ten thousand miles away, it was not ready to defend blacks at home against violence.

In mid-1965, black people in McComb, Mississippi, learning that a classmate had been killed in Vietnam, distributed a leaflet in McComb:

> No Mississippi Negroes should be fighting in Viet Nam for the White man's freedom, until all the Negro People are free in Mississippi.
>
> Negro boys should not honor the draft here in Mississippi. Mothers should encourage their sons not to go. . . .
>
> No one has a right to ask us to risk our lives and kill other Colored People in Santo Domingo and Viet Nam, so that the White American can get richer. We will be looked upon as traitors by all the Colored People of the world if the Negro people continue to fight and die without a cause.

In early 1966, the Student Non-violent Coordinating Committee declared that "the United States is pursuing an aggressive policy in violation of international law," and called for withdrawal from Vietnam. That summer, six members of SNCC were arrested for an aggressive invasion of an induction center in Atlanta, and were later convicted and given sentences of several years in jail. When Secretary of Defense Robert McNamara went to Jackson, the issue between civil rights and Vietnam was clearly joined by his own words, as he praised Mississippi Senator John Stennis, one of the country's archsegregationists, as "a man of very genuine greatness, . . . a man of courage and selflessness." White and black students joined in picketing him, after a march downtown "In Memory of the Burned Children of Vietnam."

The words of Eldridge Cleaver were strong, but the mood of the Black Panther leader was not foreign to that found in vast numbers of young blacks. He wrote "To My Black Brothers in Vietnam," reminding them that police had murdered Fred Hampton, the Panther leader in Chicago, in his bed:

> We appeal to you Brothers to come to the aid of your people. Either quit the army, now, or start destroying it from the inside. Anything else is a form of compromise and a form of treason against your own people. Stop killing the Vietnamese people. You need to start killing the racist pigs who are over there with you giving you orders. Kill General Abrams and his staff, all his officers. Sabotage supplies and equipment, or turn them over to the Vietnamese people. Talk to the other Brothers and wake them up.

How widespread and popular black antagonism was to the war, and how greatly the attitude of the black population had changed since World War II, was illustrated by the case of Muhammad Ali (Cassius Clay). He was the hero-successor to Joe Louis, heavyweight champion at the time of World War II. Louis had urged blacks to fight for their country. Now Muhammad Ali set an example for other blacks by refusing to serve in a "white man's war," and took the risk of years in prison for doing so. Martin Luther King, by 1967, was speaking out powerfully against the war in Vietnam. That April, from a pulpit in New York, he declared:

> Somehow this madness must cease. We must stop now. I speak as a child of God and brother to the suffering poor of Vietnam. I speak for those whose land is being laid waste, whose homes are being destroyed, whose culture is being subverted. I speak for the poor of America who are paying the double price of smashed hopes at home and death and corruption in Vietnam. I speak as a citizen of the world, for the world as it stands aghast at the path we have taken. I speak as an American to the leaders of my own nation. The great initiative in this war is ours. The initiative to stop it must be ours. . . .

The black protest against the war separated blacks still further from the country and its behavior. They were not ashamed to shun patriotism. Alice Walker, a young black poet from Georgia, put it lightly but firmly in verse:

> then there was
> the
>   picture of
> the
> bleak-eyed
> little black
>   girl
> waving the
> american
> flag
> holding it
> gingerly
> with
> the very
> tips
> of her
> fingers.

One of the most sustained and effective forms of antiwar protest was the draft-resistance movement. Most poor whites and blacks stayed out of this movement; they found their own quiet ways of avoiding the draft, or they went into the service, despite a lack of enthusiasm for the war, because it was expected of them, because for many it meant economic and training opportunities that were closed to them in civilian life. White middle-class students formed the core of draft resisters.

As early as May, 1964, the slogan "We Won't Go" was heard, and the following year young men who refused to be inducted were put on trial. For the next several years, the public burning of draft cards became a dramatic way of declaring refusal to fight in the war, and the prosecutions multiplied. In October, 1967, there were organized draft-card "turn-ins" all over the country; in San Francisco alone, three hundred draft cards were returned. On the eve of the great demonstration of tens of thousands of people at the Pentagon that month, a sack of draft cards was presented to the Justice Department in a gesture of defiance—one of the acts that led to the indictment the following year of Dr. Benjamin Spock, pediatrician and author; Yale chaplain William Sloane Coffin, Jr.; author Mitchell Goodman; Marcus Raskin of the Institute for Policy Studies; and Harvard graduate student Michael Ferber for interfering with the Selective Service system.

From mid-1964 to mid-1965, according to Justice Department figures, 380 prosecutions were begun against those who refused to be inducted; by mid-1968, the figure was 3,305. Mass protests were held outside induction centers with many of the demonstrators attacked by police and many arrested. The number of people trying in one way or other to avoid induction was much larger than the number prosecuted. In May, 1969, the Oakland induction center, which had jurisdiction over draftees for all of northern California, reported that more than half the young men ordered to report for induction did not show up (2,400 out of 4,400), and that 11 per cent of those who did show up refused to serve. A graduate student in history at Boston University wrote on May 1, 1968, to his draft board in Tucson, Arizona:

> I am enclosing the order for me to report for my pre-induction physical exam for the armed forces. I have absolutely

no intention to report for that exam, or for induction, or to aid in any way the American war effort against the people of Vietnam.

I fully realize the consequences of my decision, there will be a trial, and then prison. I regret the suffering this will mean for my family and friends. But even more I realize what the war has meant for the Viet Namese people. It has meant six years of ceaseless and often senseless slaughter, largely of civilians. It has meant continual hunger, fear, unspeakable atrocities, and unimaginable suffering for a people, whose only dreams are for Land, Unification, and Independence. . . .

At the height of the Spanish Civil War, that country's greatest philosopher, Miguel de Unamuno, condemned the Fascist intervention [of Italy and Germany] (who were also trying to "save" that country from Communism) and declared: "Sometimes to be Silent is to Lie." . . .

Hoping, praying, for a just and early Peace, I am,

Respectfully yours,
Philip D. Supina

Supina was sentenced to four years in prison.

As the war went on, draft resistance grew, and general support for it increased. By February, 1968, a poll among Harvard graduate students showed that 40 per cent of them would either go to jail or leave the United States if called for induction. A Harris poll among just-graduated seniors revealed a sharp reversal in attitude in just one year: whereas in 1969, 50 per cent of those polled said they would not respect persons who refused to go into the armed forces, only 34 per cent felt that way in 1970, and many more declared their respect for draft resisters.

By 1970, it was becoming more evident that this horror of a war was very much the product of the "liberal" leaders of national politics. What Carl Oglesby, an SDS leader, had told peace demonstrators in Washington on November 27, 1965, was, five years later, more widely recognized: that the war was not an aberration from normal American liberalism, but was its expression. Oglesby had pointed out:

The original commitment in Vietnam was President Truman's—signer of the first civil-rights act. That commitment was seconded by the moderate liberal, President Eisenhower— who mobilized the National Guard to integrate Central High

School in Little Rock—and intensified by President Kennedy, who gave us the Peace Corps, the Alliance for Progress, and the beginning of the anti-poverty program. Think of the men who now engineer that war—those who study the maps, give the commands, push the buttons, and tally the dead: Bundy, McNamara, Rusk, Lodge, Goldberg, the President himself.

They are not moral monsters.

They are all honorable men.

They are all liberals.

But so, I'm sure, are many of us who are here today. To understand the war, then, it seems necessary to take a closer look at this American liberalism. Maybe we are in for some surprises. Maybe we have here two quite different liberalisms: one authentically humanist, the other not so human at all. . . .

Not only did passive support of antiwar activity grow throughout the country, as shown in polls and city referendums, the activism of the handful in 1965 became adopted by all sorts of people to whom overt signs of protest were not familiar. In August of 1965, it was a few hundred protesters who joined David Dellinger, who had formed the National Mobilization Committee to End the War in Vietnam; historian Staughton Lynd; and SNCC leader Robert Moses in Washington to protest the war. Opponents splattered them with red paint as they marched down the Mall to the Capitol. By May, 1971, twenty thousand people would come to Washington committed to acts of civil disobedience in trying to stop the war.

As the sixties came to a close, denunciations of the war emanated from all sides. Peace Corps volunteers by the hundreds protested against the war; in Chile, ninety-two volunteers were threatened by the Peace Corps director with punitive action if they did not dissociate themselves from a circular protesting the Vietnam War. Eight hundred former members of the Peace Corps also denounced the war. Poets and writers refused to attend White House functions. Robert Lowell was one, Arthur Miller was another. Miller's telegram to the White House read: "When the guns boom, the arts die." Singer Eartha Kitt scandalized Washington society by her criticism of the war during a White House affair. Teen-agers called to the White House to accept 4-H Club prizes expressed their displeasure with the war. In Hollywood, local artists erected a sixty-foot Tower of Protest on Sunset Boulevard to symbolize opposition to the war.

At the National Book Award ceremonies in New York, fifty authors and publishers walked out on a speech by Vice President Humphrey in a display of anger at his role in the war.

In London, two young Americans gate-crashed the American ambassador's elegant Fourth of July reception, and, calling for attention, proposed a toast: "To all the dead and dying in Vietnam"; they were carried out by guards. In the Pacific, two young American seamen hijacked an American munitions ship to divert its load of bombs from Thailand to Cambodia in protest against the war. (At the time, Cambodia, headed by Prince Norodom Sihanouk, was in sympathy with the Communist cause.) For four days, they took command of the ship and its crew, eating amphetamines to stay awake, until the ship was in Cambodian waters.

Middle-class and professional people who had never engaged in overt protest before began to act. In May, 1970, the *New York Times* reported 1000 'ESTABLISHMENT' LAWYERS JOIN WAR PROTEST. The lawyers were on their way to Washington to urge immediate withdrawal from Indochina. Only with the acceleration of public protests did Congress begin to react in any meaningful way against the war; resolutions were introduced in both houses to put a definite date limit for American withdrawal, though as late as June, 1971, such resolutions still could not pass.

The crumbling of support for the government was exemplified also in the wave of "defections" by former government officials, who now, out of office, criticized the war they had supported or been silent on while in office: Humphrey, presidential adviser McGeorge Bundy, Professor Roger Hilsman, U.N. Ambassador Arthur Goldberg, Ambassador Edwin Reischauer. The war was unpopular now. There was at least one much more rare phenomenon: that of a person high up in the war bureaucracy who left his job and not only criticized the war, but became an active member of the antiwar movement, to the point of civil disobedience. This was Daniel Ellsberg, a former aide to Secretary of Defense McNamara, who had spent years with the Rand Corporation doing war research for the government, two years in Vietnam with the pacification program. Joining him in his rebellion against the war establishment was a former Rand colleague, Anthony Russo.

In June, 1971, defying a possible penalty of many years in

jail, Ellsberg turned over to the *New York Times* and other news-papers part of a ten-thousand-page study of the history of American involvement in Vietnam, a study he had worked on while at the Rand Corporation, ordered by the Pentagon, and labeled "Top Secret." Its publication in the *Times* caused a national furor, with the government charging "security violation." What was at stake was no one's security, only the government's embarrassment at having its plans and deceptions disclosed to the public: its planning for military action in mid-1964, while Johnson, campaigning for president, was talking peace; its control over the Saigon government; its opposition to peace negotiations; its use of bombing for psycho-political purposes; its violations of the Geneva Accords; its covert military operations against North Vietnam long before the 1965 escalation.

In the fall of 1967, a new constituency was added to the antiwar movement—Roman Catholic priests and nuns, and Catholic lay men and women. Again, here was evidence that the Vietnam War was causing tumultuous changes in all parts of American society. On October 27, Father Philip Berrigan, veteran of World War II and a Josephite priest, anguished over the killing in Vietnam, joined David Eberhardt, Thomas Lewis, and James Mengel in the invasion of a draft board office in Baltimore. They drenched the board records with blood, waited to be arrested, were tried, and sentenced to prison terms of two to six years.

The following May, Berrigan—out on bail on the Baltimore charges—was joined by his brother Daniel, a Jesuit priest, and seven other priests and lay men and women in the destruction of draft records at Catonsville, Maryland. They became famous as the Catonsville Nine, were tried, convicted, and sentenced to prison. Two of them, Mary Moylan, a former nun, and Daniel Berrigan, refused to surrender and became "fugitives from injustice." After four months in a strange kind of underground, in which he spoke from a church pulpit, gave interviews to reporters, and met with groups of people to discuss the war and civil disobedience, Daniel Berrigan was captured by the FBI. Mary Moylan remained at large.

The war troubled the church. The priests and nuns who resisted shook a whole generation of Catholics, particularly the young, who began to rethink the heritage of Christ, the meaning of patriotism, the message of the Cross, the value of resistance. As Daniel Berrigan put it:

> The madness goes on, it proliferates mightily. Behind a façade of sobriety and temperate action, the worst instincts of man are armed, rewarded, and set loose upon the world. An unthinkable Asian war, once a mere canker on the national body, a scratch on the tegument, undergone heedlessly and borne without a second thought—it has festered and flowered, a wasting fever, a plague, a nightmare rushing into full day and again into night, and on and on for months and years, until only Jeremiah and Kafka could encompass its irrational horror.

At his sentencing in Catonsville, Philip Berrigan tried to explain to the court why he and Lewis, while still on bail after Baltimore, had again broken the law:

> As a Christian, I must love and respect all men—loving the good they love, hating the evil they hate. If I know what I am about, the brutalization, squalor and despair of other men, demeans me and threatens me if I do not act against its source. This is perhaps why Tom Lewis and I acted again with our friends. . . .

The Catholic Resistance (sometimes joined by Protestants and Jews) spread, in draft board raids across the country: the Boston Two, the Milwaukee Fourteen, the DC Nine, the Pasadena Three, the Silver Springs Three, the Chicago Fifteen, the Women Against Daddy Warbucks, the New York Eight, the Boston Eight, the East Coast Conspiracy to Save Lives, the Flower City Conspiracy. Some went to jail, some fled; what was called the "ultra-resistance" dramatized the change in a former stronghold of American conservatism—the Catholic Church and its constituents.

Anger against the war thus moved up and down through the layers of American society, across faiths, from class to class, race to race, well-to-do to poor. By 1969 and 1970, this anger also emanated from those involved in the war itself, from the GIs in the armed forces, from the soldiers and sailors in Vietnam, from the young men who had returned from the war as veterans. Whether or not their bodies were still whole, their sensibilities had been changed. Nothing like it had happened in American history: soldiers and veterans of a war turning against that war while it was still going on.

At first, there were individual and sporadic protests. As early as June, 1965, Richard Steinke, a West Point graduate in Vietnam, refused to board an aircraft taking him to a remote Vietnamese village where a Special Forces team was operating. "The Vietnamese war," he said, "is not worth a single American life." Steinke was court-martialed and dismissed from the service. The following year, three army privates, ordered to embark for Vietnam, denounced the war as "immoral, illegal, and unjust" and refused to go. They were court-martialed and sent to prison.

In early 1967, an army doctor at Fort Jackson, South Carolina, Captain Howard Levy, refused to teach Green Berets, members of the elite Special Forces; Levy argued that they were "murderers of women and children" and "killers of peasants." He was court-martialed on the ground that he was trying to promote disaffection among enlisted men by his statements on the war. The colonel who presided at the trial ruled out truth as a defense for Levy. "The truth of the statements is not an issue in this case," he said. Levy was convicted and sentenced to prison.

There were others: a black private in Oakland refused to broad a troop plane to Vietnam, although he faced eleven years at hard labor. A navy nurse, Lieutenant Susan Schnall, was court-martialed for marching in a peace demonstration while in uniform and for dropping antiwar leaflets on navy installations from a plane. In Norfolk a sailor opposed to the war refused to train fighter pilots because he believed the Vietnam War was immoral. An army lieutenant was arrested in early 1968 in Washington, D.C., for picketing the White House with a sign that said "120,000 American Casualties —Why?" Two black marines, George Daniels and William Harvey, were given long prison sentences (originally six and ten years each, later reduced) for talking to other black marines against the war.

Desertions from the armed forces mounted as the war went on. Thousands went to Western Europe, and estimates on how many GIs crossed over into Canada ranged from fifty thousand to one hundred thousand. A few deserters made a public demonstration of their act, by openly taking "sanctuary" in a church or other place, where, surrounded by antiwar friends and sympathizers, they waited for capture and court-martial. At Boston University, a thousand students kept a vigil for five days and nights in the chapel surrounding an eighteen-year-old, Ray Kroll, who, when hauled into court on a charge of drunkenness, had been inveigled into the army by the judge. On a Sunday morning, federal agents arrived at the chapel, stomped their way through aisles clogged with students, smashed down doors, and took Kroll away. From the stockade, he sent a poem to the friends he had made in the Marsh Chapel sanctuary:

My Dream

They told me I got to go off to war
Just to get rid of the big red sore

Well they got me all wrong
Me? I wanna live a happy song

I wanna live and love
and hold that peace dove

Oh you mean ole Turnkey
Why don'tcha just set me free

You keep me hanging on
You really don't love me

I ain't gonna kill
It's against my will

When they gonna let me live in peace
and all wars come to a cease?

He wrote: "Marji gave me some books with some sayings in them. . . . 'What we have done will not be lost to all Eternity. Everything ripens at its time and becomes fruit at its hour.' "

As the GI antiwar movement grew, it became more organized. Near Fort Jackson some enterprising young men and women set up the first GI coffeehouse, called The UFO, a place where GIs could have coffee and doughnuts and find literature about the war and current affairs. It was a low-key, deliberate attempt to encourage discussion among GIs about the war. The UFO was closed by local harassment and court action, with the coffeehouse declared "a public nuisance." In the meantime, however, many GIs at Fort Jackson had come to know and like it, and the GI coffeehouse idea grew. A half-dozen coffeehouses were opened across the country, and at least two bookstores (to avoid the ruse of closing them for "health" reasons), one near Fort Devens, Massachusetts, and one at the Newport, Rhode Island, naval base.

Underground newspapers sprang up at army and navy bases across the country; by 1970, more than fifty were in operation.

Among them: *About Face* in Los Angeles; *Fed Up!* at Tacoma; *Short Times* at Fort Jackson; *Vietnam GI* in Chicago; *Graffiti* in Heidelberg, Germany; *Bragg Briefs* in North Carolina; *Last Harass* at Fort Gordon, Georgia; *Helping Hand* at Mountain Home Air Base, Idaho. They printed antiwar articles, revealed harassment of GIs, gave practical advice on the legal rights of men in the service, told how to resist military domination. In June, 1970, twenty-eight commissioned officers of the army, air force, navy, and marine corps, including some veterans of Vietnam, saying they represented about 250 other officers, announced formation of the Concerned Officers Movement to protest the war.

Anger among those in the armed forces against the war was mixed with bitter resentment against the cruelty, the dehumanization of military life. And nowhere was this more true than in Army stockades. In 1968 at the Presidio stockade in California, after a guard had shot to death a disturbed prisoner for walking away from a work detail, twenty-seven prisoners decided to show their outrage by sitting down during a work detail, and singing "We Shall Overcome." They were court-martialed, found guilty of mutiny, and sentenced to terms of up to fourteen years, later reduced after much public attention and protest.

The antiwar dissidence spread to the war front itself. When, on October 16, 1969, the great Moratorium demonstrations were taking place, some GIs in Vietnam wore black armbands to show their support. A news photographer reported that in a platoon on patrol near Da Nang, about half of the men were wearing black armbands. One soldier stationed at Cu Chi wrote to a friend on October 26, 1970, that separate companies had been set up for men refusing to go into the field to fight. "It is no big thing here anymore to refuse to go." Earlier in 1970, the Saigon correspondent for *Le Monde* had written:

> Indifference, rancor, disgust, hostility: the war less and less pleases the Americans who wage it. In four months, 109 soldiers of the First Cav, America's first air cavalry division, have been charged with refusal to fight. At Saigon, as at Danang, the security services pursue deserters. In most units, more than half the soldiers smoke marijuana. A common sight is the black soldier, with his left fist clenched in defiance of a war he has never considered his own. . . . Yet most of the troops fight well.

More and more, in military units in Vietnam, there were cases of "fragging"—incidents in which servicemen rolled fragmentation bombs under the tents of officers who were ordering them into combat, or against whom they had other grievances. The Pentagon reported 209 fraggings in Vietnam in 1970 alone.

By early 1970, many veterans back from Vietnam joined together in a group called Vietnam Veterans Against the War. In December, 1970, hundreds of them went to Detroit for the "Winter Soldier" investigations; there they testified publicly about atrocities they had participated in or seen in Vietnam, committed by Americans against the Vietnamese. In April, 1971, more than a thousand of them went to Washington, D.C., to demonstrate against the war and discard the medals they had won in Vietnam; they passed before a wire fence around the Capitol, threw their medals over the fence, and made impassioned statements about the war. One of them, a former navy lieutenant in the Mekong Delta, John Kerry, testified before the Senate Foreign Relations Committee. He told what GIs had seen in Vietnam: rapes; the random shooting of civilians, prisoners of war, and livestock; torture; the burning and sacking of villages; the forcible relocation of the civilian population. "It seems," Kerry said, "that someone has to die every day so Richard Nixon doesn't have to be the first President to lose a war. How do you ask a man to be the last soldier to die for a mistake?" When Memorial Day came around in 1971, the outburst of GI resentment against the war continued. A thousand American servicemen stationed in Britain announced their opposition to the war in petitions handed into the United States embassy. Circulating among them was an underground military newspaper called PEACE—People Emerging Against Corrupt Establishments.

It was on that Memorial Day weekend that several hundred veterans against the war camped out on the green at Lexington, Massachusetts, the cradle of the American revolution. They were joined by three hundred local citizens, and then all were arrested for refusing to leave the green. After getting out of jail, the veterans went to Bunker Hill, spent the night, and held an antiwar rally on the Boston Common the next day. This defection from violence, from war, this rebellion against authority, this suspicion of government, this independence of spirit, came twenty-five years after the passive acceptance by American soldiers in 1945 of the dropping of the atomic bomb on the men, women, and children of Hiroshima and Nagasaki. Something important was happening to the spirit and mind of many people in the United States.

Was a revolution—at least the first stirrings of one—taking place in postwar America? Many with a strong sense of history were dubious. Historians in the fifties, such as Richard Hofstadter and Louis Hartz, stressed the continuity in American politics and values, despite reforms in race and economics and politics and civil liberties. Would not the United States bounce back from the Vietnam War to its ordinary, if somewhat masked, injustices at home, and a quieter imperialism abroad?

And yet, there was something qualitatively different this time. Perhaps it was because Americans had now gone through the New Deal reforms, and knew these were inadequate in dealing with the gross waste and destruction of their resources. Perhaps it was because Americans had passed all those civil-rights bills, and found they failed to touch the core of the race problem. Perhaps it was because Americans had defeated McCarthyism and made many procedural changes in the judicial process, and yet realized, particularly the many thousands who had experienced courts and jail, that the whole system was still essentially unjust.

In short, perhaps by the 1960s Americans had exhausted the deceptions of mild reforms at home, and, with Vietnam, had learned enough about foreign policy for many to be dissatisfied with the old excuses for war, for military and economic domination of other parts of the world. Perhaps the nation really had run out of all that time and space it had when other countries were the great imperial powers of the world. Now Americans were right up against a wall on all sides, and they had to tear it down, or climb over it into a new world, because they could no longer get along by meandering within its limits.

It was hard to be sure, in 1971, but there were signs of hopeful changes in America. They appeared first among the black people of the country, who so often in its history have been the key to understanding the level of American humanity or inhumanity. Blacks in the sixties got their civil-rights bills and their token payments, but it was exactly as this was happening that they broke out in the greatest black rebellion in the nation's history. They then embarked on a cultural revolution of sorts, to change the *minds* of blacks and whites on the race question, while trying to figure out a way to change the basic relations of wealth and power, beyond laws and tokens.

There were indications that this more fundamental approach to changing American society, early and tentative as it was, was spreading to other problems besides race. Perhaps it was the concentration of so many crucial issues in one decade—race, education, the war— but sharper questions were being asked, a revolt was under way against not just a specific policy, but against ways of thinking, ways of life.

The most personal, most intimate of human relationships began to be examined. It was an attempt to pierce the many layers of artifice piled up by "civilization" and rediscover the root needs of man and woman, to hear again that primeval cry for companionship and freedom. That cry had been stifled by modern technology, by unnecessary things, by false relationships, money, success, status, superiority; all these things had replaced genuine affection. At the pinnacle of American success—unprecedented wealth, power, resources—people suddenly felt a failure at the core. Some were unhappy and distraught, others vaguely, confusedly dissatisfied, but almost everywhere in the country, Americans were uneasy about what they were and where they were going.

Parents and children found themselves in a conflict. Some called it "the generation gap," but there had always been a chronological difference; the conflict in the sixties was deeper. It both intensified hostility and speeded up changes in attitude, as crises and conflict tend to do. A woman named Marina Matteuzzi wrote to the *Boston Globe* one day in 1967 about how that conflict had changed her:

> Last week my 20-year-old son left home. He put on some old clothes, beads, a pair of granny sunglasses. He took no bags, little money, told me goodby, he had to go to Frisco to see the beautiful people. He said, "Mama, don't cry." So I didn't cry. I cried the day after. I cried for my dead dreams, to see my only son drop out (as he put it). I wanted him to be a doctor, teacher, something I never had the opportunity of being.

Then she told of a Negro friend, about to be sent to Vietnam, who looked for housing for his wife and two children, and was turned away again and again from one community after another.

> I was angry and so was he. This country is like a South Africa underground. They are scared stiff of the Godless Communists, when they themselves are Christians without God.
>
> So today I don't cry for my son dropping out. Let him stay out. I will write to him to ask if among the 300,000 men like him there is room for a 43-year-old hippie woman—me!

Both the parents and the children spoke of "a sick society," but it was the young who rebelled, probably because they had more space and freedom to do so. The young had not yet taken their proper places in the order of things, had less to lose, and were closer not only to their own childhood but to the yearnings of all people.

The dropouts—young people leaving the family, leaving their home towns, leaving their schools—became a mass phenomenon among the youth. They began to gather in urban centers around the country—San Francisco or Cambridge or Manhattan—and in rural enclaves in Vermont and New Mexico. The new folk music and rock music and country music of the postwar period connected them esthetically with one another and with something transcendental in a society they wanted desperately to escape.

Perhaps the degree to which the political disaffection of the thirties had become a much broader cultural phenomenon in the sixties is shown in the difference between the innocuous songs of sentimental love that dominate the popular culture of the thirties, and the more biting, vital, serious lyrics of folk-rock in the sixties. Bob Dylan became a hero because he expressed what so many felt:

> Come mothers and fathers throughout the land,
> Don't criticize what you can't understand.
> Your sons and your daughters are beyond your command,
> Your old road is rapidly aging.
> Please get out of the new one if you can't lend your hand,
> For the times they are a-changing.

Why were the young rebelling? It was hardly because of intellectual political analyses. No, it was more because of images and sounds that poured in on them in this intense period of history and stirred some inner recollection that life was supposed to be different, according to the precepts of the Bible, the Declaration of Independence, or the Communist Manifesto. On television they saw weeping Vietnamese women watching American soldiers burn down their

huts and aim rifles at their children. As teen-agers, they had seen
police hose down and club blacks in the streets of Birmingham.

The new mood of freedom, of defiance, caused the young to rethink everything about their lives. They remembered—because it
was yesterday—their classrooms, which even an older, cooler observer, after three years of observation and study, found horrifying.
Social critic Charles Silberman wrote:

> It is not possible to spend any prolonged period visiting
> public school classrooms without being appalled by the mutila-
> tion visible everywhere—mutilation of spontaneity, of a joy in
> learning, of pleasure in creating, of sense of self. . . . what grim,
> joyless places most American schools are, how oppressive and
> petty are the rules by which they are governed, how intellec-
> tually sterile and esthetically barren the atmosphere, what an
> appalling lack of civility obtains on the part of teachers and
> principals, what contempt they unconsciously display for chil-
> dren as children.

The rebellion of the young was the most visible, the most trou-
bling, but not the only, defection from culture. Older people, too,
were moving out of their accustomed lines, and in parts of life so
close to the heart of American culture that the move could not be dismissed as ephemeral or superficial. When Catholic nuns and priests
moved out of line, when 4-H Club youngsters did the same, when
young doctors and lawyers formed communes, then something important was happening. Even superstars of the football and baseball
worlds began to challenge their coaches and their publics, the cult of
competition, dollars, success. A professional football linebacker,
Dave Meggysey of the Saint Louis Cardinals, announced he was
retiring from the game early in his career, explaining: "It's no accident that the most repressive political regime in our history is ruled
by a football freak, President Nixon." Another linebacker, Chip
Oliver of the Oakland Raiders, left football at one point to live in a
California commune, saying:

> Pro football is a silly game. It dehumanizes people. They've
> taken the players and turned them into slabs of beef that can
> charge around and hit each other. But where is their esthetic
> soul, the feeling they can accomplish higher things? . . .
> I quit pro football because I felt I wasn't doing anything
> positive toward making this world a better place to live. The

world I was living in, the world of making money, was leading me nowhere. . . .

In the late sixties, a new force joined in the cultural upheaval, the revolt against authority, the search for human relationships. This was the Women's Liberation Movement, which, in a few years and on a wide tactical front ranging from violent denunciations of male supremacy to more moderate insistence on equal rights, made millions of Americans conscious of the subordinate position of "the second sex." (Simone de Beauvoir's book of that title was a pioneering statement of the issue.)

Women's Liberation pointed to the exploitation of women— crippling their education, consigning them to the household, denying them jobs in "men's work," paying them less than men for the same work, leaving them to deal alone with childbirth and children as their particular sphere, while men went off to work, or to play, or to other women. The new feminists also pointed to the way modern culture poisons the minds of men and women, from the time they are children, so that women are sex objects, weak, dependent, while men are leaders, heroic, strong. Evelyn Leo described the result of this socialization:

> The course of her entire adult life, from beginning to end, is determined by her choice of a husband because she is culturally obligated to allow him to take the lead in career, geographic location, friends, entertainment, interests, and her so-called comforts in life.
> Something is terribly wrong with this dependent status of women. They are bound up with another human being in a closely intertwined relationship, yet they are carried along in a parasitic manner, never reaching their full potential as human beings, never using their own free choice or functioning as an individual within the marriage relationship. Something must be done to change this unequal, unfair, and oppressive situation in marriage.

And so women organized. They were not centrally directed. The forms of organization, the ideology, the tactics, the emphases, differed enormously. There seemed to be special stress on avoiding authoritarian leadership and elitist direction, as if to illustrate in action what it meant to be free from man's customary authority. To win reforms, to gain recognition, to make people think, women picketed Miss America contests, formed caucuses in professional organizations, published underground newspapers, held sit-ins and demonstrations.

A counter-culture was developing in America, something more profoundly revolutionary than the political changes that followed the American Revolution and the Civil War. Along with the political struggles against racism, against war, against police brutality, there was an inchoate movement to declare for change by simply living in a different way. Some spokesmen for cultural change emphasized changing people's minds as a more fundamental act than merely engaging in political actions that could easily be absorbed by a shrewdly reformist America. Historian Theodore Roszak argued in *The Making of a Counter Culture* that "the process of weaning men away from the technocracy can never be carried through by way of a grim, hard-bitten, and self-congratulatory militancy, which at best belongs to tasks of ad hoc resistance. Beyond the tactics of resistance, but shaping them at all times, there must be a stance of life which seeks not simply to muster power against the misdeeds of society, but to transform the very sense men have of reality."

In those varied currents, although it was written in no one declaration, no one manifesto, the rough vision of some future world could be detected:

It would have to be an international society, for the nation-state —with its tight boundaries, its strangling flags, its cacophonous anthems, its armies, its hatred of others, its passports, its pledges of allegiance, its prisons, its addiction to violence—was obsolete. It was one planet; man would be embarrassed to get to Mars and explain to the green people there the Vietnam War, or the Israeli-Arab border dispute, or the Pakistani-India argument, or the Russian invasion of Czechoslovakia, or the president's latest speech on television.

The resources of the world would have to be taken away from private corporations, which exploit them for profit, and from centralized socialist states, which exploit them for political or nationalist purposes. These resources would be managed for the public good, with priority given to the production of people's most vital needs, striving for some union of social requirements and personal pleasure. Yes, socialism, some might say, but like no socialism yet seen on earth. It would retain the original socialist idea of rational use of resources for urgent needs, equitably distributed. But it would avoid national selfishness and centralized bureaucracy; it would try to give decision-making power to consumers, to those who work, with hands and brains, in the economy—to create the kind of economic democracy that has not yet existed anywhere.

Political democracy would have to go far beyond the rule of parties, whether in one-party or two-party systems, and far beyond representative government. Parliaments and congresses everywhere in the world have become a façade behind which men of power make decisions, while all other men delude themselves into thinking they control their own destiny because they go to the ballot boxes to make their puny choices, on prepared-in-advance ballots. People would have to be drawn into active, day-to-day participation in decision-making, instead of pulling a lever once in two years, or once in four or seven years, or once in a generation. People most affected by decisions would have the strongest voice in making them, and those with special knowledge would offer it to those with special interests. Administrators would be in perpetual communication with the people, and subject to immediate recall.

The circulation of ideas would have to be completely free, with no excuses of "security" to stand behind the creation of secret police, detention centers, political trials. And prisons would have to be abolished, not only because the "best" of them constitutes "cruel and unusual punishment"—unusual in the sense that the greatest perpetrators of fraud and violence, the men in charge of government and business, go unpunished—but because punishment itself is the greatest crime. No civilization worthy of respect can lock people in dungeons, deprive them of the most essential needs of human beings, and deserve to stand. It would take imagination, ingenuity, and risk to try to minimize individual acts of cruelty or violence, but that imagination and ingenuity could never come forth unless absolutely required by the elimination of imprisonment. The abolition of prisons would press Americans to speed up the transformation of the whole society—its distribution of wealth, its set of values, its human relations; it would be a good prod.

Authoritarianism in personal relations, involving blind obedience, hierarchy, arbitrary rule, control, humiliation, would have to fall away—in the family, between old and young, between man and woman, white and black, skilled and unskilled. Democracy on the personal level would be recognized as the crucial accompaniment of democracy on the social level. Americans would have to stop assigning marks of superiority to surgeons over sweepers, poets over carpenters. People would work at what most pleased them, and differences in biological or educational or cultural attributes would still leave all people equal in the most basic sense of retaining their self-respect. The ideas of cooperation, kindness, and equality would spread, by persuasion and example, firmly and vigorously.

Such, more or less, is the vision of a future society represented by the new currents of political and cultural change. How to achieve that vision, given the realities of present power and present consciousness, has been much more difficult to figure out. Many have come to believe, however, that it is not so much a matter of theorizing as of making a start. The tactics of such a change, even making a start toward change, have to be informed, both by a vision of the future and by an accurate assessment of the structure of the present. Understanding the present situation could give at least some clues to the necessary processes of change.

In postwar America it became increasingly apparent that the structure of its society differed from traditional societies—Tsarist Russia and Mandarin China, for example—not in the fact of oligarchical control, but in the mode of that control. In the traditional societies, revolution was staved off by a combination of force, tradition, and simple folk belief in obedience to authority. In the United States—as in other technologically developed societies of this century—the mode of control contained the same ingredients, but in different proportions, with different degrees of sophistication. Modern society was still held together by force—indeed, such force as could hardly be imagined in olden times—but by a much more complicated, much more effective structure of deception than in traditional societies. Control was now internalized in the masses of the citizenry by a set of beliefs inculcated from early age, by all the techniques of modern education and mass communication.

In the modern liberal scheme, there was more flexibility; partial defects could be acknowledged, so long as the whole system was considered legitimate and good. Each group that saw a tarnished side of the social structure was taught that all the other sides were clean. But most important, modern society strained the cruelties of the past through such an elaborate network of mystification as to keep the fairly educated, fairly resourceful, potentially dangerous population pacified.

Economic exploitation, for instance, has not been as obvious in liberal capitalist societies as in peasant cultures, where the lord simply took half the produce; it has been disguised by a labyrinth of contractual relationships and market interchanges that bewilder even the economists. Political tyranny has been masked by representative bodies, regular elections, and the ballyhoo of free choice. Freedom of expression, granted in theory, has been denied at crucial moments, and rationed according to wealth; the powerless have the legal right to shout into deaf ears, and the powerful have the right to pipe their message into every living room in America. Due process of law and the formalities of judicial procedure conceal inequality before the law between rich and poor, black and white, government and citizen.

All this deception is distributed through a system of compulsory education, and reinforced in home and church, so that school, church, and parents have become instruments of control. And just as the coin of the marketplace has had its value determined by powerful corporations and the government, the coin of communication, language itself, has been controlled in schools and in the mass media. Words like violence, patriotism, honor, national security, responsibility, democracy, freedom, have been assigned meanings difficult to alter.

For those seeking basic change, the main problem in liberal societies, with such a structure of control, would not be to organize military units for a violent revolution in the classical sense, but to pull apart the web of deception. What has been needed is a set of tactics aimed at exposing the gap between words and reality, a set of tactics proving that the liberal system failed to fulfill its own professed goals, that it violated its own asserted values, that it destroyed what it said it cherished, wasted what it said it revered.

The history of the postwar world demonstrated that such learning about reality did not take place in the home, the classroom, and the Sunday school, or from lecture and political platforms. Learning took place most forcefully, most dramatically, most promptly where people took direct action against an evil policy, for a desired goal. In the struggle with power that such action inevitably produced, deceptions were exposed, realities revealed, new strengths discovered. Out of such struggles, people might begin to develop new forms of working and living—the seeds of a future cooperative society. The civil-rights movement, the student movement, the peace movement, the women's liberation movement revealed how rapidly Americans could learn.

Not everyone was deceived in the wealthy liberal state. Many knew that it was a rich man's society, that politics were corrupt, that justice was a farce. But they remained quiet, and played the game, because they also were very practical people; they knew they were powerless and saw the futility of rebellion. Yet for such people, organized action could give a sense of confidence, and occasional small victories could show that resistance is not always futile. Action could lay bare the potential power of the presumably powerless. It could show that money and guns are not the only ingredients of power. For whatever progress has taken place in the world, wherever revolutions or reforms have even temporarily succeeded, has it not been where some special, indefinable power was assembled out of the will and sacrifice of ordinary people?

The politics of protest in the sixties gave at least suggestions of this power. Minorities of organized blacks won gains here and there. Students drove the ROTC off fifty campuses, and changed many academic programs. Antiwar demonstrators made life impossible for Johnson and Nixon, determined the geography of their speeches, forced them to renege, if slowly, on their military policies in Asia. And there were many other examples, not always successful in attaining their immediate objectives, but showing the possibilities of action:

   • In East Harlem, a group of young Puerto Rican activists, the Young Lords, seized a mobile chest X-ray unit and brought it to work in an area where the tuberculosis rate was high.

   • In Boston, elderly residents organized and crowded into public hearings to get fare reductions for old people on the public transportation system.

• In Michigan, an elusive group of "billboard bandits" managed to remove 167 billboards along highways to restore the quiet beauty of central Michigan.

• In Upstate New York, a small group of volunteers guarded the home of an American Indian family being harassed by neighbors who wanted them to leave the area.

• Ten welfare mothers held a "shop-in" at Macy's department store in New York, taking clothes openly, without paying, to publicize the fact that they had no money to buy the clothes.

• An antiwar group raided a small FBI office in Media, Pennsylvania, and distributed documents to the press to publicize the way in which the FBI was acting undemocratically to suppress civil liberties.

• Poor people showed up at lavishly financed national conferences on welfare to interrupt traditional speeches and demand action.

• Protesters appeared at stockholders' meetings to ask that auto companies take measures to stop polluting the air, that banks remove investments from South Africa, that the Dow Chemical Company stop manufacturing napalm.

• Poor blacks in Greenville, Mississippi, occupied an empty air force base to demonstrate their lack of housing and their need for jobs and land.

• Doctors defied orders to close a hospital in the South Bronx, and set up voluntary clinics; residents later broke into the hospital and reopened it to let two doctors treat patients in the emergency room.

• Indians on the West Coast occupied Alcatraz Island to dramatize neglect of their problem; Indians in South Dakota stationed themselves on top of the Mount Rushmore memorial to pressure the government to honor an 1858 treaty giving land to the Sioux.

• In Berkeley, California, radicals succeeded in getting their candidates elected to half the seats of the city council.

• In Milwaukee, members of a tenants' union invaded a housing authority meeting and succeeded in stopping evictions of two families.

The significance of these acts lay outside their immediate demands. They represented attempts to act out a fuller form of democracy, beyond the limitations of the ballot box and the political party, in which aggrieved people would make their statements directly to the public, and show directly what their needs were. Sometimes this meant bold confrontations, sometimes it meant hit-and-run tactics. One citizen, pondering the relationships of power, told a student: "No, you can't fight city hall, but you can shit on the steps and run like hell." His was one idiosyncratic approach. Significant change, however, required more permanent forms of action and organization, people moving in concert but without hierarchy. It was necessary to reach, to organize, to stir into action, large sections of the working population that had hitherto been absent from the movement of the sixties.

Some people found it necessary to act out new ways of living, to show the possibilities of cooperation. Thus, around 1970, communes became a widespread phenomenon in America, with tens of thousands of people across the country, in various living and working arrangements, trying to prove that people did not have to live competitively, that they did not have to live in small, segregated families, that a larger, warmer notion of "family" might be possible, in which children would grow up better, and adults would have a richer, freer life.

Some of these communes were based on cooperative living arrangements, with the members going off during the day to work at their regular jobs. Others were working communes, in which a group of lawyers or doctors, living where they chose, set up cooperative work forces with social need, not private profit, as the chief motivation.

In December, 1970, there were at least two thousand communes across the country, but the *New York Times,* which had made the survey, acknowledged that this was a conservative estimate. Women's liberation groups set up communes. So did radical political organizers, living together in the communities where they worked. The *Times* survey found living together: Cincinnati Health Department employees campaigning for a more efficient administration; former nuns and Appalachian whites working together with mining families in the mountains of Kentucky and Tennessee; young men in Maine developing programs to save the state's open lands and shores.

A common type of commune in many cities consisted of the staff of the local underground newspaper. Near a number of military bases, antiwar organizers—civilian and GI—lived and worked together, operating a local coffeeshop or a bookstore. Rural communes sprang up in Vermont, in the Rocky Mountain states, on the West Coast.

In the tactics of social change in postwar America, one problem was constant: how to work for immediate, urgent reform, without succumbing to the American system's customary way of avoiding drastic change by granting piecemeal reforms to pacify the population. No theoretical answer to this problem seemed to exist; it was a question of working hard, without losing a larger vision of change. Some were able to do this. In 1969, in Dorchester, a white working-class section of Boston, eight young people of different backgrounds —including a former student at Harvard, a local fellow just back from Vietnam, a girl who had left her high school after leading the antiwar movement—moved into a house together, opened up a storefront, and organized a food cooperative in which many local residents joined. They collected thousands of signatures on a petition to remove a particularly oppressive local judge, and they published a community newspaper. The paper was called *tpf*—the people first. It told about landlord-tenant disputes, discussed reasons why police should be hired and supervised by the community, gave special attention to the problems of women, offered practical advice to those on welfare, advertised the food co-op, explained the effects of the Vietnam War on the cost of living in Dorchester.

These eight people wanted revolutionary change in American society. They expected to get it, not by some massive military confrontation in Washington, but by groups like themselves, working all over the country to assemble the splintered power of people into forces so diverse, so widespread, so ingrained in their communities and their workplaces as to become irrepressible. The stability of the old order rested on widespread obedience. It required everyone to stay in place. Perhaps enough sensibilities could be affected, enough confidence built up, so that some day people, acting together, would refuse to obey, refuse to do their jobs on the assembly line of violence and waste, and build their own organizations, on the job and in the neighborhood. Then the government, with all its arms and money, would be impotent. Then, through free associations of people, engaged over a long period in difficult struggles with entrenched power, democracy would come into its own at last.

In postwar America, it was beginning to be recognized by a small but growing part of the population that the special qualities of control possessed by the modern liberal system demanded a long revolutionary process of struggle and example. The process would have to be long enough, intense enough, to change the thinking of people, to act out, as far as possible, the future society. To work for the great ends of the Declaration of Independence, for life, liberty, and the pursuit of happiness, did not mean looking for some future day of fruition. It meant beginning immediately to make those ends real.

Bibliographical Notes

1. THE BEST OF WARS

Peter Berger's words come from the *Christian Century,* October, 1968.

Truman gives his account of the use of the atomic bomb in Harry S. Truman, *Memoirs,* vol. 1, *Year of Decisions* (1955), p. 419. For Oppenheimer's testimony, see Atomic Energy Commission, *In the Matter of J. Robert Oppenheimer* (1954), p. 34. Arthur Compton and Farrington Daniels report on "A Poll of Scientists at Chicago" in *Bulletin of Atomic Scientists,* February, 1948. Compton's own interpretation of the poll is in his book *Atomic Quest* (1956), pp. 242–243. The delay in the forwarding of opposition views by scientists on the use of the atomic bomb is discussed by Fletcher Knebel and Charles Bailey, "The Fight Over the A-Bomb," *Look,* Aug. 13, 1963. The Szilard petition is reprinted in Morton Grodzins and Eugene Rabinowitch, ed., *The Atomic Age* (1963), pp. 28–29, and in Barton Bernstein and Allen Matusow, *The Truman Administration: A Documentary History* (1966), pp. 17–18. Groves' account is in Leslie R. Groves, *Now It Can Be Told: The Story of the Manhattan Project* (1961), pp. 265–266. General George Marshall's views are cited in Knebel and Bailey's article. The estimate of a million casualties in the event of an invasion of Japan is made in James Byrnes, *Speaking Frankly* (1947), p. 262. Hanson Baldwin's appraisal of the need to use the bomb is in his book *Great Mistakes of the War* (1950), pp. 89–90. The report of the U.S. Strategic Bombing Survey is published in *Japan's Struggle to End the War* (1946), edited by Walter Wilds; the conclusion is on p. 13. Truman's August 9 statement is contained in *Public Papers of the Presidents* (1945), p. 212. The statement of the naval officer on military targets in Vietnam can be found in the *Naval Review* (1969), p. 214, and is quoted in Noam Chomsky's article "In North Vietnam," *New York Review of Books,* Aug. 13, 1970. Leahy offers his viewpoint in William D. Leahy, *I Was There* (1950), p. 441.

The political uses of the atomic bomb are discussed in Gar Alperovitz, *Atomic Diplomacy* (1965); see also his essay "The Use of the Atomic Bomb," in *Cold War Essays* (1970) and P.M.S. Blackett's *Fear, War, and the Bomb* (1948), p. 135. The article by Norman Cousins and Thomas Finletter, which Blackett cites, appears in the *Saturday Review of Literature,* June 15, 1946.

The effectiveness of the bombing in Europe is analyzed in *U.S. Strategic Bombing Survey 3 (The Effect of Strategic Bombing on the German War Economy)* (1945), p. 2; Allied strategy in the bombing is discussed in the *U.S. Strategic Bombing Survey (Overall Report, European War)* (1945), p. 3. It is quoted in Blackett, pp. 21–22. On the bombing of Dresden, see David Irving, *The Destruction of Dresden* (1964). For a smaller-scale discussion of Allied bombing policy, see the essay "Hiroshima and Royan" in Howard Zinn, *The Politics of History* (1970). The testimony of Daniel Ellsberg and Adam Yarmolinsky in *No More Vietnams?* (1968), edited by Richard Pfeffer, describes the psychological element in U.S. bombing policy in Vietnam. The official approach to postwar atomic bombing policy is presented by Herman Kahn, *On Thermonuclear War* (1960). The poll of people willing to risk atomic war appeared in *Time,* July 7, 1961.

For the international politics of the wartime period, an indispensable source is Gabriel Kolko's *The Politics of War* (1968). See also Isaac Deutscher's essay "Myths and Legends of the Cold War" in David Horowitz's *Containment and Revolution* (1967); Martin F. Herz's *Beginnings of the Cold War* (1966); and Milovan Djilas's *Conversations With Stalin* (1962). Arnold Offner has written on American policy during early Fascist aggression in Europe, *American Appeasement: U.S. Foreign Policy and Germany, 1933–1939* (1969). United States policy on the Jews in Germany is outlined by Arthur D. Morse, *While Six Million Died: A Chronicle of Jewish Apathy* (1968). For an academic specialist's candid support of American imperial power, see George Liska, *Imperial America: The International Politics of Primacy* (1967).

Cordell Hull's statement on international investment capital is on p. 1,177 of his *Memoirs* (1948). The American quest for economic power during the war is related in detail by Lloyd Gardner in his *Economic Aspects of New Deal Diplomacy* (1964). The quotation from Archibald MacLeish is reprinted in Gardner, p. 264. Herbert Feis's statement appears in his book *Sinews of Peace* (1944), pp. 137–138. Averell Harriman's statement on the political value of economic aid is in Kolko, p. 259. Much of the material on wartime economic policy appears in Kolko, especially in chapter 11.

Wartime job discrimination is briefly summarized in the *Report of the National Advisory Commission on Civil Disorders* (1968), especially p. 223. For an account of the wartime march on Washington, see Herbert Garfinkel, *When Negroes March* (1949).

Eric Goldman's picture of the postwar economic scene is in his book *The Crucial Decade and After* (1960). A critical view of the wartime jockeying for power in Washington, and the failure of the war's highest ideals, is found in Bruce Catton, *The War Lords of Washington* (1948).

Morton Grodzins tells the story of the evacuation of the Japanese in *Americans Betrayed: Politics and the Japanese Evacuation* (1949). See also, Norman Jackman's "Collective Protest in Relocation Centers," *American Journal of Sociology,* November, 1957, and Walter Murphy's "Civil Liberties and the Japanese American Cases: A Study in the Uses of Stare Decisis," *Western Political Quarterly,* March, 1958.

2. EMPIRE

An excellent account and analysis of the Yalta Conference is by Diane Clemens, *Yalta* (1970). Frederick Merk makes some sound comments on American expansionism in *Manifest Destiny and Mission in American History: A Reinterpretation* (1966). Arthur Schlesinger's remarks are in *No More Vietnams?* (1968), edited by Richard Pfeffer.

Hugh Seton-Watson's statement on the British role in Greece appears in *The Pattern of Communist Revolution* (1961), p. 217. William McNeil's *The Greek Dilemma* (1947) is recommended for a general discussion of the Greek civil war; McNeil also describes the use of American planes to fly in two British divisions. Howard K. Smith's observations on British policy are offered in his *The State of Europe* (1949), pp. 232–234. Churchill's instructions to General Scobie are quoted by Martin F. Herz, *Beginnings of the Cold War* (1966). A good overall account of the American intervention in Greece is by Richard Barnet, *Intervention and Revolution* (1968). See also Joseph Jones, *The Fifteen Weeks* (1955). Dean Acheson's role is also noted in Barnet, p. 115. That the United States drafted the Greek request for aid is pointed out in Jones, p. 77. The text of the Truman Doctrine is given by Barton Bernstein and Allen Matusow, in *The Truman Administration: A Documentary History* (1966). Isaac Deutscher takes up the role of the Soviet Union during this period in "Myths and Legends of the Cold War," in *Containment and Revolution* (1967), edited by David Horowitz; so does Milovan Djilas in his *Conversations with Stalin* (1962). The significance of oil in the Grecian intervention is noted in Stephen Xydis' *Greece and the Great Powers* (1965). General Van Fleet's counter-insurgency policies are discussed in Edgar O'Ballance's *The Greek Civil War* (1966), p. 215. Todd Gitlin has an excellent essay on the subject, "The Mythology of Counter-Insurgency, The Case of Greece," in Horowitz's collection. Barnet's summary analysis of United States postwar policy toward Greece is on pp. 127–128. Torture in Greece during the late sixties was reported by Christopher Wren, in *Look,* May 27, 1969. For more on the military rule, see the *New York Times,* September 20, 1970. The secret dispatch of arms by the United States to Greece, despite a publicly proclaimed arms embargo, is reported in an Associated Press dispatch of Oct. 5, 1970.

James Byrnes's statement on Asia "as a great smoldering fire" is from his book *Speaking Frankly* (1947), p. 204. Kenneth Latourette's explanation for Chiang Kai-shek's defeat is in his book *The American Record in the Far East, 1945–1951* (1952), pp. 106–123. The Department of State publication *United States Relations With China, 1944–1949* (1949) tells much about American policy during the civil-war period.

Allen Whiting's *China Crosses the Yalu* (1960) recounts China's entrance into the Korean War. The description of the effects of napalm bombing in Korea is from the *Manchester Guardian,* March 1, 1952. I. F. Stone's *The Hidden History of the Korean War* (1952) is a dissenting view from the usual defense of American policy in that war.

Material on the CIA operation in Guatemala is in David Wise and Thomas Ross, *The Invisible Government* (1964). The quote from Eisenhower defending the Guatemalan intervention is from Wise and Ross, p. 166. The description of reform in Guatemala before the U.S. intervention is from Ronald Schneider, *Communism in Guatemala, 1944–1954* (1959), pp. 302–303. John Foster Dulles' deception on the Guatemalan intervention is recorded in the *New York Herald Tribune,* July 1, 1954, and quoted in Barnet's *Intervention and Revolution,* p. 234.

An account of the United States intervention in Lebanon is also given in Barnet's book, pp. 132–151.

The text of the Platt Amendment on Cuba is reproduced in Ruhl Bartlett, *The Record of American Diplomacy* (1954), pp. 535–536. Material on American economic interests in Cuba is from David Horowitz, *The Free World Colossus* (1965), p. 201, while information on U.S. military aid to the Batista regime can be found in Edwin Lieuwen's *Generals Vs. Presidents* (1964), p. 24. Castro's article in *Cuba Libre* is reprinted in the *Nation,* November 30, 1957. Arthur Schlesinger discusses the Castro visit to the United States in *A Thousand Days* (1965), p. 221; another viewpoint on the visit and Castro's attempt to get a loan is that of William Appleman Williams', *The United States, Cuba, and Castro* (1962), p. 102. Wise and Ross also portray the CIA's role in Cuba, page 24; so, too, does Schlesinger, p. 240. George Sokolsky's quote is printed in Tad Szulc and Karl E. Meyer, *The Cuban Invasion* (1962), pp. 71–72. State Department duplicity on Cuba is described by Wise and Ross, p. 34. Theodore Sorensen summarizes the results of the Cuban invasion in his book, *Kennedy* (1966), p. 329. The *Manchester Guardian*'s comment appeared in the *New York Times,* April 23, 1961. The Kennedy press conference on April 12 is mentioned by Sorensen, p. 334, and Kennedy's part in the deception on Cuba, pp. 335–336. Schlesinger's account of the White House meeting is in *A Thousand Days,* p. 271. He relates how editors agreed to kill their stories on the Cuban invasion, p. 261.

The similarities between the U.S. invasion of the Dominican Republic and the earlier intervention in Nicaragua are outlined by Neill Macaulay in his book *The Sandino Affair* (1967). Trujillo family holdings in the republic are given by Barnet, p. 155. Schlesinger, p. 769, tells about Kennedy's fear of a Castro regime in the

Dominican Republic, and George Smathers' point on U.S. investments in the republic is from the *Congressional Record,* May 31, 1966, quoted in Barnet, p. 166. John Bartlow Martin's book *Overtaken by Events* (1966) gives an American diplomat's inside view of that intervention. The surge of American investment after the intervention is reported by Barnet, p. 177.

Figures on postwar American economic and military aid come from the *New York Times,* international edition, April 5, 1963; they are also quoted in *Containment and Revolution,* p. 215. The Marshall Plan is discussed critically in several chapters in Joyce and Gabriel Kolko's *The Limits of Power* (1972); the quotation from Marshall is on p. 376. Acheson's view on the Marshall Plan is quoted by Horowitz, *Free World Colossus,* p. 76. Lieuwen's statement on military aid to Latin America is in *Generals Vs. Presidents,* p. 129. The Rockefeller presidential mission to Latin America in 1969 produced *The Rockefeller Report on the Americas* (1969). Harry Magdoff assesses American economic activity abroad in his book *The Age of Imperialism* (1969); on pp. 48–49, he talks of America's growing need for raw materials.

United States military policy after World War II is evaluated, and its myths noted, by Edgar Bottome, *The Balance of Terror* (1971). His comment on American responsibility for escalating the arms race is on pages pp. xv–xvi. Herbert York's *Race to Oblivion* (1970) is also valuable; his statements on U.S. military power are on pp. 228, 229, and 230. The concentration of war contracts in a few corporations is reported in the *New Republic,* April 25, 1970. Sen. William Proxmire's investigation is summarized in *Report from Wasteland: America's Military-Industrial Complex* (1971).

The best overall account of United States policy on Vietnam in the postwar period is by George Kahin and John Lewis, *The United States in Vietnam* (1967). The Vietnamese Declaration of Independence is reproduced in *Vietnam* (1965), edited by Marvin Gettelman. The Ho Chi Minh letters to Truman are mentioned in the first volume of Sen. Mike Gravel's four-volume edition of *The Pentagon Papers* (1972), p. 17 (hereafter cited as *Papers*). State Department instructions on Vietnam to American diplomats abroad are in *Papers,* vol. 1, pp. 31–32. The figures on United States aid to the French are in *Papers,* vol. 1, p. 77. Truman's radio talk on the

eve of the Korean War is in *Public Papers of the Presidents, 1951.*
The State Department memoranda on Ho Chi Minh and Moscow
are in *Papers,* vol. 1, pp. 33–34. Eisenhower's news conference of
Feb. 10, 1954, is in *Public Papers of the Presidents, 1954,* p. 253,
and is quoted in *Papers,* vol. 1, p. 593. His talk to the Governors'
Conference is on p. 540 of *Public Papers of the Presidents, 1953.*
The State Department memorandum on the "domino theory," on
the eve of Dienbienphu, is in *Papers,* vol. 1, p. 405. The Joint Chiefs
of Staff intelligence estimate on free elections is in *Papers,* vol. 1,
p. 448, and the American encouragement of Ngo Dinh Diem to
reject elections is mentioned on p. 183 in that volume. The quote
from the Pentagon analyst on South Vietnam as the creation of the
United States is in the *New York Times* one-volume edition of *The
Pentagon Papers,* p. 25. The figures on military appointees as province chiefs under Diem is in *Papers,* vol. 1, p. 323. The quotes from
Douglas Pike are from his book *Viet Cong,* chapter 6. The Kennedy-
Eisenhower conference on the eve of Kennedy's inauguration is in
Papers, vol. 2, pp. 635–636. The secret plan for covert actions in
Indochina of May, 1961, is in *Papers,* vol. 2, pp. 637–642. For ma-
terial on the United States involvement in the Saigon army coup, see
Papers, vol. 2, p. 780 and p. 793. The Gulf of Tonkin events are
detailed by Joseph C. Goulden, *Truth is the First Casualty: The
Gulf of Tonkin Affair—Illusion and Reality* (1970). For details
on the My Lai massacre, see Seymour Hersh, *My Lai 4, A Report
on the Massacre and Its Aftermath* (1970). The quote from Colonel
Henderson on the massacre appeared in the *Boston Globe,* May 25,
1971. For figures on the tonnage of bombs dropped on Indochina
by the United States, see *The Air War in Indochina,* a report by the
Center for International Studies, Cornell University.

3. DEMOCRACY AND PROFIT

The statement by economist Harold G. Vatter on the American
postwar economy is in his book *The U.S. Economy in the 1950s*
(1963). The 1968 Citizens' Board of Inquiry into Hunger and
Malnutrition in the United States has its findings reported in *Hunger, U.S.A.* The figures on stability of income distribution through

the postwar years are taken from the U.S. Bureau of the Census, *Historical Statistics of the United States, Colonial Times to 1957,* p. 166, and from Herman P. Miller, *Rich Man, Poor Man* (1964), p. 35. The statistics on the concentration of corporate stocks and bonds come from the essay by Robert J. Lampman, "Changes in the Share of Wealth Held by Top Wealth-Holders, 1922–1956," in *The Review of Economics and Statistics,* November, 1959. Information on equal opportunity for college education is contained in a State University of New York publication, *Crucial Questions About Higher Education,* and those on the concentration of military contracts and profits in war-related industries appeared in the *New York Times,* June 17, 1968. Data on actual tax rates paid by high-income categories was published by the *Saturday Review,* March 22, 1969; the *New York Times,* March 8, 1970, printed the figures on the cost to consumers of government subsidies to the oil industry. The report on Hubert Humphrey's speech to the Citizens Crusade Against Poverty was in the *New York Times,* April 13, 1966. John Kenneth Galbraith's comment on the American economic system is in his book, *Who Needs the Democrats?* (1970). The statement by Andrew Shonfield on the pace of American capitalism appears in his book, *Modern Capitalism* (1965), p. 11.

The figures on the cost of style changes in the auto industry are given by Paul Baran and Paul Sweezy, *Monopoly Capital* (1966), pp. 136–137. The estimate by the Federal Water Pollution Control Commission was noted in an Associated Press dispatch Oct. 14, 1969. Adelle Davis' statement about bad beef was published by *Look,* Dec. 15, 1970. Business opposition to air-pollution control was reported in the *New York Times,* May 20, 1967, and the role of Stewart Udall in the off-shore oil drilling in the *Boston Globe,* Feb. 9, 1969. The material on price-fixing in the drug industry is in the Dec. 11, 1959, publication by the U.S. Senate Subcommittee on Antitrust and Monopoly, *Transcript of the Proceedings on Administered Prices in the Drug Industry;* see p. 31 for the point on the drug prednisone. *I.F. Stone's Weekly* in late 1959 and early 1960 carried a good deal of material on those hearings.

Points of view of more than passing interest on American political democracy are expressed in C. Wright Mills, *The Power Elite* (1956); Robert Dahl, *A Preface to Democratic Theory*

(1956); Henry Kariel, *The Decline of American Pluralism* (1961). See also the essay by Robert Paul Wolff in Barrington Moore, Herbert Marcuse, and R. P. Wolff, *A Critique of Pure Tolerance* (1965). The statement on universal suffrage not being a threat to property interests is made by Kenneth N. Vines and Henry Robert Glick, "The Impact of Universal Suffrage: A Comparison of Popular and Property Voting," *American Political Science Review*, December, 1967. On voting, see Bernard R. Berelson et al., *Voting: A Study of Opinion Formation in a Presidential Campaign* (1964) and Angus Campbell et al., *The American Voter* (1964). For a sharp analysis of Dahl and others, see Jack L. Walker, "A Critique of the Elitist Theory of Democracy," *The American Political Science Review*, June, 1966. Duane Lockard's comments on the concentrations of power are in his *Perverted Priorities of American Politics* (1971), p. 314.

4. SOLVING THE RACE PROBLEM

The report of Truman's Committee on Civil Rights is contained in a government publication, *To Secure These Rights* (1947). Loren Miller's bitter comment on the Supreme Court's "all deliberate speed" postulate is in his book *The Petitioners* (1967), p. 352. The Little Rock school incident is described by Daisy Bates, *Long Shadow of Little Rock* (1962). The young black girl's recollection is presented in dramatic form by Martin Duberman in his play *In White America* (1964), p. 64. Eisenhower's statement after his dispatch of troops to Little Rock appeared in the *New York Times*, Sept. 25, 1957. The quotations from the Mississippi Constitution, used for voter registration, are cited in *The Reporter*, March 26, 1964. James Forman describes the Tuskegee incident in *Sammy Younge, Jr., The First Black College Student to Die in the Black Liberation Movement* (1968), pp. 186–187.

Malcolm X's comment on the March on Washington is reprinted in *Malcolm X Speaks* (1965), pp. 14–15. On the Watts riot, Robert Conot's *Rivers of Blood, Years of Darkness* (1967) is recommended; his comment on its significance is on p. ix. On the

Newark riot, see Tom Hayden, *Rebellion in Newark* (1967); the taxi driver's quotation is on p. 10. The essay by Julius Lester appeared in a newsletter of the Student Non-violent Coordinating Committee, and can be found in August Meier, Elliott Rudwick, and Frances Broderick, *Black Protest Thought in the Twentieth Century* (1971), p. 482. Burke Marshall's defense of federal inaction is in his book *Federalism and Civil Rights* (1964), pp. 71–72. Richard Wasserstrom's scathing critique of Marshall's book was printed in *The University of Chicago Law Review,* Winter, 1966. On the killing of black students at Orangeburg in 1968, see Jack Nelson and Jack Bass, *The Orangeburg Massacre* (1970), pp. 83, 99, 227. The *New York Times* report on the Augusta, Georgia, shooting of May, 1970, was published on May 14, 1970. On the 1967 urban upheavals, see the *Report of the National Advisory Commission on Civil Disorders* (1968); the quotations are from pp. 10–11. Quotations from Kenneth B. Clark's *Dark Ghetto* (1965) appear on pp. 1-6. James Baldwin's description of black anger in his *The Fire Next Time* (1963) is on pp. 132–133.

5. JUSTICE

For a complacent view of American civil liberties in the postwar period, see Milton Konvitz's *Expanding Liberties* (1966). For a comprehensive picture of constitutional rights, see Thomas Emerson, David Haber, and Norman Dorsen, *Political and Civil Rights in the United States* (1967). The essay by Richard Drinnon is as yet unpublished. The reactions of the U.S. Senate, especially its liberal members, to the McCarthy phenomenon is reported in depth by Robert Griffith, *The Politics of Fear* (1970); on the State Department's reaction, pp. 215–216; on McCarthyism as a "natural expression," p. 30; on those who fought McCarthyism, p. 269; on the Washington worker, p. 309. The statement of John F. Kennedy to the House of Representatives on the fall of China to the Communists is in the *Congressional Record,* Jan. 25, 1949, pp. 532–533, and is quoted in the essay by Daniel Ellsberg, "The Quagmire Myth and the Stalemate Machine," *Papers on the War* (1972). For the role of Harry Truman in the creation of the McCarthy atmosphere, see Alan D. Harper, *The Politics of Loyalty: The White House and the Communist Issue, 1946–1952* (1970). On the Rosenberg case, see Walter and Miriam Schneir, *Invitation to an Inquest* (1965). The *Scientific American* quotation on the Greenglass bomb is contained in its May, 1951, issue. James Beckerley's speech was reported in the March 17, 1954, issue of the *New York Times*. Irving Saypol's comments to the jury are in Schneir, pp. 120 and 155; Kaufman's comment to the jury, p. 167; and Saypol's remarks before the sentencing, p. 168. Robert Carr's *The House Committee on Un-American Activities* (1952) is helpful; it cites the quotation from John Rankin and the Stripling-Mrs. Rogers exchange. Much transcript material on the hearings of the committee appears in Eric Bentley's *Thirty Years of Treason* (1972); p. 148 gives Gary Cooper's testimony. An indispensable book on the sedition laws of the First and Second World Wars is Zechariah Chafee's *Free Speech in the United States* (1941). Irving Feiner's experience is related in *Political and Civil Rights in the United States,* p. 532. The Langston Hughes poem read to his class by Jonathan Kozol is in Kozol's *Death at an Early Age* (1967), pp. 235–236.

The incident involving the distribution of the Declaration of Independence to military personnel is told in John V. H. Dippel, "Getting Nowhere through Channels," *New Republic,* May 22, 1971. The report on the 1968 Chicago police riot is in the publication, known as *Rights in Conflict: The Walker Report* (1968), of the National Commission on the Causes and Prevention of Violence; cited quotations are from pp. 1 and 10. Jerome Skolnick's comments on police violence are in his report *Politics of Protest* (1969), p. 247. On the Kent State shooting of 1970, see I. F. Stone's *The Killings at Kent State* (1970) and various issues of his *Bi-Weekly;* the Nov. 2, 1970, issue contains Sen. Stephen Young's comment. Milton Konvitz's observation on crimes of status is on p. 272 of his *Expanding Liberties* (1967). The Supreme Court decision on the banning of public gatherings in Philadelphia was reported in the *New York Times,* May 25, 1970. E. S. Corwin's statement on the traditional limitations on the right of assembly is from his *The Constitution and What It Means Today* (1963 edition), pp. 203–204. The Gideon case has been amply treated by Anthony Lewis in his book *Gideon's Trumpet* (1964). The weak impact of Supreme

Court decisions on the right of suspects is noted in John Kaplan's review in the *New York Times Book Review,* Nov. 22, 1970, and the problem of bail is discussed carefully in Ronald Goldfarb's *Ransom* (1965).

The statement by criminologist Richard Korn appears in an article by Goldfarb, "Prison: The National Poorhouse," *The New Republic,* Nov. 1, 1969. The comment on state prisons appeared in *P.I.C. News,* March, 1971. The Karl Menninger statement comes from his book *The Crime of Punishment* (1969), p. 28. The American Friends Service Committee publication *Struggle for Justice* (1971) has much sound information on the problem of punishment.

On United States violations of international law in Vietnam, see Richard Falk, *The Vietnam War and International Law* (1969), Telford Taylor, *Nuremberg and Vietnam: An American Tragedy* (1970), and the publication of Clergy and Laymen Concerned About Vietnam, *In the Name of America* (1968). Falk's comment appears in his preface to the publication of the Lawyers Committee on American Policy Toward Vietnam, *Vietnam and International Law* (1968). The Lawyers Committee publication also reproduces the text of the U.S. government's defense of the legality of the war; in this connection, see also Falk, Kolko, and Robert Lifton, eds., *Crimes of War* (1971).

The instances of governmental immunity come from the article by Ronald Goldfarb, "Legal Nonsense," in *The New Republic,* Aug. 16, 1969. The failure of Attorney General John Mitchell to prosecute the fund-raising committees in the 1968 presidential campaign is reported in an article by Washington correspondent Fred P. Graham, in the *New York Times,* June 7, 1970. Alan Westin's *Privacy and Freedom* (1967) is an excellent source on the subject of wiretapping; his quotation on the Coplon case is on p. 177. The reports on tapping by the Internal Revenue Service were printed in the *New York Times,* July 28, 1965. The limitations of the 1968 Omnibus Crime Control and Safe Streets Act were discussed in the article "New Taps on Freedom" by Sally Fly in *The Nation,* June 2, 1969. On the tapping of defendants' wires in the "Chicago Conspiracy" trial, see the *New York Times,* June 14, 1969. On April 9, 1971, the *Times* also reported the government's admission of illegal wiretapping in the "White Panther" case. Victor Navasky's comments on illegal wiretapping were printed in the *New York Times,* April 10, 1971; see also his *Kennedy Justice* (1971). The FBI's use of dossiers is covered by Eleanor Bontecou, *The Federal Loyalty-Security Program* (1953). The FBI interviews of professors at Kent State were reported in the *New York Times,* June 10, 1970. The FBI agent's criticism of the bureau was published in the *Boston Globe,* Jan. 30, 1971. Pilot Donald Cook's comment on the FBI appeared in the *New York Times.*

6. BUNKER HILL: BEGINNINGS

The quotation from Joan Didion is from her book, *Slouching Towards Bethlehem* (1968). Albert Bigelow's sailing trip into the atomic testing area of the Pacific is reported in his article "Why I Am Sailing Into Pacific Bomb Test Area," *Liberation,* February, 1958; it is reprinted in *Seeds of Liberation* (1964), edited by Paul Goodman. For material on the early postwar peace movement, Lawrence S. Wittner's *Rebels Against War: The American Peace Movement 1941–1960* (1969) is helpful.

The statement by Rosa Parks on the Montgomery bus boycott comes from the anthology by Joanne Grant, *Black Protest* (1968), pp. 277–278. The dispatch by Wayne Phillips on the bus boycott is reproduced in *Portrait of a Decade* (1964), pp. 62–63, by Anthony Lewis and the *New York Times.* Material on the Student Non-violent Coordinating Committee comes from my book, *SNCC: The New Abolitionists* (1964); quotations here from Ruby Doris Smith are on pp. 18–19, 44, 48; from Stokely Carmichael, p. 57. Bayard Rustin's comment on Birmingham appeared in *Liberation,* June, 1963. Jerome Skolnick's observations on black activism are on p. 170 of his task force report *Politics of Protest* (1969); the black man's testimony before the National Advisory Commission is in Skolnick, p. 171. Malcolm X's exhortation to a group of black students is from *Malcolm X Speaks* (1965), p. 153.

The statistics on student rebellion in 1969 appeared in the *New York Times,* Jan. 14, 1970. James Kunen's comment on "the Biggies" appeared in the *Atlantic.*

The report on changes in students' thinking in the Columbia uprising is from Richard Rosenkranz, *Across the Barricades* (1971), pp. 41-42. The two commencement stories in the *Boston Globe* appeared in May, 1970. The student's observations on radical movements are contained in an unpublished paper by Miriam Elmer. Figures on underground high-school newspapers come from Marc Libarle and Tom Seligson, *The High School Revolutionaries* (1970).

Polls showing antiwar sentiment on the West Coast were reported in *The Nation,* Nov. 30, 1970. See also the report on the Gallup poll in the *New York Times,* Nov. 4, 1970. The vote in Madison, Wisconsin, was reported in the *New York Times,* April 8, 1971; the poll on loss of public trust in the government appeared in the *Times,* May 24, 1970.

On black protest against the war, see my book *Vietnam: The Logic of Withdrawal* (1967), Michael Ferber and Staughton Lynd's *The Resistance* (1971), and Alice Lynd's collection, *We Won't Go* (1968). Eldridge Cleaver's open letter to his "black brothers" was printed in an unidentified leaflet in 1970, and Martin Luther King's antiwar stand is quoted in *Black Protest,* p. 423. The poem by Alice Walker appears in her book *Once* (1968). On the Spock trial, see Jessica Mitford, *The Trial of Dr. Spock* (1969). The Daniel Berrigan quotation is from his introduction to Philip Berrigan, *Prison Journals of a Priest Revolutionary* (1970), p. xv; see also Daniel Berrigan, *The Trial of the Catonsville Nine* (1969). The quote from the Howard Levy trial appeared in the *New York Times,* May 18, 1967. The Presidio stockade uprising is described in Fred Gardner's book, *The Unlawful Concert* (1970). The *Le Monde* correspondent's report on disaffection in the American military was quoted in *I.F. Stone's Bi-Weekly,* Feb. 23, 1970; it appeared in the Jan. 24, 1970, issue of *Le Monde.* Pentagon figures on fragging incidents in Vietnam were given in the *Boston Globe,* April 21, 1971.

The statement on joylessness in the public schools is by Charles Silberman, in his book, *Crisis in the Classroom* (1970). The Dave Meggysey quotation is on p. 147 of his book *Out of Their League* (1970). The analysis of women's dependence on their husbands is in an essay by Evelyn Leo, "Dependency in Marriage: Oppression in Middle-Class Marriage," in Leslie B. Tanner's *Voices from Women's Liberation* (1971). The Theodore Roszak argument is made in his book, *The Making of a Counter Culture* (1969), p. 267.

Index